Mass Intellectuality and Democratic Leadership in Higher Education

Perspectives on Leadership in Higher Education

Series Editors:
Camilla Erskine, Tanya Fitzgerald and Jon Nixon

Perspectives on Leadership in Higher Education provides a forum for distinctive, and sometimes divergent, ideas on what intellectual leadership means within the context of higher education as it develops within the twenty-first century. Authors from across a number of nation states critically explore these issues with reference to academic and research-informed practice and development, institutional management and governance, the remapping of knowledge as well as sector-wide policy development.

Forthcoming in the Perspectives on Leadership in Higher Education series
Leadership for Sustainability in Higher Education, Janet Haddock-Fraser, Peter Rands and Stephen Scoffham

Also available from Bloomsbury
Academic Identities in Higher Education, edited by Linda Evans and Jon Nixon
Academic Working Lives, edited by Lynne Gornall, Caryn Cook, Lyn Daunton, Jane Salisbury and Brychan Thomas
Cosmopolitan Perspectives on Academic Leadership in Higher Education, edited by Feng Su and Margaret Wood

Mass Intellectuality and Democratic Leadership in Higher Education

Edited by Richard Hall and Joss Winn

BLOOMSBURY ACADEMIC
LONDON • NEW YORK • OXFORD • NEW DELHI • SYDNEY

BLOOMSBURY ACADEMIC
Bloomsbury Publishing Plc
50 Bedford Square, London, WC1B 3DP, UK
1385 Broadway, New York, NY 10018, USA

BLOOMSBURY, BLOOMSBURY ACADEMIC and the Diana logo
are trademarks of Bloomsbury Publishing Plc

First published 2017
Paperback edition first published 2019

Cover design: Louise Dugdale
Cover image © Jobalou / Getty Images

A catalogue record for this book is available from the British Library.

Library of Congress Cataloging-in-Publication Data
Names: Hall, Richard, 1971- editor. | Winn, Joss, editor.
Title: Mass intellectuality and democratic leadership in higher education / edited by Richard Hall and Joss Winn.
Description: London ; New York : Bloomsbury Academic,2017. | Series: Perspectives on leadership in higher education | Includes bibliographical references and index.
Identifiers: LCCN 2017004883| ISBN 9781474267588(hardback) | ISBN 9781474267601(epdf) | ISBN 9781474267595 (epub)
Subjects: LCSH: Education, Higher–Aims and objectives–Great Britain. | Educational leadership–Great Britain. | Educational change–Great Britain. |Universities and colleges–Great Britain–Administration | BISAC: EDUCATION/ Higher. | EDUCATION / Leadership.
Classification: LCC LA637 .M3543 2017 | DDC370.110941–dc23 LC record available at https://lccn.loc.gov/2017004883

ISBN: HB: 978-1-4742-6758-8
PB: 978-1-3501-0064-0
ePDF: 978-1-4742-6760-1
ePub: 978-1-4742-6759-5

Series: Perspectives on Leadership in Higher Education

Typeset by Integra Software Services Pvt. Ltd.

To find out more about our authors and books visit www.bloomsbury.com and sign up for our newsletters.

Contents

Series Editors' Foreword

What are universities for in the twenty-first century? This is a question that is now debated not only within universities themselves but also within wider society and across the political spectrum: we can no longer assume a consensus regarding the ends and purposes of higher education or the role of universities in fulfilling those ends and purposes. Consequently, leadership within higher education cannot simply be a matter of managing the *status quo*: leadership necessarily involves an understanding as well as analysis of the twenty-first-century world and of how the university might contribute to the economic, social, cultural and political challenges that we face. In short, it requires leadership that is both visionary and programmatic: visionary in its understanding of the past as well as present and future impacts of globalization and programmatic in its grasp of how universities might respond to that impact.

What might such leadership look like? This series aims to address that question with reference to academic practice and development, institutional management and governance, the remapping of knowledge and sector-wide policy development. Central to each of these areas of concern is the importance of interconnectivity in a context of increasing institutional and global complexity: interconnectivity within and across institutions, regions and cognate fields. The gathering of agreement is one of the prerequisites of leadership at every level – and that requires an understanding of different viewpoints and opinions some of which may be in direct conflict with others. The capacity to balance, respect and contain these differences is what constitutes leadership. This inevitably raises important ethical questions regarding leadership in a more complex and subtle setting, where leadership goes beyond the 'command' model of telling others what to do and expecting them to do it. The twin themes of interconnectivity and ethics cut across the series as a whole.

Mass Intellectuality and Democratic Leadership in Higher Education focuses these twin themes on the notion of *democratic* leadership as developed in a variety of higher education settings and extra-mural contexts. The central argument of the book is that the institutions comprising the higher education sector have become increasingly financialized and marketized; that the idea of 'the public university' is – as a result – under severe threat; and that the practice of 'mass education' needs, therefore, to be re-imagined. That re-imagining, argue the contributors to this book, requires new and emergent forms of academic leadership that may as yet be embryonic, but could – given the political will – revitalise the higher education sector as a whole, re-energise those working and studying within it, and lead to a radical reconceptualization of the higher education curriculum.

Richard Hall and Joss Winn have brought together a group of authors whose work is theoretically informed and challenging, whose ideas are grounded in innovative forms of institutional and pedagogical practice, and whose agenda for change is clearly articulated and evidenced. The book points to a renewed vision for 'mass' higher education: a vision that places collaborative ways of working and cooperative modes of pedagogical practice as its focal point of concern. Neither the editors nor the authors are starry-eyed regarding the problems they face in realising that vision. But the arguments they put forward for the radical democratisation of higher education – and the critique of the *status quo* upon which those arguments are premised – are of vital importance in any consideration of what leadership means in the rapidly changing landscape of higher education.

Notes on Contributors

Gordon Asher is an educator/learner, researcher/writer, editor/proofreader, 'activist' and cultural worker based in Glasgow, UK. A member of the burgeoning academic precariat, his main employment is as a Learning and Curriculum Developer at the University of the West of Scotland, UK. He studied for a Master's degree in Adult Education at the University of Glasgow, UK, and is currently working towards a PhD by publication, within a broad framing – 'In, Against and Beyond the Neoliberal University'; linking critical educational theories and practices within the academy with radical education outwith the academy. Amongst other commitments outwith the university he is the co-editor of Variant magazine(http://www.variant.org.uk/), a board member of Strickland Distribution (http://strickdistro.org/), a member of the Social Science Centre (http://socialsciencecentre.org.uk/) and a founder member of the Centre for Transformational Learning and Culture (http://utlc2016.wix.com/home). His 'bag' is critical pedagogy/popular education/critical academic literacies for radical democracy/eco-social justice.

Birmingham Autonomous University is an independent group of a dozen university students, graduates, activists and workers committed to developing viable popular and radical education programmes in the city of Birmingham, UK. Founded in 2013, BAU has delivered talks, workshops and critiques to students in movement, and is keen to build links with pedagogues engaged in struggle. Its sessions have focused on unorthodox Marxism, and its members have co-organized participatory events with the British Sociological Association 'Activism in Sociology Forum'. BAU is also interested in the initiative to develop a sustainable social, legal and business model for Co-operative Higher Education, and in the longer-term project of developing intellectual capacities and critical faculties beyond capitalism.

Joyce E. Canaan is Professor of Sociology at Birmingham City University, UK, and Visiting Professor of Applied Linguistics at UECE, the State University of Ceará in Fortaleza, Brazil. Her research and writing has focused on critical pedagogy and popular education in and outside the neoliberal university. As capitalism devours more of the planet and immiserates its people, Joyce is engaged with creative activists and popular educators, in nurturing bottom up activism at home. She is also learning with and from Brazilian popular educators and cultural workers.

Jonathan Owen Clark is an artist and academic, and currently Head of Research at Trinity Laban Conservatoire of Music and Dance, UK. He has previously held lecturing positions at the University of Newcastle, UK, and Brunel University, UK, and has research interests in critical theory and aesthetics.

Martin Paul Eve is Professor of Literature, Technology and Publishing at Birkbeck, University of London, UK. In addition to many journal articles, he is the author of four books – *Pynchon and Philosophy* (2014), *Open Access and the Humanities* (2014), *Password: A Cultural History* (Bloomsbury, 2016), and *Literature Against Criticism* (2016). Martin is also heavily involved in policy debates around open-access to research work and is a founder and co-director of the Open Library of Humanities.

Richard Hall is Professor of Education and Technology at De Montfort University, Leicester, UK. At DMU he is Co-Director of the Institute for Education Futures. Richard is a UK National Teaching Fellow, a co-operator at the Social Science Centre in Lincoln, UK, and a Trustee of the Open Library of Humanities. He writes about life in higher education at: http://richard-hall.org.

Thomas Henfrey is senior research fellow at the Schumacher Institute (Bristol, UK) and research fellow in the Centre for Ecology, Evolution and Environmental Change at Lisbon University. His main current role is providing research support to the ECOLISE network of European community-led sustainability initiatives. This builds on prior work at the interface of research and practical action for sustainability, equity and social justice, particularly within the permaculture and Transition movements.

Louise H. Jackson is Head of Learning Enhancement at Trinity Laban Conservatoire of Music and Dance, UK, and is a National Teaching Fellowship of the Higher Education Academy. Her areas of interest in research include how Widening Participation enacts and promotes notions of Neoliberalism, and the development of Educational Fundamentalism within Music in Higher Education.

Joel Lazarus completed his PhD at St Anthony's College, University of Oxford, in 2011. Since then, he has joined the ranks of the 'precariat' academic, teaching on short-term contractual bases at Oxford, Reading University and SOAS. Over this period, his research focus has gradually metamorphosed from the political economy of democracy promotion to critical pedagogy and social transformation through radical popular education.

Sara C. Motta is a mother, feminist writer, critical educator and currently senior lecturer in Politics, University of Newcastle, Australia. She is committed to the co-creation of an emancipatory autonomous and decolonising politics for the twenty-first century. She has run numerous women's empowerment workshops working particularly with the power of the body, art and the sacred for personal and collective transformation and worked as a critical educator with women's and other movements in Latin America and Europe. She has also written extensively on the reimagining of emancipatory politics in the twenty-first century, in relation to Latin America, and more globally. Her most recent books are *Education and Social Change in Latin America* (ed. with Mike Cole) (2013) and *Constructing Twenty-First Century Socialism: The Role of Radical Education* (with Mike Cole) (2014). She is currently writing a decolonial feminist book *Liminal Subjects: Weaving Our Liberation* exploring such a reimagining in theory and practice.

Mike Neary is Professor of Sociology in the School of Political and Social Sciences, University of Lincoln, UK. He held a senior management and leadership role at Lincoln, where he was the Dean of Teaching and Learning 2007–2014. Mike's research is informed by Marxist value theory of labour. His current writing applies this theory to a higher education context, with a focus on student and academic labour. Mike was made an honorary life member of the University of Lincoln's Students' Union in 2014 for his work with students. He is a founding member of the Social Science Centre, Lincoln, a co-operative providing free public higher education since 2011.

Jenny Pearce is Research Professor in the Latin American and Caribbean Centre, London School of Economics. Previously, she was Professor of Latin American Politics in Peace Studies, University of Bradford. Jenny has worked for many years on issues of violence and social change in Latin America and written extensively on these topics. She has also tried to bring this learning about social change and action from the global South to the global North, particularly to work with communities in Bradford District.

Gary Saunders is a Criminology Lecturer at the University of Lincoln, UK. Part of Gary's research focuses on teaching and learning in higher education, especially assessment feedback and the design of the learning landscape. He is currently writing up his PhD thesis, 'Re-imaging the idea of the university for a post-capitalist society', which is based on research conducted with education experiments that emerged out of the student protests in 2010 to provide alternative forms of 'higher education'.

Eurig Scandrett is Senior Lecturer and Programme leader in Public Sociology at Queen Margaret University, UK, with research interests in social movement learning in environmental justice struggles. After an initial career as an environmental scientist, he spent fifteen years in adult education and community development, including as Head of Community Action at Friends of the Earth Scotland. He is an active environmentalist and trade union representative, currently co-chair of Friends of the Earth Scotland and the Bhopal Medical Appeal and elected Vice-President for Scotland of University and College Union.

Stevphen Shukaitis is Senior Lecturer at the University of Essex, UK Centre for Work and Organization, and a member of the Autonomedia editorial collective. Since 2009 he has coordinated and edited Minor Compositions (http://www.minorcompositions.info). He is the author of *Imaginal Machines: Autonomy & Self-Organization in the Revolutions of Everyday Day* (2009) and *The Composition of Movements to Come: Aesthetics and Cultural Labor After the Avant-Garde* (2016), and editor (with Erika Biddle and David Graeber) of *Constituent Imagination: Militant Investigations // Collective Theorization* (2007). His research focuses on the emergence of collective imagination in social movements and the changing compositions of cultural and artistic labour.

Joss Winn is Senior Lecturer and Programme Leader in Education at the University of Lincoln, UK. His research focuses on co-operative education, workplace democracy, academic labour and alternative forms of higher education. In 2011, he co-founded the

Social Science Centre, Lincoln, a co-operative for higher education and is a Director of the Lincolnshire Co-operative Development Agency.

Tom Woodin is a reader in the social history of education at the UCL Institute of Education, UK, where he is the programme leader for the History of Education MA. He has written on worker writers and community publishing in the UK since the 1970s and is currently producing on a book on the topic to be published in 2017. He researches co-operation and education and recently edited *Co-operation, Learning and Co-operative Values* (2015) and led a Joseph Rowntree Foundation project on the history of community and mutual ownership which resulted in a report on the topic: http://www.jrf.org.uk/publications/community-mutual-ownership. With Gary McCulloch and Steve Cowan, he wrote *Secondary Education and the Raising of the School Leaving Age – Coming of Age?* (2013). His other research interests include the social history of learning and the history of social and labour movements. He co-edits *History of Education*.

1

Mass Intellectuality and Democratic Leadership in Higher Education

Richard Hall and Joss Winn

Introduction

A series of global economic crises rooted in debt-saturation and the increasing deregulation of globalized financial markets, culminating in the Great Crash of 2008 and persistent stagnation, have formed a critical moment of contention that reframes the role of leadership within the management and governance of higher education (HE). These crises have emerged imminent to the transnational mobility and flexibility of capital, which has subsequently dispersed neoliberal governance models across the globe (Clarke 2005). They have also tended to swamp socio-environmental and sociocultural crises that have disproportionately affected the global South, and which have amplified the impacts of the ongoing coloniality and patriarchy of power.

Collectively, these form an ongoing, transnational crisis of social reproduction that amplify the tensions between leadership both as status (or metaphor) and function, alongside its relationship to vertical and horizontal forms of governance. These tensions have affected responses to the increasingly financialized and marketized idea of HE, which are conditioned by the restructuring of the university as space in which associations of transnational actors have a stake. These actors include finance capital, such as private equity firms and hedge funds, which are leveraging both student and institutional debt, for instance through the issuing of public and private bonds; technology firms and publishers, which are seeking to extract surpluses through a rentier economy; policymakers, who are attempting to reshape the terrain of HE *for-profit*; think tanks and consultancies seeking to widen the space for the market through evidence-based practice; philanthrocapitalists, who use charitable foundations to promote the virtues of the market and entrepreneurial activity to stimulate outcome-based practices; and finally, university senior managers, effectively acting as chief executive officers rather than as *primus inter pares*.

In spite of restructuring, transnational capital has been unable to reassert stable forms of accumulation (Bellamy Foster and Yates 2014; Cleaver 1993). The result has been persistent recession with low levels of growth, weak aggregate demand and high levels of underemployment or unemployment. Beyond the economy, this has amplified social divisions and tensions, including inside the HE sector. Here, antagonistic forces have emerged in opposition to: increased student fees; rising levels of student and institutional debt; increased performance management within and across institutions, through the imposition of teaching and research metrics; a lack of transparency and accountability from managers to the students and academics who labour inside the universities; the corporatization of the university and the diminution of its potential social agenda beyond the market; historic pedagogic practices that emerged from inside the public, liberal university and which are bound up with colonial power; and ideologies of students as purchasers of services (Hall 2015b; Hall and Smyth 2016).

In this context, it is clear that HE is in crisis. The idea of the public university is under assault (Bailey and Freedman 2011), and both the future of the sector and its relationship to society are being gambled (McGettigan 2013). HE is increasingly unaffordable, its historic institutions are becoming untenable, and their purpose is overwhelmingly instrumental. What and who have led us to this crisis? What are the alternatives? To whom do we look for leadership in revealing those alternatives?

This book brings together critical analyses of 'intellectual leadership' inside and outside the university and documents ongoing efforts from around the world to create alternative models for organizing HE and the production of knowledge. Its authors offer their experience and views from inside and beyond the structures of mainstream HE, to reflect critically on efforts to create really existing alternatives. In the process, the book asks whether it is possible to reimagine the university democratically and co-operatively? If so, what are the implications for leadership not just within the university but also in terms of HE's relationship to societies?

The positions taken in the book are plural, emerging from critical feminism and radical pedagogy, alongside the politics of subaltern resistance, as well as from critical theory that is informed by Marxism and anarchism. However, as a whole, the book takes forward a programme that is deliberately counter-hegemonic in conception and theoretical framing. While utilizing a number of different theoretical positions, in its analysis, the book provides a collective voice that calls for a radically different engagement with intellectual leadership. Throughout the book, such an engagement can be categorized politically as being from the left. However, in its intention, the focus of the book is on forms of leadership for social justice and liberation.

Thus, a number of the authors argue that mass HE is at the point where it no longer reflects the needs, capacities and long-term interests of global society. An alternative role and purpose are engaged with critically based upon 'mass intellectuality': the real possibility of democracy in learning and the production of knowledge, including the ways in which we know ourselves and our relationships with others.

Mass intellectuality

Throughout this book, the authors engage with the critical concept of 'mass intellectuality' from multiple perspectives. The origins of the term 'mass intellectuality' can be found within the Autonomist Marxist tradition, building on Marx's notion of the 'general intellect' (Dyer-Witheford 1999; Manzerolle 2010; Marx 1993; Virno and Hardt 1996). Marx (1993: 694) argued that the dynamics of capitalism meant

> the accumulation of knowledge and of skill, of the general productive forces of the social brain, is thus absorbed into capital, as opposed to labour, and hence appears as an attribute of capital, and more specifically of fixed capital [machinery].

Through innovation and competition, the technical and skilled work of the social individual, operating in factories, corporations or schools, is absorbed into the things she produces. Therefore, the 'general intellect' of society, that is, its general capacity for *science* in the broadest sense, is absorbed into capitalized technologies and techniques, to reduce labour costs and increase productivity. As a result, 'the human being comes to relate more as a watchman and regulator to the production process itself' (Marx 1993: 705).

With the crisis of funding, regulation and governance of HE, there is a need to understand: first, the mechanisms through which the general intellect is directed, absorbed or co-opted into the total social production process of value, to which universities contribute; and second, how leadership enables this as 'watchman and regulator', or resists such co-option. Addressing the crisis of HE in this way calls attention to the proliferation of alternative educational practices, which are themselves reimaginings of the idea of the university as a site for the production of knowledge. These alternatives are rooted in the desire and potential for reclaiming the knowledge, skills, practices and techniques that form the general intellect, to produce and circulate new forms of socially useful knowledge or ways of knowing, being in and creating the world. From this reclaiming or liberation of the general intellect, away from the valorization of capital, emerges 'mass intellectuality' as a direct, cognitive and social force of production that exists as an increasingly diffuse form of intellectuality. In this form, it circulates as a 'commons' that is pregnant with critical and practical potential but still remains marginal in the face of general commodity production (Smith 2013). As a result, it is constantly being recuperated by capital in the form of the 'knowledge economy' or 'cognitive capitalism'. Virno (2001) argues:

> Mass intellectuality is the prominent form in which the general intellect is manifest today. The scientific erudition of the individual labourer is not under question here. Rather, all the more generic attitudes of the mind gain primary status as productive resources; these are the faculty of language, the disposition to learn, memory, the power of abstraction and relation and the tendency towards self-reflexivity.

It should be made clear that the concept of mass intellectuality refers to knowledge and forms of knowing that can be and are being valorized by capital, but also refers to that same knowledge's immanent (negative) and prefigurative (positive) critical and reconstructive potential for new forms of sociality. In this way, mass intellectuality implies a struggle over the proletarianization of cognitive and affective forms of labour, and its emancipatory implications, as the embodiment of the cumulative history of science.

An engagement with the concept of mass intellectuality therefore implies a critique of subjectivity, in its relationship to the prevalent mode of (knowledge) production, the institutions where it is sited and the oversight, management and leadership that arises from these spaces. The process of liberating and reclaiming the knowledge, skills, practices and techniques that are produced inside higher educational contexts is central to moving beyond exploitation and valorization in the market, and in creating democratic, co-operative alternatives. As a result, mass intellectuality is an important concept in the critique of existing approaches to intellectual leadership, because it suggests that critical-practical solutions to global, socio-environmental problems need not be framed around economic growth and business-as-usual. It enables a refocusing on the potential for the democratic or co-operative reproduction of the university, and a level of productive, scientific and social knowledge that exists as an immanent, transgressive potential across capitalist societies.

The case studies and models of analysis in this book argue that the democratization of HE as an emancipatory project must reappropriate the means of knowledge production in the labour process (Postone 1993), and engage with leadership models that nurture the co-operation of academic and student scholarship and work. This includes questioning these relationships, alongside the forms of thought and being that they constitute and through which they are constituted. The authors ask: What kind of 'leadership' in the academy and beyond can support the liberation of the general intellect? They question whether the idea and institutions of the university can be freed from the market, to generate the kind of leadership which is self-challenging and capable of enabling the knowledge production process of others. To do the latter, it has to respect the knowledge of others and potential problem-solving through co-production, co-critique and evidential exploration. We argue that society needs 'leaders' who do not seek 'followers', but who are themselves rooted in the philosophy and ethics of mass intellectuality. By uncovering widespread, objective conditions for the alienation of the products and processes of HE from their social utility, this book also identifies the already-existing material conditions for new democratic models of knowledge production and education. It is on the basis of these objective conditions and the potential of this social subjectivity that the authors in this book engage critically with the idea of 'intellectual leadership'.

The literature on academic leadership

The translation of the crisis of capitalism into the terrain of HE has forced the sector to consider its structure and forms, alongside its regulation and governance models, with knock-on implications for leadership, in its dual nature as status and function. Reflecting the outcomes of a global literature review, Dopson et al. (2016: 7) argued that 'the current literature on leadership development approaches in UK [United Kingdom] HE appears small scale, fragmented and often theoretically weak, with many different models, approaches and methods co-existing with little clear pattern of consensus formation'. A central issue is the effect of externalities, such as socio-economic crises and demands for impact, on the ability of institutional and sectoral leaders to develop leadership capacity and capability, for instance through leadership development programmes (Marshall 2012; Pepper and Giles 2015).

For Day et al. (2014) where leadership is instrumentalized as a process that can be measured, using status or position to analyse leadership is problematic, and this may hinder any engagement with uncertainty (Barnett 2012; see also, Evans et al. 2013 for a discussion of leadership issues relating to the professoriate). The response of policymakers and senior staff has been to refocus upon organizational development agendas and performance management, which foreclose on alternative possibilities. In the global North, this has highlighted a disconnect between leading and leadership, precisely because the ideal of the university as a self-critical community of academic and student scholars with high levels of autonomy (Neary and Saunders 2011) is being disciplined by a dominant corporate agenda that incentivizes specific, impactful behaviours (Alvesson and Spicer 2012). There is also a separate question about whether these agendas should be globally generalized and whether binaries about what the university was or might be are culturally relevant.

The literature attempts to interpret the practices of effective leaders. A tension emerges between critical theory and the idea of leadership (Western 2008; Zoller and Fairhurst 2007), especially in relation to ideas of power. One mechanism that has been critiqued in relation to power is the idea that leadership can be exerted in a distributed manner through network governance. For Davies (2011), the idea of the network society is complex and contested and rests on claims about: the inability of effective command management, given the fragmentary nature of capitalist modernity; the decentred opportunities that exist for intersectional interests to challenge hegemonic power and elites; and how ubiquitous communications technology provides an infrastructure for such global connections. These precepts underpin horizontalism, as the belief that we live in a world that can only be understood if we apply network-theoretical, cybernetic concepts (Miller Medina 2005).[1]

However, what emerge are fluidly organized, technology-rich, hegemonic governance networks, rather than new forms of democratic, network governance. As a result, ethical virtues, such as trust and empowered reflexivity, are co-opted by hierarchies for command management and the anti-ethical closure of horizons. Governance becomes based on consent through coercion, and the latter demands forms of performance management and governmentality, for instance in the relentless focus on curriculum performance data or in the production of knowledge transfer (Ball 2009; Davies 2011). The distributed forms of leadership that are claimed through network governance theory (Hoppe and Reinelt 2010; Jarvis et al. 2013; King and Nesbitt 2015) ignore that networks are prone to resolving into hierarchies and incremental closure, that they reproduce and crystallize inequalities and that distrust is common.

The idea that leadership can be cultivated and distributed so that networks can be amplified connects to the entrepreneurial development of leadership as a form of human capital. This risks breeding the idea of the leader as superhero, with identifiable traits capable of generating the space and time for the accumulation of social capital by distributed others (Bolden et al. 2003). The development of coaching and mentoring practices, reflexivity, risk management, ethical leadership and so on, then tend to crystallize the idea that leadership can be instrumentalized (Morrison et al. 2003) and internalized.

Such instrumentalization downplays the gendered and racialized nature of leadership (Avolio et al. 2009) and instead emphasizes: control and transaction; accountability; individual persistence; personal performance management; self-development (rather than collective); psychometric development and so on (Fischer et al. 2015; Simmonds and Tsui 2010; Turnbull and Edwards 2005). In contrast, Deem et al. (2007) have argued for reflective leadership practices that are appropriate to both the management of knowledge workers and the public purpose of the university. The pressures on subjects who are female, feminized and/or racialized, who are attempting to lead in workplaces that have traditionally functioned as white and male, are especially problematic (Gallant 2014; James 2013; Johnson 2015; Loke 2015; Mirza 2015), and signal one of the ways in which leadership may fail to provide solutions to ongoing socio-economic or environmental crises (Bryman 2007).

These tensions reveal a further examination of the boundaries of academic leadership (Bolden et al. 2009; Noble and Pym 1970). One response is to address the scope of academic leadership in terms of citizenship (Bolden et al. 2014), as an attempt to analyse it as a bottom-up process that might become sustainable by starting from established values of collegiality and academic autonomy, rather than fetishizing missions, visions, shared goals and followership. This is important in addressing 'leadership' through the possibilities opened up by 'mass intellectuality' as a reframing of social relationships and processes. The idea of citizenship enables leadership to be analysed as a social process 'in which it is considered to be relationally constructed and embedded within communities' (Bolden et al. 2014: 756).

Thus, it is possible to see leadership as an activity rather than a form of status, and as a deliberative, social service (Macfarlane 2007, 2013) grounded in self-governance, self-regulation and self-directedness. Here, communal rights and responsibilities are immanent to one another, and the health of the organization is strengthened through institutional connections to traditional communities grounded in academic values. As a result, the university might be a site for renewed, collective, civic engagement that is negotiated communally and that may take many forms. For Bolden et al. (2014: 765), this enables individuals 'to recognise their own part within power relationships and find ways of articulating their anxieties about academic life'.

For Alvesson and Spicer (2012), dissolving the boundaries between academic leadership as a process and civil society, in order that crises can more appropriately be addressed, demands new forms of critical performativity. This moves beyond functionalist and interpretive analyses of scientific or socially constructed leadership activities, to reposition them reflexively. The concept of critical performativity questions dominant positions through: circumspect care for the views of those who are leading; progressive pragmatism in working with accepted academic discourses for emancipatory ends and uncovering present potentialities or a sense of what could be (Alvesson and Spicer 2012: 376, 377).

As a result, academic leadership is related to specific local contexts and mindful of the structural limitations of power. This enables critical performative leadership to mitigate the risk that outright resistance to, or rejection of, leadership leads to the further imposition of authority alongside the refusal to countenance democratic organizational engagement. Critical performativity recognizes leadership as a terrain of struggle that reveals and questions established and emergent social relations and forces of production inside the university. It thereby offers the space for alternatives that are co-operative and democratic.

We might then question how academic leadership restructures the everyday educational and pedagogical realities of academics and students. This demands a return to the idea of intellectual leadership as a form of mass intellectuality, to reveal the politicized and elitist (rather than normative or interpretive) nature of academic practices (Kautsky 1903). A further question is whether leadership reflects or reproduces the abstract nature of social relations (Eacott 2013), and how it might be analysed in relation to its concrete contexts, in order that crises of social reproduction might be overcome or addressed at the level of society, rather than in relation to the market. This is the purpose of the chapters that follow.

The structure of the book

Our alternative framing of intellectual leadership emerges through three sections that situate HE against the ongoing crisis of capitalism, with responses to it from inside and outside the university. This articulates the limits of formal HE, including the binaries of public and private, in a range of national contexts. Here, there is a connection to traditions of critical pedagogy in which critical knowing has always been existential, collective and transformative, to challenge the hegemonic framing of learning as separate from society and everyday life. The opening section focuses on *Power, History and Authority* inside formal HE. It asks what and who has led us to this crisis of HE? What forms of resistance are taking place inside the university and how are these being led? This section seeks to situate certain functions of the university against distributed leadership at the level of society, rather than it being rooted in a professional cadre. Stevphen Shukaitis begins this work with an analysis of struggles inside the classroom over the labour of students and academics and the potential responses that are enabled through critical pedagogy. Shukaitis situates this against networked or free labour and enables an exploration of the idea that academic labour becomes a form of self-exploiting entrepreneurship. This in-turn needs critique if the university is to be repurposed for wider, communal benefits. Tom Woodin then situates these emergent realities historically, through the lessons to be taken from the development of co-operative HE. This enables an alternative analysis that emerges from the specific historical context of public versus private educational provision in the UK.

This historical and material focus has implications for academic leadership on a transnational scale, and this is addressed through Mike Neary's analysis of the voices of those who both work inside the university and who have opposed the subsumption of academic labour to financialization and the market. Neary's interviews with those who have demonstrated leadership in resisting the neoliberal restructuring of HE in the global North begin to articulate a theoretical understanding of public intellectualism, as a form of mass intellectuality. To extend this cultural, public intellectual analysis and in similar transnational contexts, Martin Eve then explores the ways in which positive rhetorics and projects that extend the open and public reach of HE research have been recuperated by neoliberal governance systems. By addressing the co-option of open access, the section ends by questioning the societal value of business-as-usual models for public HE, and what forms of leadership practice might enable alternatives to emerge.

The second section examines *Potentialities* for change and radical experiment in various transnational contexts, alongside their ramifications for reimagining leadership as a distributed, democratic activity. This section asks whether it is possible to reimagine the university democratically and co-operatively? If so, what are the implications for leadership not just within the university but also in terms of HE's relationship to society? Joyce Canaan outlines her engagement with Brazilian resistance to extreme neoliberalism in the pedagogic practices of the Landless Movement. She uses this to discuss the impossibility of being an intellectual worker in the neoliberal university and questions whether the concept of mass intellectuality enables a meaningful analysis of democratic leadership outside the global North. The argument then moves to examine social movements rooted in pedagogy, through forms of resistance inside the university. Eurig Scandrett questions the specific, enhancement-driven space of Scottish HE with reference to case studies of environmental justice, resistance to gender-based violence and trades union activity. Scandrett situates the experience of the knowledge worker against that emerging from within social movements, to address the possibilities for alternative forms of leadership.

Developing this approach, the section then looks at the germination of two specific strands of academic leadership as forms of struggle to reclaim HE. In the first, Jenny Pearce engages with strands of mass intellectuality as they emerged historically in Bradford University's Peace Studies curriculum and the CommUNIty project, as they were infused with a material and cultural analysis of sociability in Latin America. In this work, Pearce questions the relationships between academics and social movements, revealed through the curriculum and the possibilities that emerge. Clark and Jackson then develop a theoretical/practical case study grounded in performing arts, which questions the place of HE in the production of artistic and cultural leadership. This analysis develops the meaning and purpose of arts education in its relationship to societal leadership as it emerges in the global North.

The final section is rooted in *Praxis* and looks at practical, alternative initiatives that are rooted in critical pedagogy and physical places beyond the university. It asks whether a focus on mass intellectuality as a form of distributed, democratic leadership enables alternative reimaginings of HE. The section begins with the Birmingham Autonomous University's (BAU) six theses on the collective failings of the hegemonic university, and the possibility that exists for creating a co-operative form of societal engagement. The Birmingham, UK, collective shapes its response as a means of striking against the methodological university. Joel Lazarus then develops an auto-ethnography of an alternative education project in Oxford, UK, which looks at leadership and managerialism, framed by the idea of the organic intellectual in society.

Lazarus uses the experience of the People's Political Economy (PPE) as a case study of what might be achieved.

The wider global and transnational context of resistance to marketization and financialization in HE is then situated against a critique of the Lincoln Social Science Centre, UK, by Gary Saunders. This is an established alternative that offers a means of analysing the governing principles and leadership modes of other, transnational alternatives, to frame questions about their co-operative and democratic, practical and theoretical viability. Tom Henfrey then develops the idea of alternative responses to leadership in the face of global, socio-environmental crises, through an eco-critical, thematic approach to mass intellectuality, rooted in the ethics of environmentalism. This enables the alternatives discussed in this book to connect to a wider environmental and transition/resilience agenda and its relationship to formal HE. The section then concludes with Sara Motta's comparative analysis of indigenous communities and women of colour in the Escuela Política de Mujeres Pazifica (Political School of Pazifica women) in Cali, Colombia, and the Family Inclusion Strategy Hunger (FISH) collective based in the Hunter Valley, Australia. This analysis specifically relates co-operative, inclusive educational practices of creating ourselves, our relationships and communities differently. It challenges the coloniality of knowing-being as it is reproduced in the geopolitics of knowledge production of contemporary capitalism and Higher Education. The potential for mass intellectuality to be decolonized by feminized and racialized subjects on the margins enables a unique analysis of educational leadership that is embedded within political-pedagogical, emancipatory horizons.

Finally, the book is rounded off with an evaluation and systematic critique of the collaborative approach adopted in its production. Gordon Asher analyses the ways in which co-operative writing and publishing inside the university might enable voices to be heard that are against and beyond the valorization of academic labour. Uncovering the production processes of this book and the methods through which its ways of knowing the world are articulated, then becomes a mechanism for analysing the possibility for distributed leadership. Here, co-production, deliberation and negotiation in and through writing are potentially a form of mass intellectuality that affects our perceptions of democratic leadership.

A thematic critique of leadership

These chapters also connect with a series of themes related to the critical study of academic leadership.

The relationship between hegemonic leadership and academic labour

In enabling an exploration of this hegemony, Shukaitis focuses upon the development and management of pedagogical labour, to articulate how education reproduces a specific social field, in particular through free labour and entrepreneurialism. Meanwhile, Neary focuses upon dissent and the articulation of academic freedom that emerges in response to a perceived lack of senior leadership and sector-wide fragmentation. For Eve, this fragmentation is amplified through open access, by corporate finance and the instantiation of capitalist social relations across academia, in his case through the commodity form of research material.

For BAU, the exploitation of academic labour by managers and the potential for engaging in struggles within the university related to overwork are central. This is situated through a project of reimagining independent, working-class education against the methodological university. This is echoed by Lazarus, in his focus on *post*-capitalist, critical HE that can be prefigured in the ends *and* means of public HE projects. Motta problematizes this space of struggle, by asking us to consider who is silenced and who is spoken-for and what kind of knowing-subjectivities are reproduced and curtailed. In attempting to describe this struggle, Clark and Jackson identify how theory relates to practice, and they couple the teaching of technique with both critical thinking and sociocultural awareness.

The realities of hegemonic leadership

For Canaan, there is a risk that the dominant discourses about HE catalyse forms of leadership and governance that 'kettle' or predefine subjectivity. Clark and Jackson analyse this in terms of the development of sites for the production of the 'cultural entrepreneur' or 'artistic leader', as alternatives. Saunders argues that such sites demand new approaches to the university governance, in its structures and organizational cultures, as a response to new public management. This involves a redistribution of power through a negative rather than an affirmational critique that exposes or unmasks elite perceptions.

Alternative models of leadership as forms of counter-hegemony

Shukaitis highlights the importance of articulating multiple positions inside the classroom and enables an appreciation of the impact of pedagogical struggles on normative leadership discourses. This is situated inside the relationship between counter-hegemony and critical pedagogy, as a process of decolonizing the classroom. Neary then describes the relationship between counter-hegemony and public intellectuals, to open up a space to discuss the dualities of abstract/academic and concrete/intellectual. For Canaan, the Brazilian landless movement offers a way to move beyond imposed 'fences', for instance those related to literacy, and to imagine new models for leading. She argues the need to address concrete experiences, rather than to impose abstracted models of leading from the global North.

In terms of developing new forms of leading as a social process, BAU argue for militant research and the importance of workers' enquiry, to nurture the Commons. Both Scandrett and Pearce look at historical and material spaces for resistance that enable the reproduction of liberating praxis in the university. They argue, akin to Canaan and Motta, that these come from the margins and position intellectual leadership in its interface with dialogic emancipatory movements. Where this coalesces, it might start to build a counter-narrative. For Clark and Jackson, this counter-narrative connects to the idea of a suitable 'aesthetic education' and the 'artistic leader', which requires a whole context of critical thinking as its accompaniment.

Lazarus uses the case study of the PPE to link alternative models to social movements and community projects that are engaged in participative action research. Saunders argues that these kinds of methodologies also enact democratic pedagogy and democratic self-organization, which also expose the contradictions of the current model of HE. He positions the Social Science Centre somewhere between reform and revolution, as a moment of popular education that creates the possibility of a social, co-operative university. Henfrey views permaculture as a separate form of popular education with potentially transformative power for formal education and wider society, through its celebration and practical use of diversity. Motta uses the examples of FISH and the Escuela, as social movements that are committed to practices of epistemological prefiguration, to expose the epistemological blindness of coloniality reproduced in the concept of Mass Intellectuality itself.

The attributes of counter-hegemonic leadership

Neary argues that intellectual leadership and public intellectualism are moments of resistance to dominant forms of cultural conformity among academics. He positions this against the efficacy of student protest, to develop the idea of public intellectuality. For Eve, this work rests on ideas of co-production and the mutual harnessing of intellectual labour, while for Scandrett, the experience of engagement with social movements promotes dialogic characteristics in leading problem-solving. From these different contexts, there emerges a moment of leadership, rather than a focus on leaders, that is rooted in a critique of consent through conflict.

Pearce also highlights the importance of academics contributing to a process that aspires to generate democratic exchange between the academy and the community. This is a form of experimentation with 'horizontal' rather than 'higher' education. The BAU's theses connect to this idea of democratic exchange through mutual recognition, good conversation and practical reflexivity, as the basis for a new 'sensibility'. Such reflexivity underpins Henfrey's focus on highly distributed and networked contributions to communal educational projects. This collective work questions the methods and institutional forms that are appropriate, and is a moment of subversion in developing and operating alternatives with explicit ethical roots. Motta also sees a commitment to deep epistemological listening that implies a disruption of the established coloniality of knowing. Storytelling using multiple literacies forms a part of this and can be an active process of developing subjectivity and critical epistemological practice that is transformative.

Articulating the problems with alternative forms of leadership

Shukaitis argues that there is a tendency towards the gifting of free labour across networks based on distributed leadership, such that individuals become self-exploiting. Pearce situates her analysis of CommUNIty around the tensions that exist in the multiple motivations, expectations and backgrounds of participants. These are heightened through the subjective effects of the prevailing knowledge production system, which can be both empowering and disempowering. She argues for an 'articulating movement' that can acknowledge and repurpose the knowledge that emerges from experience. For Lazarus and Saunders, sustaining alternatives is impeded by the very foundational constituents of capitalist reality – space, money, personal energy and particularly time.

Contradictions in developing mass intellectuality as form of resistance

For Scandrett, mass intellectuality emerges through resistance-as-praxis. This is especially important because in the ongoing crisis, universities are spaces in which the structural contradictions of neoliberal capital are so explicitly being played out. Clark and Jackson see one response as being a return to curricula and practices that stress the underlying features of human perceptive capability. For Lazarus, meaningful engagements with crisis lie beyond the simple emancipation of academic labour, since intellectuality is a component of all labour and of all humanity. He argues that the democratization of the general intellect necessitates the cultivation of mass intellectuality across society.

Eve argues that capitalism transforms academic labour into productive labour, and that any democratic hopes for open access tend to be subsumed by its co-option and recuperation, for instance inside systems of individualized incentivization. In Lazarus's terms, this opens up the immanent contradiction between *mass* intellectuality as a useful form of practice and *higher* education as a positional good with exchange-value. Canaan and Motta argue that the concrete contexts that generate new forms of human capacity and collective agency need to be viewed from the perspective of the global South. Motta also argues that new emancipatory subjects emerge out of the historic and contemporary experiences in which they are produced as the non-subjects of modernity. Their critique as living and lived praxis thus decentres the knowing-subjectivity enmeshed within the public university, opening our horizons to other onto-epistemological visions of mass intellectuality.

Our final, crucial question for academics and students who labour inside the university then becomes, what is to be done? Neary argues for a new form of higher learning that emerges out of the negative dysfunctionality of the capitalist university. He asks 'what do we wish for?' and this forces us to consider how the corporate university disables self-direction and self-governance. Motta wishes to see emerge the conditions for participants' reoccupation of their colonized selves, as the space from which decolonizing emancipatory practices of mass intellectuality might flourish. She argues however that these experiences, also, shine a light on the ways in which we are all wounded in differentiated ways by coloniality and thus open possibilities for alternative intellectual practices more generally. Pearce shapes her answer to this through shared and co-operative 'public' spaces and forms of provision, which align with the BAU demand for the abolition of the methodological university. Both Lazarus and Saunders situate such an abolition against the generation of a social, co-operative university. This is a space that serves a democratic, emancipatory agenda, rooted in collective ownership and co-operative participatory governance. This is founded on a radical reconceptualization of labour.

Institutionalizing democratic leadership

We conclude this chapter by addressing the 'crucial question' posed by the book ourselves: What is to be done? One critical response discussed in some of the chapters and already found in both the global North and global South focuses on the co-operative. This is a constitutionally democratic organizational form with a long history in progressive international politics and that holds education as one of its core principles. Since the mid-nineteenth century, 'Co-operators' have built a worldwide social movement of member-led organizations based on the common ownership of property and its democratic governance (Yeo 1988). Education has always been a core principle, alongside open membership, autonomy and independence, solidarity with other co-operatives and concern for community. The internationally agreed co-operative values are self-help, self-responsibility, democracy, equality, equity and solidarity (MacPherson 2007).

Since 2010, a growing body of research into co-operative HE (Winn 2015a) has emerged that points to three routes to a 'co-operative university': first, the formal *conversion* of existing universities into co-operatives through legal and constitutional means; second, the *dissolution* of our institutions into de facto co-operatives by constituting research centres as co-operatives, embedding co-operative values and principles into institutional strategies and leadership roles, establishing taught programmes of study along co-operative values and principles and so on; and third, the *creation* of new co-operative forms of HE alongside the existing system of universities. Whichever route that might be opted for – and we should pursue them all – there are no quick fixes. Co-operatives are not a panacea for the forces of neoliberalism or the personal ambitions of some academics, managers and administrators. However, there are deep historical and social resources to draw upon within the co-operative movement that can help us rethink the way our universities are run, the institutional form that they take and the nature and role of leadership within a democratic organization.

Critics of the 'co-operative university' might question our commitment to the idea of the 'public university'. Indeed, co-operatives are antithesis, but they also exceed the idea of 'public ownership' with that of 'common ownership', a social form of property that is the anti-thesis of the right of free alienability which distinguishes capitalist private property. In short, co-operative HE is entirely compatible with the idea of the 'public' if we reconceive it as a 'commons': an academic commons, democratically controlled by academic and support staff, students and others.

Although the co-operative form of member-owned and democratically controlled organization has historically been adopted primarily for the benefits of an exclusive single member type (e.g. workers or consumers), a more recent form of co-operative that is becoming widely adopted around the world is that of 'social co-operatives' (also called 'solidarity' or 'multi-stakeholder' co-ops). This historically recent form of association emerged in the 1970s has been gradually obtaining legal status in different nation states. In 2011, the 'World Standards of Social Co-operatives' was ratified after a two-year global consultation process. We emphasize that this is a new form of association, one that was not available to the founders of most twentieth-century universities. To-date, the best example is Mondragon University in the Basque region of Spain, where its membership is comprised of workers (academics and non-academic employee-owners), students and 'collaborators' (members of the community, local business, etc.). In its current form, Mondragon University, which is in fact a 'co-operative of co-operatives', itself only dates back to 1997. Each of its four Faculties is an autonomous co-operative with elected positions of leadership that represent the democratically determined interests of their organization's members (Wright et al. 2011).

According to the World Standards of Social Co-operatives, there are five defining characteristics of social co-operatives, at the heart of which is the multi-stakeholder membership structure. Each of the stakeholder groups is formally represented in the governing structures of the organization on the basis of one-person one-vote. The multiple forms of membership reflect the combined interests of the organization within its social context and not surprisingly, such co-operatives typically pursue social objectives through the provision of social services, such as healthcare and education. For example, since 2011, over 850 schools in the UK have become multistakeholder co-operatives, following other countries where co-operative schools already exist (Woodin 2015). This particular model of democratic ownership and governance is an increasingly popular form of co-operative organization with successful examples of different sizes and services being provided, demonstrating its flexibility as a modern organizational form (Ridley-Duff and Bull 2014).

The literature on university governance in the UK shows clearly that a number of incremental policy changes have led to a more hegemonic corporate form of university governance: first, the Jarratt report (1985), which established the Vice Chancellor as Chief Executive; second, the Dearing report (1997), which reduced the number of members on the governing body; and third, the Lambert report (2003), which stated that participatory governance by a community of scholars was not 'fit for modern times' and recommended a voluntary code of governance for the HE sector (Shattock 2006; 2008). Each of these government-sponsored reviews and subsequent policy and regulatory changes has been conducted in response to the changing historical development of the corporate form in general, most notably the Cadbury report (1992), the Hampel report (1998), the Higgs report (2003) and the development of the current UK Corporate Governance Code (Shattock 2006). Thus, a history of the development of the university governance and management has to be seen in the broader context of changing corporate forms and the underlying dynamic of political, economic and social contradictions. The intellectual and academic leadership that arises from and is supported by the particular corporate form of the university is similarly affected by the changing nature of the body corporate. Hence, it is no surprise that with the changing corporate form of the university, academic leadership itself becomes morphed into more managerial and entrepreneurial forms. The university as a social and institutional form demands it.

As many of the chapters in this volume indicate, a critique of intellectual leadership in HE also implies a critique of its corporate (i.e. organizational) form. As a historically new form of institutional governance, the 'social co-operative' appears to be compatible with traditional collegial structures (Cook 2013) and speaks to many of the concerns raised over increased corporate governance structures and hierarchical management of universities (Bacon 2014) by providing an alternative for existing governors, academics and students to consider. It also has much to commend for more radical, popular and community-based forms of education. As all the chapters argue, we need to encourage a different way of thinking about the role, value and form of HE institutions in society. Such thinking is not as 'public' or 'private' forms of HE, but as 'social' organizations sustained through solidarity and co-operation among their members. To address this, one task is to compare forms of governance and leadership in both HE and social co-operatives and use this learning as a stimulus for critical reflection on the practical and contemporary issue of democracy in HE. Such a task does not address the wide range of critical issues highlighted in this book, but a better understanding of practices that create and sustain co-operative organizations could support the critical, intellectual forms of association that are discussed throughout.

Note

1 The theoretical lineages of horizontalism are multiple and emerge from positions, places and times that are exterior to the traditional centres of global power (the periphery), as well as from immateriality and the centre.

Part One

Power, History and Authority

2

Pedagogical Labour in an Age of Devalued Reproduction

Stevphen Shukaitis

While Bill Hicks is often remembered as a comedic genius, he is much less commonly thought of as a pedagogical thinker, labour theorist or management guru. Despite that, there are moments in his dark humour where he points to key issues for these areas. For instance, describing his experience a night after a performance (2001), Hicks finds himself eating in a waffle house, where he is reading a book. While waiting for his food, Hicks is interrupted first by someone who declares, 'Well look here we have ourselves a reader', and then a question from the waitress, 'What are you reading for?' Hicks is perplexed by this, responding that while he's used to being asked *what he is reading* he's stumped by the question *what is he reading for*. After taking a second to respond, he answers that one of the reasons he's reading is so that he doesn't end up as a waitress in a waffle house.

True, this is a joke, but, carrying on in a long satirical tradition, Hicks diagnoses what is one of the key contradictions of academic labour today, particularly for academic workers who think of themselves as encouraging skills of critical reflection and engagement as part of their pedagogical practice. What does Hicks' answer to the question really say? Basically, his reply is founded on the notion that he is engaging in reading, or one might say in a broader sense in education, so that he is not caught working in a low-waged job with little prospects for promotion, higher pay, job security and so forth. In short, Hicks here responds that what he is doing is part of gaining some form of social advancement. But in responding this way Hicks, unfortunately, is not indicating that he is taking up a position of leading the struggle for better access to education or social advancement, but rather that his actions are based on a personal investment in the future. This is an understandable and long-standing trope, one that underlies much of the rise of the university in the post–Second World War era as a mass experience, namely that education is a pathway to material security and advancement out of the working conditions of low-waged, industrial capitalism. But is this the case today, if indeed it ever was? There are likely to be multiple issues this anecdote points towards, but I use it as an introduction to thinking about the relation between pedagogical practice and a broader sense of the labour process. This starts from the realization that students are already workers. It is this pedagogical labour, both of students and teachers, that has been devalued as the social contract reframed it as a matter of personal investment rather than as a social good. If there is to be a critical pedagogy for today that is worthy of the name then it must start from examining the relationship between mass intellectuality in the labour market and the devaluation of education as a form of social reproduction.

Learning to Labour, labour of learning

Paul Willis, in his classic book *Learning to Labour* (1982), describes the way that it is precisely the rejection of education by working-class British lads that slots them into their continued role as future factory workers. By refusing to engage with the knowledges and skills developed within education, and the concomitant opportunity for advancement this offered, the lads refusal means that they have little other choice than taking the low-skilled, low-paying factory jobs (ironically enough the very jobs that would shortly be disappearing in the rise of post-Fordist capitalism). But this is not to blame them, as much as that might appear to be the argument developed at first glance. What Willis makes clear is that it is hard to imagine how such working-class students would choose otherwise, or more precisely why they would want to. This is due to the heavily class-structured nature of the educational system, one that is based around a certain kind of class elitism about what constitutes the proper objects of knowledge and their study, and all that goes along with this formation. Willis is arguing that the very habitus of the working-class lads is such that *not to refuse* the opportunity for advancement through education would precisely be a betrayal of the working-class community from which they come; a betrayal of the bonds of solidarity and community in which they are formed.

What we see here is a kind of refusal of pedagogical labour and of academic achievement, which ends up forming the lads for their place in the working of the economy. Why engage in this working upon yourself, this attempt to improve your condition through educational labour, if it means betraying where you came from? In short, it still ends up reproducing the class relationship. One of the interesting dynamics that emerges here, despite Willis' attention to the relationship between education and labour more generally, is the way that they are still conceived of as separate spheres. Students are students precisely because they are not yet workers. That is a role they are being trained for in the future. This goes along with the assumed sharp division in knowledge and planning formed the assumed operating format of Fordism: Management held the knowledge and planned; workers executed the tasks set for them. Conversely, today within the conditions of post-Fordist flexible labour, such a distinction breaks down precisely because of the rise of mass intellectuality (as explored in this book), which Paolo Virno describes as 'not so much a specific stratum of jobs, but more a quality of post-Fordist labour power' (1996: 193). While it is debatable whether these spheres were ever separate, or whether the division of planning and execution was ever that clear, today these realms have blurred into each other. If Willis were to be studying such lads today he would find that they are already immersed in the flows of ideas, practices and labours happening within the dispersed networks of the digital economy that their future managers are enmeshed in as well, even if from different positions within them.

As both Marc Bousquet (2008) and the EduFactory Collective (2009) observe in reflections of social struggles in the classroom, there are also strains of thought that understand this relationship between labour and pedagogy differently, arguing not that students are training to become workers, but that they already are workers. While Bousquet does not draw explicitly on the autonomist traditions or concepts of mass intellectuality in framing it this way, his arguments make similar points. This is both in the more literal sense (students, particularly within university settings, are already working part-time or even full-time jobs), but also that that there is labour involved in taking part in an educational process; labours that in various ways are integral to the working of the economy in a more general sense. This mirrors certain approaches to understanding the labour of teachers, particularly coming out of the Marxist tradition, that argue that their labour is not directly productive of value for capital. Thus, the labours of education might indeed be understood as part of training future workers, but they are not an integral part of the circuits that constitute the economy proper.

While this might seem a rather abstract point to work from, it is important on several counts. What this line of thought points towards is the way that both students and teachers are engaged in what can be described as a circuit of reproductive labour. Education is a form of reproductive labour in how it is integral to the reproducing of the social field. It is this wealth of sociality that is broken down by neoliberalization, as education is shifted from being understood as part of renewing the fabric of society, as a collective gain, to being that of individual investments and benefits. Bill Hicks seems agreeable to getting ahead of menial labour through educational advancement, while Willis' lads end up exhibiting a more advanced degree of class consciousness precisely through their rejection of it.

The argument about the productivity of that reproductive labour becomes crucial in how it provides a way for thinking about a common and shared condition, a similarity across the places occupied by students and teachers. This is important for identifying a common ground or space from which to work in the educational process. As David Harvie argues, it is quite common for teachers to regard the labour they are engaged in as 'a "natural" part of themselves' (2006: 9). Similarly, it is quite possible for students to regard the labours they are involved in as students, or to support their existence as students, as part of forming themselves as future subjects who are capable of achieving forms of social recognition. In both cases our perception of these labours is that they are individualized, and separate from broader economic questions. This prevents us from connecting our understanding of these practices across multiple contexts. They are regarded as individual investments rather than as common conditions that can be struggled over or transformed through common effort.

Here we can see parallels with the analysis put forward by autonomist and socialist feminists, arguing the assumptions that certain forms of labour are not actually labour. If there are forms of labour, that as Harvie suggests, mean teachers regard their work as part of themselves, then this is even more the case for reproductive and care work. This is traditionally gendered as a feminine task that is part of their being, that is to say as part of the feminine condition, rather than as a form of work to be undertaken (Dalla Costa and James 1972; Malos 1980). This gives the context that a movement such as Wages for Housework had to start from, that all the work involved in domestic labour was in fact work at all, but rather a naturalized part of the feminine condition (Weeks 2011). As Silvia Federici (1980) has argued putting forth a demand for wages for housework then was not necessarily one that aimed to actually accomplish its stated goal, but rather was a strategic framework that made these labours visible and thus possible to struggle over, in an attempt to refuse and reduce such work rather than to embrace it.

But let us now rise to the concrete, namely the way that thinking of the multiple positionalities within pedagogic labour creates a space for engagement. Or perhaps more fittingly how not thinking through these issues prevents the emergence of a shared engagement around them. This has been my most common experience, and precisely why I have been reflecting upon these concerns in such a fashion. The implicit assumption that carries through in relating to students is that they are not workers. This is meant not just in a conceptual sense, but also literally. Take for instance how much time it is assumed that students have to engage in study outside of the classroom setting. If the student is enrolled within a full-time programme, there are certain allocations of hours that are expected of them in terms of time spent on that programme. I would argue that if one were to assign an amount of reading or work that took the given allocation of time seriously, it would easily result in the crafting of assignments that would likely not be followed anywhere near the level expected. The students simply would not accept it.

Rather there is something of informal levels of expectations regarding workloads and what can be expected from both students and teachers that emerge through a constant push and pull of demand and response. These are the struggles of the classroom that David Harvie discusses in relation to the value they produce. But this value is not to be realized by a proclaimed or implicit leadership which is uniquely skilled to harvest it, rather it is held in common through the productivity of common labours. The value produced in these classroom struggles emerges not from a preset plan, but rather from the social wealth of what Stefano Harney and Fred Moten theorise as the 'undercommons' (2013) The difficulty is that this often does not find formal acknowledgement, except in instances where something intervenes formally to acknowledge different situations (for instance, in the filing of an extenuating circumstances). The problem is that, if there still exists the shared fiction of a certain level of conditions and expectations, it becomes hard to engage with the reality of how things are actually working on the ground. This has been very much my experience when I discuss with students the conditions they find themselves in, and often how they are finding it difficult to cope with their workload, precisely because of having to manage other commitments of work, family and life more generally. In short, figuring how to balance other commitments is not optional.

In the UK, this is a condition that has been intensified with the introduction of tuition fees in recent years. This is also frequently paired with the realization that all the energy that is being put forth to attaining a degree might not actually translate into the kinds of security or stability that it did previously. To borrow an argument from 'Communique from an Absent Future,' a pamphlet from student protests in California:

> We work and we borrow in order to work and to borrow. And the jobs we work toward are the jobs we already have. Close to three quarters of students work while in school, many full-time; for most, the level of employment we obtain while students is the same that awaits after graduation. (Research and Destroy 2009: 8)

Students realize that they're working towards what could end up being the same crappy jobs they already have rather than 'advancing' in any meaningful sense. It could be argued that the debt produced by education is just as much a part of fitting the student into a larger labour process than the content of the education they are receiving. If before students invested themselves (in multiple registers) in the promise of education to escape from dead-end jobs and livelihoods, today's lesson is that this guarantee is off, and instead they face a potential lifetime of debt just in order to 'run in place' in the work they already find themselves. In this sense, what we have seen is a shift in how pedagogical labour functions as a form of social reproduction. Rather than building an informed citizenry, or perhaps more glibly an educated elite, as the previous model of liberal education aspired to do, what we see today is the rise of a 'pedagogy of debt' (Williams 2009). As a result, students and faculty are schooled in the devaluation of their labours as anything other than forms of personal investment and educational entrepreneurialism, with all the associated risks shifted onto themselves.

Network culture and labour pedagogies

In considering the relation between labour and pedagogy, it is important to note that while the institutional space in which formalized teaching occurs is indeed a prime space for how that relation is formed, it is far from the only one. This is what Tiziana Terranova (2004) points towards in her exploration of labour involved in the functioning of what she describes as 'network culture'. For Terranova this means that various information technologies, from mass media to the Internet, interactive and participatory media, have congealed together into one integrated media system. This is not necessarily a new argument in itself. What is unique about the angle Terranova takes is in arguing that such an integrated network culture can only function through an immense supply of the 'free labour' of participation, which can range anywhere from the building of websites and running of listservs, to generating content through social networking sites, to writing open source code. While Terranova was writing before the rise of web 2.0 to hegemonic cultural status, the argument she makes about the forms of labour necessary to sustain it is prescient. Terranova's analysis thankfully does not simply say that interactive media is run on exploited labour and therefore is bad in some sort of reductionist manner. Rather she is quite careful to point out the ambivalent nature of such activities, how they are willingly taken on and enjoyed, but also exploited.

It is precisely this ambivalent nature of free labour that is integral to the devaluing of education as social reproduction. If people are always already involved in the production of culture, ideas and images, why bother to train them for it, especially if they're willing to pay for the privilege? Education might have previously been thought of as a form of social development, as a marker of progress, but today it functions more as a kind of what Stefano Harney (2002) describes as state work, or the labours of governance that hold together culture and production. For Harney this state work is

> at once the domination of the general intellect by capital and the place to find the trail of a mass intellectuality that is the basis for social cooperation within capital's governmentality... [it] has become an attempt to organize the 'raw material' of what Maurizzio Lazzarato calls immaterial labor. That raw material was subjectivity. (2002: 21)

Thus, one could say that the vast majority of university students entering the college classroom today have been engaged in some form of labour, even if they have never held a waged job, precisely because of the ubiquity of these modalities of free work in media networks and communication. They are always already enmeshed in state work as they mould their subjectivity according to the needs of post-Fordist capitalism, self-organizing and producing without being commanded, being invested in their own self-production with no guarantees attached. But what is interesting about this is that these are precisely the forms of labour that are least recognized as labour. I have found this quite often in discussing the dynamics of network culture and media labour in the classroom. In particular, students are quite hesitant, and even resistant, to thinking about these forms of interaction as work. Perhaps, it is that they would prefer to keep thinking of them as play, or as pleasurable activities, so as not to have to think about them as work. But that has the interesting effect that a good portion of how students come to experience themselves as workers is not recognized as such and cannot be because of the combination of those activities not being understood as labour, and students not being understood as workers. The sociologist and pedagogical theorist Stanley Aronowitz (1983) has made a similar argument about the role of mass media in blocking off spaces for critical reflection about the conditions in which we find ourselves. For Aronowitz, this constitutes 'the major event of social history in our time' (1983: 468). Given when Aronowitz was writing, we could argue that the intensification of media flows that Terranova describes only intensifies this same dynamic.

Educational theorist Peter McLaren argues that critical pedagogy should become a strategic and empowering response 'to those historical conditions which have produced us as subjects, and to the ways we are inserted on a daily basis into the frontier of popular culture and existing structures of power' (1995: 21). Popular culture in this sense can be quite ambivalent, providing space for contestation and the maintenance of hegemony. But this approach too reaches a limit that one chafes against, and this is precisely the kind of limit formed by the pedagogy of a networked labour that disguises itself. Or perhaps, it does not really disguise itself per se, as students will often admit in discussion that there is a good deal of sense in

Terranova's case, but nevertheless they would prefer not to think about it that way. Perhaps, students' refusals to see themselves as labourers, and their free and enjoyed participation in networks of free labour as labour, is precisely because to think about the exploited element contained within it strips them of the agency and enjoyment they currently take from it.

This points towards what my teaching experience also highlights as a key concern, although one that can often be the most difficult, namely getting students to reflect critically on their own position, not just in the present, but also what they aspire to, what they desire, and why they desire what they desire. One of the difficulties in adopting a critical approach to the subject matter in question is how this can in itself be taken by the students as 'a threat to their general ideological commitments. Critical pedagogy becomes, for many students, an uncomfortable and self-contesting exercise' (McLaren 1995: 19). While McLaren's take on this fits with some experiences I have had in the classroom, it is perhaps also as much wrong as it is correct. What McLaren is arguing here is that critical educational approaches are threatening to the student's ideological commitments. However, I have found this to be less the case. My classroom experience has been marked less by students clinging to an ideological attachment to any particular relationship to business or management. Rather they are threatened where they fear a critical angle that will undercut the prospects they have for a future becoming of their labour and living conditions. This is indeed a version of what McLaren calls a 'self-contesting exercise' but not the exercise that McLaren describes. The attachment exhibited by students in my experience has not been of an ideological nature and for that reason cannot be engaged with as an ideological question. It is not the case that once the student has been informed, and thus relieved of their 'false consciousness', they will be relieved of this condition. Rather it is this orientation to a self-in-potential becoming operational at an affective level, which amplifies the student's experience of wanting to become more capable of acting in the world. For McLaren, it is precisely the task of critical pedagogy as a form of intellectual labour that can have transformative effects by enabling a deconstruction of these affective investments. This is, as McLaren himself admits, a challenge for critical pedagogy that is 'a daunting one at this time of historical amnesia' (1995: 25)

Pedagogy of the imagination

To conclude, let's return to Bill Hicks. In the anecdote I opened with Hicks points to very much the question I wanted to think through, this relation between what one actually reads and thinks for, and how this relates to pedagogy and labour. Hicks thinks that he's reading so that he can achieve a better and more secure standard of living. And the rise of mass education and support for it has been underpinned by much of the same sentiment, although it is questionable whether this will continue to be the case in the future. But in this anecdote, Hicks also hints at another problem that is important to thinking through my practice. In his trope of the 'flying saucer tour', Hicks is playing on a common cultural trope of the southern United States being filled with people who are too stupid to know better, are culturally backward, and generally idiotic: in short an area filled with *hicks*. As Hicks description goes on, he makes a joke about someone who would show up to a UFO landing with a shotgun. For Hicks, this is the height of stupidity, the idea that when truly encountering the Other the only way to do so in by bringing along one's weapons, perhaps desiring to treat it as some sort of intergalactic skeet shoot. The problem here is that Hicks is engaging in the same process of Othering the people in the waffle house that he is mocking in their behaviour. The population who abide in the territory covered in this flying saucer tour might be suggested not to know how to relate to an alien intelligence other than with the protection of their shotguns, but arguably Hicks is no more capable of meeting and appreciating the terrestrial life that actually is directly in front of him.

When we laugh with Hicks, when we laugh at the people in the waffle house, this risk is recreating the kind of division and preventing a space of engagement. Perhaps, the question for Hicks would have been how to laugh with the people he met in the waffle house rather than laughing at them. Perhaps the neoliberal restructuring of social relations acts to make this change in perspective seem impossible. If so what would the method of intervention be, pedagogical or otherwise, to reverse these transformations? It is very much a form of what Chela Sandoval (2000), taking up the work of Paulo Freire, talks about as methodology of the oppressed, or 'a set of processes, procedures and technologies for decolonizing the imagination' (1970: 69). In this context, the imagination to be decolonized is the imagination that cannot perceive the forms of labour that form it as labour, or to recognise the intelligence held by students who hold on to such position precisely because it is in the interest of their self-conceptions to do so.

A postcolonial education, one that would exist in and after this liberation of the imagination, would help in the education of what Cornel West calls 'a new kind of cultural worker' capable of exercising a 'politics of difference' that will enable students to 'interrogate the ways in which they are bound by certain conventions and to learn from and build on these very norms and models' (1990: 107). This is precisely what I've been trying to think through in this chapter. In that sense, I would agree with Peter McLaren when he suggests that the role of critical pedagogy is not to work toward some grand and pregiven ideologically endpoint but rather to 'to explore other models of sociality and self-figuration that go beyond dominant language formations and social organisations' (1995: 225). Where this actually ends up is hard to say exactly, but this is precisely the point. In the same way that the challenge for Bill Hicks is to find it within himself to appreciate the intelligence of those around him on his UFO tour as he can for the possible existence of extraterrestrial intelligence, this approach to critical pedagogy and its labour is based around keeping open a relationship to possible futures that emerge within the classroom, whatever they may be.

3

Co-operation, Leadership and Learning: Fred Hall and the Co-operative College before 1939

Tom Woodin

The Co-operative College, established in 1919, provided a model for other co-operative colleges around the world. In Britain, it was, and remains, a unique organization with links to a democratic movement of consumer co-operatives (on the wider movement see Gurney 1996; Wilson et al. 2013). For the interwar period, the 'College' was a partial realization with classes being run out of the Co-operative Union in Manchester, which was the central democratic arena for the movement. The project was led by Fred Hall, adviser of studies at the Union from 1914 (Bellamy and Saville 1972: 145–148). Following the Second World War, the movement purchased Stanford Hall, a country house which became the home of the College until it was sold in the early twenty-first century at which time it returned to Manchester. Concentrating upon the early years of the College helps us to understand the complex role of leadership within a working-class movement. The work of Hall illustrates opportunities and difficulties of operating with an alternative vision of education for social change.

The College was formed at a time of educational ferment when there was a growing interconnection between the working-class movement and the universities. From the late nineteenth century, new universities were developing in major cities while Oxford and Cambridge had nurtured university extension and tutorial classes arranged with the Workers Educational Association (WEA). The co-operative movement (or 'co-op') had helped to initiate university extension and hosted extension lectures. Many co-operators were also involved in the WEA, not least its founder, Albert Mansbridge, who had worked for the Co-operative Wholesale Society (CWS). New areas of research and courses of study were developed but, ultimately, the pre-eminence of the Oxbridge system was defended with adult education kept at bay, as 'extra-mural', beyond the walls (Goldman 1995).

The process of change in academic knowledge finds parallels today, most obviously with the idea that contemporary social issues require an interdisciplinary approach. One such area also in need of attention is the history, theory and practice of co-operation which does not easily fit into traditional subject boundaries. Since the 2008 financial crisis and ensuing period of austerity, co-operative ideas and educational initiatives have been re-evaluated. This can be seen in work being done on co-operative higher education (Winn 2015a; Yeo 2014), and most visibly with the mushrooming of co-operative schools of which, by 2016, there were over 800 in existence. These schools have asserted the relevance of co-operative values and principles as an alternative to the current educational framework (Woodin 2015, 2017). Moreover, the present context provides an opportune moment to examine historical examples of higher education and leadership. Internationally, universities are in a state of flux and have become sites where learning and knowledge are actively contested. In Britain, the division with further education has become blurred as this 'Cinderella' service has been colonized by universities (Wolf 2015: 74). At the same time, commercialism, differentiation and marketization have entrenched wider social divisions into the sector.

Emergence

The roots of the co-operative movement stretch back to the early nineteenth century, at a point when liberal economics was spreading its wings. From the 1840s, the consumer co-operative movement witnessed almost uninterrupted growth in terms of both business turnover and membership. By the turn of the century, there were just under 1,500 independent co-operative societies while membership had grown to three million by 1914 and, on paper, eight million by 1939. The Co-operative College itself would arise out of a broad range of educational activities. For instance, a number of journals were published both nationally and locally by individual societies including the *Co-operative News* (weekly circulation over 100,000), the *Co-operative Educator* (circulation around 6,000), and the *Wheatsheaf* (circulation in the hundreds of thousands). Young people were catered for through groups such as the Woodcraft Folk and British Federation of Co-operative Youth as well as publications, story books and junior classes on co-operation. For adults, classes and examinations were held on the history of co-operation, economics of co-operation, industrial history and more. Employees benefitted from technical and vocational learning (Vernon 2011). In addition, the co-op became an early innovator in correspondence courses for their dispersed membership and, at one point, all courses were available to be studied in this way (Hall 1928: 10). For much of the period, over 50,000 students were enrolled upon Co-operative Union courses each year. Formal classes were complemented with a range of informal educational activities, and social events for families, often with entertainers and speakers, after were a regular feature of most societies. In addition, the Women's Co-operative Guild was a hive of learning and campaigning on issues such as maternity.

As this structure was built, co-operators turned to the question of higher education. Ideas for a co-operative college had been simmering for some time and stretched back to the Owenites, such as William Pare. Edward Owen Greening proposed a co-operative university at the 1905 Conference at Stratford while co-operators held meetings with universities and sat on various committees. In 1912–1913, Hall and others established the College Herald Circle with the intention to create a college. Their enthusiasm emerged out of various weekend and summer schools that brought together like-minded people in an intellectual and social milieu conducive to the development of co-operative ideas. Summer schools had proved an effective means of harnessing both 'formal instruction' as well as 'informal talks ... on the walks, on the picnics, at the dining-table, and in the innumerable talks in the little groups that form...' (Hall 1915: 4). Moreover, the college idea met with sympathy from the wider movement. In 1912, Hall read a paper on the formation of a co-op college and, in 1914, the Union organized a conference on the subject and passed a supportive resolution. Following the War, in 1919, the Co-operative Congress passed two resolutions in favour of a college, requesting that societies contribute to a fund of £50,000. It was envisaged that the college would serve as an apex organization for the diverse range of co-operative activity. It would provide leadership and guidance and be 'a crowning piece for our educational edifice' (Hall 1923a: 8)

> Such a college would be the headquarters of the educational life of the movement; and its academic and ethical centre. It would give greater vitality to all our class work as well as to the less formal educational work of the Guilds and fellowship branches. We provide elementary classes for juniors; we provide more advanced classes for adults and the Co-operative College is needed to complete the scheme.... (Hall 1919: 4)

It was affirmed that the college was to provide 'a centre for higher education in the specialized subjects required for the full equipment of the co-operator and the further development of efficiency in the Co-operative Movement' (*College Herald* 1916: 2). Structure, specialization and 'efficiency', a keyword of the early twentieth century, were evident in co-operative thought as they were in the educational zeitgeist of the time.

There were attempts to make the proposed college a war memorial. During the war, the movement had been marginalized by the joint power of the state and capitalist business which was a major reason behind the formation of the Co-operative Party. The Walsall Society resolution to Congress held that 'no worthier memorial of the Peace and of those co-operators who have served and fallen in the war could be established than an institution for the dissemination of the principles of co-operation and harmony in industrial and international relationships' (Hall 1918a: 8; Walsall Co-operative Society 1919: 46–47). Indicative of co-operative thinking, the 'Peace' was capitalized while the 'war' remained in lower case. However, co-operators were also engaged in hard-headed business and the attempt to create an educational memorial was not completely successful. Subsequently, the slump in trade during the 1920s led to the suspension of the appeal for funds (Hall 1928: 6–7). Nevertheless, the College was started by following 'an evolutionary method' with classes at Holyoake House in Manchester while a hostel was acquired which could house up to forty students (Co-operative Congress 1919: 4).

The perceived need for a college derived from the nature of co-operative education itself which did not fit easily into existing divisions of knowledge. Education was understood in both practical and liberal aspects. The education department of the

Rochdale Pioneers had included reading rooms, classes, laboratories and a wide range of educational practices, which would later be characterized as 'a university and technical college combined' (Redfern 1939: 218). The sympathetic commentator and member of the Edmonton Men's Guild, Leonard Woolf, could see the need for both technical and liberal education:

> We do not employ engineers in the great C.W.S. factories until we have proof that they have knowledge of engineering; and we cannot do our work within the Co-operative Movement without a real knowledge of politics, economics, and finance, of business structure, of industrial and social problems . . . there is still more knowledge which is required, if they are to be Co-operative citizens, to enable them to deal intelligently with the wider problems of their class and their nation. (Woolf 1914: 2)

In the tradition of adult education, liberal education was seen in practical terms, in relation to the working classes gaining power. Yet, the movement also challenged the prevailing dichotomies found in the adult education movement (Harrison 1961; Taylor et al. 1985; Woodin 2007). Indeed, the interconnection between the vocational and the humanistic would be a recurring theme and co-operators would claim that technical education could be the basis of the education of the whole person (Woodin 2011). From the inception of the movement, activists pointed to the importance of educating members as a basis for progress. The co-op was a business driven by the impulse to improve people and society. The definition of co-operative education carried a dual conception of internal and external change: 'primarily the formation of co-operative character and opinion, and secondarily, though not necessarily of less import, the training of men and women to take part in industrial and social reforms and municipal life generally' (Hall and Watkins 1937: 168).

The other significant division within adult education was that between humanistic and political education, the latter supported by the Plebs League and labour colleges which pursued independent education committed to the political aims of the labour movement. These divides also found some parallels in the co-operative movement but, again, they were redefined in co-operative terms. The College was to 'teach men how to apply their knowledge to definite social ends', to create 'a burning desire for social justice, inspire a willingness to work for it, and provide the knowledge how best to attain it' (Hall 1919: 5; also Tawney 1912: 3). For Thomas Anderson, of the York society educational committee, the College was going to provide training and knowledge to challenge the current competitive economic system, and build 'liberty in place of industrial slavery by making us a real democracy' (Anderson 1913: 9). The discussions relating to the formation of a college stimulated new courses that addressed the learning needs of the movement. These included 'co-operation and social problems', 'the welfare of the group' and 'after-war problems', the latter a correspondence course (Hall 1918a: 3). Research organized by the Co-operative Union focused upon co-operative issues and it was hoped the College would take further steps in this direction (Hall 1918a).

Leaders and visions

Leaders in the co-operative movement worked at the intersection of vision and practical reality. Historically, wide-ranging visions of change had gone hand-in-hand with prosaic, detailed actions in building forms of self-help (Woodin 2011). A spiritual faith in the capacity of working people to create the 'co-operative commonwealth' represented not only a continuation of Owenite themes in the movement, but also helped to maintain and motivate loyalty and enthusiasm for the co-op. The confidence in co-operative ideas constituted a secular devotion that drew upon religious traditions. Leaders actively sought new members but, as they arrived in greater numbers, a corresponding concern arose about the danger of diluting the co-operative message. This combined with the fear that elected representatives might themselves be apathetic and that a mutual indifference between these two groups could potentially debilitate the movement. The College was responding to an implicit sense that the movement was falling behind:

> Among our leaders there seems to be a lack of confidence in the success of a forward movement and an apprehensiveness about the result. As a result of this over-cautiousness, our advance towards the social ideal is disappointingly slow... we are without a conscious and continuous policy for the redemption of co-operators from the social and economic ills that surround them. It might not be the place of a college to provide such a policy, but it could give us light on some of our problems and direct our attention to fundamentals; and it would put more life and confidence into us if it gave us an increased number of men and women trained in the interpretation of social phenomena. (Hall 1919: 9)

At the same time, leaders looked askance at the inactivity of many members: 'the apathy of the rank-and-file and their indifference to the fuller objects of the movement are frequently lamented by co-operative leaders' (Hall 1923b: 4).

The College represented an attempt to respond to these challenges. It was to bolster faith with a deeper understanding of facts and principles and instil conviction in the co-operative ideal. In outlining aspects of co-operative education, Hall underlined the necessity to look forwards:

> There must be a vision, or the co-operative movement will perish; co-operators must have imagination, or they will fail; the worker must have confidence in his schemes for social redemption, and must have patience in working them out, or he will always be a victim of the less scrupulous people who look farther ahead. (Hall 1923b: 3)

It was claimed that the college would also provide a centre for 'the cultivation of the co-operative spirit' (*College Herald* 1916: 2) and an avowal of co-operation as a collective force was a necessity:

> the common life of the college would do much to develop the feeling of common interests and sympathy between co-operators and to keep alive the idealism which

> inspired the founders, but which at times seems likely to be swamped. (Hall 1919: 4)

In this sense, co-operative education would not be like other educational institutions where the 'principal object is to train students so that they may become more efficient to compete with one another'. Instead, the College was to promote the 'common welfare':

> Instead of education for private gain and 'getting on', we stand for education for use and for service. We want education to develop all the potentialities of the individual; but we wish his powers to be used for public good, not for individual aggrandisement. We want education to have a moral purpose as well as an intellectual purpose. We want our students to become not only more intelligent and more clever, but to employ their cleverness for the attainment of desirable ends. (Hall 1918a: 10)

The injunction applied to the leaders who were answerable to the movement. While paid employees such as Hall tended to be appointed by elected committees, other leaders were directly elected and everyone had to justify their actions and ideas through the accepted democratic channels. The management of the College was itself to 'be vested entirely in the movement, either in the Central Education Committee or in a specially-constituted committee' (Hall 1928: 12).

Moreover, co-operators were infused with the expectation that the movement was to move as a whole. Leaders would be representative of the 'best type of members' and this only made sense in an environment where individuals would be

> limited in their leadership by the intelligence of their co-workers, which may be insufficient to enable the rank-and-file to recognise the merits of good proposals, or insufficient to recognise the capacity and disinterestedness of their leaders. This will cause them to be unwilling to trust and follow these leaders. In any case, the progress of the group will depend upon the intelligence of the mass, and upon the existence, among those who are co-operating, of a group spirit as contrasted with an individualistic spirit. This means that the whole of those who are co-operating must be educated to develop their intelligence and foster the group spirit. (Hall 1923b: 4)

The prominence given to higher education was related to the learning of everyone. Education was conceived as a social and economic investment for the common good – an early incarnation of what later become known as the 'knowledge economy'. In this vein, the restrictions facing leaders were celebrated by Hall and W.P. Watkins who remarked on the danger for the movement should the business get 'beyond the understanding of the rank and file, it would get beyond their control' and would rapidly lose its 'democratic character':

> In the long run, the direction of the journey is more important than the speed of the journey… the only way of speeding up the co-operative achievement is to

> quicken the intelligence and increase the co-operative determination of the rank and file. (Hall and Watkins 1937: 90)

Marshalling the great body of co-operators behind the vision was indispensable to success. Leaders thus had to tailor their responses not only to the political, economic and social context but also the collective constituencies within the co-operative movement.

Engaging the dispersed individuals committed to co-operative education raised another problem for co-operators. In part, co-operation was to be developed and managed through democratic structures but these comprised a plethora of fragmented autonomous parts. In working through this co-operative labyrinth, Hall and others had to develop a canny sense of strategy in convincing activists of the worthiness of their cause while acting as role-models. Flair and flourish were not enough to bring the College into being. Protracted campaigning work was necessary to amass a threshold of supporters convinced of the value of co-operative education. The College Herald Circle aimed to accomplish its task

> by spreading a knowledge of the proposals in the movement (1) by distributing copies of that paper [A Co-operative College]; (2) by securing the reading of the paper at conferences and meetings of the various branches of the Guilds, Students' Fellowship, and A.U.C.E. [Amalgamated Union of Co-operative Employees]; (3) by bringing the proposals to the notice of general and educational committees; (4) by articles in the 'Records,' 'Wheatsheafs,' etc; and (5) in other ways that present themselves. (Hall 1919: 13)

This represented hard graft and the active engagement of a significant group of people working on a voluntary basis. With this in mind, Hall implored activists not to shun the 'dry details' of educational organization. They were often fighting against the 'lack of determination among co-operators to will that "these things shall be"' (Hall 1918b: 7).

However, the Survey Committee, which carried out a review of the movement and published its final report in 1919, fretted about 'a large amount of educational zeal in the movement which has hitherto been insufficiently enlisted for our educational work' and for this reason, it was recommended that individuals interested in education were to be brought into membership. All too frequently, it was found that these men and women were 'drawn off into other reform movements' (Hall 1918b: appendix; Co-operative Union 1919). The response, paradoxically, was the creation of additional organizational structures, the Co-operator's Educational Fellowship and the College, which it hoped might help to enlist individuals in this cause who would become active propagandists and teachers. Hall aimed to assemble a force of 10,000 enthusiasts able to teach and keep alive the spirit of co-operation among the rapidly expanding membership. Co-operative education was nonetheless caught up in a catch twenty-two situation: the fixed structure of the movement acted as a break upon the development of co-operative spirit and activism but was a problem that could only be addressed through structural innovation which added to the already extensive and intricate machinery.

Public engagement

The arguments in favour of a college encompassed not only internal co-operative issues but looked outward to the development of civic democracy. For instance, when speaking at the 1912 Co-operative Congress, the educationist and historian, R. H. Tawney contended that the co-op should act as a catalyst for continuing progress in higher education as it had previously in other areas: 'you have won your way into Elementary, Secondary, and Technical Education, and it is time that you turned your attention to Universities' (Tawney 1912: 12). He wanted an inquiry on educational endowments and urged the movement to take on a 'special responsibility' to act as pioneers in 'removing what is undoubtedly one of the greatest evils in education to-day, the restriction to a privileged few of the opportunities for advanced study which should be open to all' (Tawney 1912: 6).

By contrast, the urge for a distinct identity was a priority for those who argued for 'a self-contained movement, Co-operative Commonwealth, in order to be our own employers, and thus bring about a fairer distribution of wealth…' (Laws 1915: 2). In 1890, Lord Rosebery had described the movement as a 'state within a state', a phrase which captured the imagination of many co-operators. Co-operatives had pioneered new economic and social forms in the nineteenth century such as libraries, reading rooms, scientific education as well as classes on liberal and technical subjects. Each of these social innovations was gradually taken on by the state and represented a growth of educational provision. But there were also drawbacks as the co-operative content of libraries and classes was quietly removed over the passage of time. The neglect of co-operation in mainstream education angered those who argued for the need to keep control of learning and ensure that co-operative knowledge remained relevant to the movement's vision of social change. The resulting frustrations nurtured the opinion that alternative examples of higher education had to be constructed by the movement itself. In 1909, W. R. Rae, the chair of the Co-operative Union educational committee, reasoned that the evolving education system might offer benefits to working-class children but it was a path with many dangers for the co-operative message:

> Too often these travellers, keep too closely to the old road, and imbibe the old prejudices, the old errors. What we want and seek to obtain is a co-operative journey that will end in a co-operative university… So long as the State does not provide it, we must do, as we have in the past, the best we can to provide it ourselves. (Rae 1909: 29)

It was a tricky process to navigate because the extension of state activity liberated of funds for direct co-operative purposes but was tied to a declining public influence (Gurney 1996; Rae 1904).

Paradoxically, each step in this direction meant that co-operatives became more isolated from wider streams of activity within the working-class movement and in the educational system as a whole. The expansion of public education unavoidably marginalized the movement somewhat. In 1927, Honora Enfield, in an overview of the movement, revealed the contradictory nature of these developments. The concentration upon co-operative education meant that 'those who intend to devote themselves to the Movement' would 'get exactly the training they want' but it had

> a tendency to restrict the place given to Co-operation in other educational institutions of the workers' movement, and so to separate Co-operation and its problems from the rest of the Labour movement.

Enfield advocated a workers' college on the Belgian model which embraced the whole labour movement and allowed for both general and specialist courses. She felt that the strong identity of the British movement could also lead to an element of insularity and lack of direct engagement with universities:

> It is curious that in Great Britain co-operation has no recognized place in the public educational system, though Paris and Brussels Universities have their Chairs of Co-operation provided and maintained by Co-operative Societies, and in several countries Co-operation forms a subject in the curriculum of certain types of schools. (Enfield 1927: 41)

For instance, the noted co-operator, Louis de Brouckère, held the chair in co-operation at the University of Brussels from 1926 to 1938 where he lectured widely on the topic (Barbier 1951).

It is possible to identify an oscillation between the desire to impact upon mainstream institutions and the necessity to build up internal co-operative structures. The latter impulse worried about dissipating co-operative identity and this could be evident among outsiders who nevertheless argued for large scale social change. Partly in tune with the position of Enfield, and perhaps contrary to Tawney's ideal of progress, Woolf hoped that the movement might indeed establish a 'working class system of education'. It was something the co-op was eminently well-placed to do:

> It is no use imitating the systems of the Universities, the Public Schools, and the Board Schools. These are the old academic systems of the upper and middle classes. Those classes have had their chance. Why should not we show what can be done by a working class system of education, younger, fresher, and more living? The Co-operative Movement provides an opportunity such as exists nowhere else in the world. We have the money; we have the skeleton of an organisation; we are not educating with the object of fitting our pupils to earn so many pounds sterling a year; we are not competing with other schools and colleges. (Woolf 1914: 5)

It was the very physical presence, achievements and resources of consumer co-operatives that permitted Woolf to dream up such revolutionary ideas about an alternative education system, the beginnings of which could be forged from the considerable materials available to the movement. However, Woolf's educational vision was contained by the hard and fast class barriers of the early twentieth century. He hoped that co-operation 'should enter into the life of men and women completely, changing their view of what the construction of society should be, making them more useful members both of their class and of the State' (Woolf 1914: 1). An apparent acceptance of class divisions could thus go hand in hand with a willingness to countenance fundamental change. It was a predicament shared by co-operative leaders who worked within a system while aiming to transform it.

Limitations

The dilemmas facing co-operative leaders could not easily be solved and the aspiration for a co-operative commonwealth met with enduring problems. At times, the concerns about the conservatism of leaders seemed to be justified by actual results. The limited number of students at the College indicated a lack of progress and this could be wearing. In 1939, John Thomas, the new director of education at the Co-operative Union, lamented that the College had only thirty students who were mainly holders of scholarships from individual societies as well as a few private students from South Africa, Ceylon, India, Egypt and the United States Some strongholds of co-operation were hardly represented and he identified a significant imbalance:

> *Think of the hundreds of thousands that pass through British Universities and Colleges to serve capitalist enterprise. Shall British co-operators with a membership of over eight millions* [sic] *be content with 20 to 30 students training annually at their College?* Not if I can rouse my fellow co-operators to see a new vision of co-operative education! (Thomas 1939: 200, emphasis in original)

His method for stimulating the movement again related to the importance of the vision. With enthusiasm and belief on the part of members, and a realization of the great potential they held in their hands, change might come. However, the heavy structures of the movement could act as a brake upon concerted action.

Working out coherent programmes on the basis of voluntaristic and democratic action proved problematic. This was compounded by the fact that, on the left, planning and state action were coming to be seen as the major way of addressing social problems. In addition, the formation of the College paralleled debates about a national co-operative society and the 'overlapping' of societies which meant they were competing with each other rather than the capitalist world. Local autonomy of individual societies was a cardinal principal that was jealously guarded. Alongside the Co-operative Union, federal co-operative bodies had been built to handle insurance, banking and wholesaling. But in general, the movement remained grounded in its local societies that only reluctantly ceded power to federal organization after much experimentation. The growing independence of the CWS would be an issue of concern to some societies and may have inhibited the development of other federal bodies. This pattern was replicated in relation to education. Some local leaders were wary of the exhortations of those who called for more expenditure on education. Even within societies, education committees were not everywhere in existence and, where they were, some of them laid on minimal provision and were frequently isolated from the central management committees. Common action became much less possible where power and responsibility were so diffused and where funding for formal educational activity remained marginal.

This helps to explain the partial response to the initial proposal for a co-operative college. From one perspective, supportive statements could be made because the central congress and other educational bodies had little power to act upon them. Sympathetic outside commentators had the freedom to express their frustration at the limited achievements given the scale, spread and wealth of the consumer movement. Woolf complained at how little was spent on education (Woolf 1914: 3–4) and Mansbridge also voiced his exasperation at the lack of co-ordination. Resources could not easily be funnelled up the movement in order to develop new ideas. In 1912, he highlighted the 'ridiculous' condition of the Central Education Committee of the Co-operative Union getting by with a grant of £712 while the rest of the movement devoted over £100,000 to education (Mansbridge 1912: 490). Although the College was envisioned as a co-ordinating body, it was not to receive a lion's share of the resources during the interwar years.

In addition, the restriction of funds created an environment in which an expectation of overwork became the norm. The co-operator, S. Fairbrother, opined that staff were working ten to twenty hours overtime each week: 'the wages were practically sweating wages ... they were sweated from the point of view of overwork, and that could not go on without a deteriorating effect upon the whole work of the Educational Department' (Fairbrother 1919: 16). This reflected an ambivalence in the co-op about the treatment of its staff who were not immune from the labour struggles found in capitalist enterprises (Gurney 1996). Rather than share profits or power with employees, they were encouraged to join as consumers. T.W. Mercer, hoped that the proposed college might solve grievances that were often the result of misunderstanding; it might equip workers 'for the final struggle between capital privately controlled and labour co-operatively organised' (Mercer 1919: 2). To some employees, these arguments had a whiff of hypocrisy about them.

Activists promoting the College also grappled with the role of women. The Co-operative Women's Guild actively campaigned for women's participation. Many societies had allowed women to become members in their own right. Further, it was planned that the College should do 'something to repair the deficiency' in relation to women's role:

> The co-operative movement has been built up by women as well as by men; and educational opportunities for women are as necessary as for men, yet the provision of facilities for the education of women in social science has been notoriously neglected. (Hall 1919: 12)

But this concern exposed the continuing marginalization of women in the movement. Special subjects directed at women, such as 'Women's Place in Society', often assumed fixed and gender differentiated roles (Woodin 2011). One commentator claimed to have an 'open mind' on the topic of women on educational committees but worried that they would not be able to handle 'rough work' and emphasized difference in order to undermine claims of equality:

> In every great movement – religious, philanthropic – women have been of the greatest service; but still none of us likes the pushing woman, anxious to take the place of men. If women insist upon having all the rights of men, they must necessarily lose the privileges of women. Is this desirable? (Laws 1915: 2)

Similarly, sustaining a belief in the common welfare came under pressure from other social forces. As in broader educational and social developments, difference and differentiation were visible and it was claimed that there would always be leaders who had 'wider vision and greater intelligence' (Hall 1923b: 4 check). Co-operative education had to address the differentiation and hierarchy that pervaded mainstream education. The notion of a 'broad highway' rather than a socially restrictive ladder, championed by the WEA, was actively supported by co-operators. But the position was more difficult to uphold given varying levels of enthusiasm, knowledge and standards. One report on the 1915 summer schools observed a need to recognize prior experience: 'varying grades of students; some students have not previously been class students, and others have been studying systematically for a few years… more differentiation is required' (Summer Schools 1916: 4). The College itself was based upon a need for students to pursue a more 'advanced stage' in their studies (Hall 1928: 4) and those with 'low mental power' were expected to benefit from general education (Hall 1923b: 3).

These debates spilled over into the value and meaning of higher forms of education. Various scholarships to Oxford and elsewhere, which were made available for co-operators, following bequests by supporters like E.V. Neale and Thomas Hughes, had proved to be a means of channelling potential students out of the movement. Scholarships and opportunities to study at the College were awarded for a variety of motives which might not be related to the priorities of individual societies. On introducing the idea of the college, Hall himself had been quizzed that it might provide a home for the 'sons and daughters of the aristocratic and middle classes of the co-operative movement… the officials, managers, and secretaries of the co-operative movement… the well-to-do members and employees…' (Hornsey 1919: 499). Hall strongly rebutted the claim and argued that everyone would have access to the College. In 1928, he was still at pains to underline that the College was serving the movement; its ex-students were now

> managers and secretaries of societies, secretaries of educational committees, organisers and canvassers for societies, members of the staff of national organisations like the Co-operative Union, the Wholesale Society, and the Co-operative Party; whilst others are serving as co-operative journalists and in other capacities, many now acting as teachers of evening classes for local societies. The fear of some critics that the College would educate students who would then leave the Movement has not been justified. (Hall 1928: 7)

These activists had become what Antonio Gramsci would later refer to as 'organic intellectuals' (Gramsci 1971). Educating students from around the world was also having an international impact. Yet, it could feel a world away from the life of the average member.

In part, these reservations reflected the fact that the very idea of a 'college' was alien to many in the movement: 'they had the idea that colleges were only for the rich, and that a co-operative college would only be a means of lifting a few students out of their class at the expense of the Co-operative Movement' (Hall 1928: 4). In fact, the 'college' label posed a challenge. In forging plans for a college, there were historical models to draw upon such as the working men's colleges in London, Sheffield and elsewhere (Dent 1928). Nevertheless, there was a palpable nervousness about taking on this mantle and an ambiguity about the type of institution that it should become. This became evident over the debates about the ideal, potentially rural, location of the college. As a result, activists were not always completely sure whether their proposals constituted a 'real' college or not. For instance, in 1914, Hall argued that, 'One takes it for granted that the college would be established in some country district, where the work could be carried on under the best conditions.' But he prevaricated on this point and later shifted his position in noting the advantages of working in the heart of the movement:

> The presence of the College in Manchester has had certain advantages, such as proximity to the warehouses and many factories of the C.W.S., and contact with the day-by-day life of co-operators and co-operative societies. These advantages are much appreciated by the students, particularly by employee-students, who are attending the College in order to increase their knowledge of the trade, and the technical subjects bearing upon it. (Hall 1928)

Such ambiguities were indicative of the way that the co-op traversed the boundaries and expectations that were being erected in the wider society. After the Second World War, the purchase of a country house in a rural location would in turn eventually come under scrutiny as the costs and purpose of the College were re-evaluated in the twenty-first century. At each stage, there were gains and losses.

Conclusions

All leadership must be understood in relation to its social context. The Co-operative College grew out of a long and complex collective history. It came into being to address the needs of a democratic consumer movement that had grown to significant proportions. It was to provide a higher education for co-operators which cut across vocational training, liberal learning and education for social change. Although the College was expected to co-ordinate the varied educational activities of the movement, its federated structure, in which power was widely diffused, made it difficult to concentrate resources in the centre. Co-operatives had been built from the ground up and individual societies resisted centralized organization. Leaders were well aware of the resulting challenges and opportunities. Fred Hall, W. R. Rae and others developed strong visionary thinking to inspire the many societies to provide financial and moral support for a college as well as to construct networks of sympathetic teachers and learners. They built upon the everyday experience of co-operators and connected it to comprehensive social change. This was no easy task and was made more difficult in times of economic hardship following the First World War. Even though the College was started on a small scale, it nevertheless had to be sustained with a continuing flow of students and income. Additionally, the aspiration to educate for a co-operative commonwealth was frequently frustrated by the reality that the College could only handle relatively small numbers. Yet as leaders strove to build a college of their own, they found themselves at some distance from other labour movement initiatives as well as the rapidly developing mainstream educational system. In arguing for a democratic future, co-operators also had to handle popular ideas about difference and differentiation that were a source of continuing debate.

The implications for understanding higher education leadership today cannot be read off in a simplistic way. Very different assumptions held sway in the interwar years in comparison to the early twenty-first century. The grounded nature of the movement meant that the College was part of a extensive co-operative network. The democratic accountability of leaders made them answerable to elected committees. It did have an influence abroad wider added to the mix of experiences and internationalist ideas upon which the College was built. Education and learning was to provide the basis for building character for service as well as the expansion of a democratic model of business. In doing so, it proved necessary to think beyond the accepted divisions of knowledge. Mainstream forms of liberal education were welcomed but much College work focused upon the future of the movement. While this may have appeared overly specialized to outsiders, co-operative leaders saw it as the route to true equality, justice and democracy. Today, universities contribute to the problem of a democratic deficit in aping for-profit businesses often at the expense of their identities as public institutions. The paucity of vision is reflected in the preoccupation with defending hierarchies, organizational boundaries and market share rather than developing new learning communities as a means for social improvement. As a result, alternative models of co-operative further and higher education may still have a role to play at this present-day historical juncture.

Acknowledgements

I would like to thank Gillian Lonergan and staff at the National Co-operative Archive.

4

Academic Voices: From Public Intellectuals to the General Intellect

Mike Neary

Introduction

This has been a time of trauma and turbulence for higher education (HE) in England and around the world as it struggles to come to terms with the deconstruction of the public university now being recast as a financialized, money-making institution (Hall 2015b; Holmwood 2011; McGettigan 2013; Newfield 2013). Financialization means deregulation to attract for-profit providers, the commodification of knowledge, curtailment of collegiality, academics as entrepreneurs and the repurposing of students as consumers and proto-employees. This has been underpinned by a campaign for economic growth linked to a political strategy that criminalizes dissent in a way that undermines academic freedom (Serewizc 2015).

This chapter explores these troubles through a series of interviews with sixteen academics who have raised their voices against this assault on universities (Bailey and Freedman 2011), rising to the challenge as public intellectuals. The academics were asked about their experiences of being a public intellectual, the current quality of intellectual leadership in higher education, the culture of conformity among academics, and what, if anything, can academics learn from their students and the student movement about the politics of protest (Giroux 2011). Each had a different view on their role as a public intellectual but all complain about a lack of intellectual leadership by Vice-Chancellors and senior managers. They recognize a culture of conformity among academics based on self-interest and fear, while some sense a simmering resistance that might be ignited through targeted campaigns in which trade unions have a role to play. The student movement appears fragmented with some success at the national and local level and is strongest when connected with matters of public concern. One of the unexpected outcomes is the commitment by those interviewed to teaching as a key function of the public intellectual.

The purpose of this inquiry is not to be judgemental about the activities of academic colleagues, but to consider the nature of academic leadership in higher education and the extent to which it is possible to be a critical voice in universities, against professionalization as well as increasing financialization and the anti-democratic political culture that it promotes. At the end of the chapter, I reflect on my own experience as a senior manager inside an English university and the ways in which it connects with the matters that are raised by the academics who have given their voices to this chapter.

I will frame my inquiry about academic leadership using the notions of the public intellectual and the 'general intellect'. Public intellectuals are usually considered in terms of how much they are abstracted from the real world of practical affairs, or when they have become so involved in practical matters that they betray the disinterested function of intellectual life (Collinsi 2006: 297). The literature moves between these two polarities without fully resolving the dichotomy, so that a gap remains between theory and practical action.

The concept of the general intellect has a different starting place, not the individual intellectual but knowledge at the level of society. The gap between theory and practical action might be dissolved by the appropriation of knowledge and science by social individuals for the benefit of humanity and the natural world expressed as the possibilities of living an active, intellectual life (Marx 1993).

Critical debate

The notion of the public intellectual has been subject to much critical debate. A sample of some of the literature captures the flavour of this discussion. For Russell Jacoby (2000), the intellectual has been subsumed by the expansion of the university, with its professional academic practice and performance measures calibrated within disciplinary expertise. The result is that intellectuals 'have lost command of the vernacular': the voice of the people (Jacoby 2000: xv). Elsewhere in the academy, Henry Giroux wants to reclaim higher education as a 'democratic public sphere' (Giroux 2014: 142) and a form of critical pedagogy where educators 'function as public intellectuals…[who]…close the gap between the university and everyday life' (142). He argues that this can be done by listening to students who insist that 'the relationship between knowledge and power can be emancipatory' (145) as a way of building social movements inside and outside of the university.

For Stefan Collini (2007), the so-called retreat into the academy, when the generalist intellectual becomes the specialist academic, is not simply an historical truth but something within the nature of the concept and the role itself (58–59). Collini sees the role of the intellectual maintained through a structured set of social and cultural relations where the skills of disinterested scholarship are brought to bear 'in wider public debate' (504), to create what he refers to as 'academic intellectuals' (504), provoking a 'counterpoint' of critical and creative voices (503) against the 'bottom-line rationalism' of international corporations' (503). While Collini reminds us that public intellectual is a 'moddish term' (470) his relational concept of the intellectual implies contact with the public, not simply as an analytic concept but through engagement with a variety of publics, or, better, 'overlapping spheres of publicness in any complex society' (55). His formulation contains the possibility that we might come to see intellectuality as a non-exceptional activity and intellectuals as 'ordinary', not 'Other

People' (505), but as ourselves in a spirit of 'full historical consciousness' (505) so that we cease to be the prisoners of prejudice and tradition and take on responsibility for our own critical intellectuality.

Edward Said (1993) is inclined to the notion of the intellectual as scholar-hero speaking truth to power on the basis of universal principles of freedom and justice, not as loyalty to abstractions but on behalf of the 'weak and the unrepresented' (17). While the intellectual's voice is lonely, exiled, non-aligned and marginal, 'it has resonance only because it associates itself freely with the reality of a movement, the aspirations of a people, the common pursuit of a shared ideal' (75). He recognizes the Western University as a place that can 'offer the intellectual a quasi-utopian space in which research and reflection can go on, albeit under new constraints and circumstances' (61). For Said, the greatest threat to the intellectual today is 'not the academy… but rather an attitude that I will call professionalism' (55), by which he means 'thinking of your work as something that you do for a living – not rocking the boat, not straying outside of the accepted paradigms or limits, making yourself marketable and above all presentable, hence uncontroversial and unpolitical and "objective"' (55).

For Steve Fuller (2005), academics and intellectuals should be on the same side but 'regard each other with mutual suspicion' (136). Academics think intellectuals are sloppy in research, as well as impressionistic and parasitic (137). For intellectuals, academic research is 'comfort thinking' (136). Academics get lost in esoteric jargon and fail to engage with the public; whereas, 'intellectuals at their best can reduce complex arguments to their key point and then provide a context for them that conveys a significance that attracts a much wider audience than academics normally manage' (137). Academic training makes academics conservative and to think only within the terms of their own discipline – leading to conformity (139). Academics are set against the idea of a 'universal intellectual' (139), indeed 'the world's complexity transcends human comprehension' (140). But intellectuals are not beholden to facts, which do not speak for themselves. The very essence of the role of the intellectual is to make facts speak beyond their existence as facts, in public. In the end, to be an intellectual is to be concerned with the issue of what it is to 'become fully human' (163), or at least 'the commitment of intellectuals to the essentially public character of humanity' (166). At their most controversial 'intellectuals routinely commit a cardinal sin of academic life. They refuse to detach their thoughts from their times, or indeed their lives' (166).

Richard Posner (2003) sets out to evaluate what he refers to as academic public intellectuals within an economistic framework based on public intellectual work as a type of information and entertainment. His argument is that the output from public intellectuals is mostly shoddy as it is not regulated in any way, unlike mainstream academic work which has a system of peer review and the norms of tenure and promotions (81). The result is that academic public intellectualism is in decline, replaced by specialist academics associated with the expansion of the university sector (29). His solution is to make the academic public intellectual more accountable by encouraging full disclosure of public intellectual work as well as any conflict of interests. While spending much time on clarifying the concept of intellectual, he has almost nothing to say on the idea of the public. In fact, he holds the public in contempt 'for its short attention span, its philistinism, its embrace of a "soundbite" culture' (79). He shares this view with the intellectuals he writes about who he says 'tend to be disdainful of the general populace … This is part of their broader disdain for people less intellectually acute than themselves' (78).

Posner displays a contempt for the masses that John Carey (1992) identifies with a certain kind of English intellectual writing: modernism, in the period 1880–1939 (17). Carey argues controversially that modernism was a literary genre which could prevent the masses from accessing culture by making it too difficult to understand, so that intellectuals 'free from the limitations of mass intelligence … can communicate effectively with one another' (17) and, therefore, 'counteract the progressive intentions of democratic educational reform' (18). For Carey this amounts to 'an exclusion of the masses, the defeat of their power, the removal of their literacy, the denial of their humanity' (21). Carey argues '"the mass" is an imaginary construct, displacing the unknowable multiplicity of human life, it can be reshaped at will, in accordance with the wishes of the imaginer' (23). He maintains the aim of modernist writing is 'to segregate the intellectuals from the masses, and to acquire the control over the mass that language gives' (23). Carey argues that modernism is 'rooted in European intellectual orthodoxy' and includes the work of Hitler's *Mein Kampf*, as an exemplar of this type of written work (208). From this analysis, it is very clear that the role of public intellectual is not restricted to leftist academics.

There are more radical versions of the public intellectual, seeking to undermine the dichotomy between the abstract and the concrete as well as challenge its more elitist assumptions, expressed either as a revolutionary or proletarian intellectual. In the case of the former, Subcomandante Marcos of the Zapatistas People's Liberation Army appears as a 'revolutionary intellectual' (199) who manages to be a revolutionary hero and the expression of oppressed people at the same time. Focusing on the ski-mask that has become a feature of the Zapatista uniform, he is described as 'a faceless stand-in for all of the oppressed' (Estrada 2014: 200), with the mask as a 'subversive strategy for it simultaneously liberates and empowers' (207), enabling him to express himself through a literary style of communication, as 'an eloquent and poetic breath that speaks for the entire community' (206). In this way, Marcos presents not only 'a practical force of arms, but also a theoretical revolution' (209) where his voice is 'serving as the bridge between the western and indigenous cosmologies, or as the agitator of modernity's long history of coloniality' (209–210).

In the case of the latter, Jacque Ranciere's work on proletarian worker-intellectuals (2012) is based on archival research giving the space to nineteenth-century French workers to tell their own stories in ways that undermine the caricatures and assumptions of social and labour history. In this research, workers are revealed not simply as locksmiths, shoemakers and tailors, but as worker-intellectuals finding time to write and think, as poets, artists, metaphysicians, philosophers, humanitarians, aesthetes and *flaneurs*, in ways that challenge the accepted boundaries in the social sciences between worker and bourgeois cultures: in particular; between intellectual and manual labour. Ranciere's work is contrary to prevailing workerist and proletarian ideologies in the sociology of labour and provides a very different understanding about the nature of public and proletarian intellectuality (Reid 2012: xxvi).

This is a rich literature expressing the complexity of the issue, with a focus on the descriptive and the definitional, at its strongest when the public intellectual is discussed in terms of political, cultural and social relations. The writing is concerned with two poles of public intellectuality: the abstract and the concrete, the academic and the intellectual, the academic and the student without being able to dissolve this dichotomy. It might be that public intellectuality by its very nature can never be only a theoretical concern but demands that it be carried out in the full glare of public expectation and anticipation. In the next section, I want to explore this matter further not by writing about public intellectuality as a concept but, rather, by exploring what it is to be a public intellectual. I intend to contextualize this question with reference to the current situation in which the notion of intellectuality itself is being called into question, in the troubled turmoil of higher education. This will be done with regard to matters that have come to define this dispute: intellectual leadership; the culture of conformity among academics; and the efficacy of student protest. I will go on to suggest my own interpretation of public intellectuality, not as a definition or description but as a methodology grounded in the concept of the general intellect and my own work as a senior manager in an English University. My inquiry into the experience of being a public intellectual is based on interviews with sixteen academics who have raised their voices against the financialization of universities. While I recognize the limits of the interview method, being 'creatures of context and occasion … ultimately the product of the artful edit: careful fictions' (Osborne 1996: vii), I want, following Marina Warner (1995), to make a claim for the importance of storytelling, as a way of reclaiming the possibilities of living an intellectual life grounded in real practice.

Academic voices

Public intellectual

I asked academics who had spoken in public about the assault on higher education if they thought of themselves as public intellectuals. Chris Newfield sees himself as a public intellectual writing for *'an educated public'* not in any elitist way but on the basis that *'I just have a total instinctive precognitive unconscious trust in ordinary intelligence.'* Thomas Docherty claimed his *'public intellectual work is always concerned with matters that pertain to a more general public'* in a way that remains connected to his working-class origins. Peter Scott was more self-deprecating, describing himself as a *'hack or propagandist'*. Stefan Collini uses his writing as a way to retain an *'an idealism about intellectual inquiry'* not as a public intellectual but as an *'academic, critic and scholar'* carrying out the type of individual disinterested scholarship that is possible inside universities for *'the greatest collective rewards'*. Des Freedman had a more radical understanding of his work, preferring to be described as *'researcher, activist, teacher, scholar'* who works with others precisely to challenge the notion that there ought to be a firm intellectual division of labour: '*who, after all, is* not *capable of doing intellectual work?*'

Mary Evans felt that being a public intellectual is not a matter of choice: '*every academic is a public academic*'. Noam Chomsky felt being a public intellectual was based on more fundamental precepts:

> a fundamental feature of human nature that distinguishes us from the rest of the animal world is having language which makes us unique, as well the ability to use it in free, independent and creative ways... as the basis of classic liberalism and other libertarian conceptions... making any impediment to that freedom illegitimate.

Marina Warner was motivated by the need to speak out against the tyranny of managerialism even though it was against her natural inclination. She was '*astonished by the number of letters I received in response, expressing the depth of anguish, people had gone through hell*'. Her very public intervention was strengthened by the way she was able to connect it to her own academic writing on storytelling: '*the fairy tale material is about the voice of the people*'. Nina Power felt compelled to speak out even though it made her a '*bad academic*' in the eyes of her colleagues and senior managers. Gurminder Bhambra saw her role not in an individualistic sense but as part of a '*collective collaborative campaign*'. John Holmwood expressed a similar view, seeing himself involved in the production of '*public knowledge for democratic purposes*'.

Max Haiven refused the concept of public intellectual and saw himself as part of a group of '*common intellectuals: catalysing communities of struggle*' so that people could express their '*revolutionary brilliance*'. For Bhambra, there was a sense that writing was not enough, as she put it '*people need to get their skin in the game*'. Haiven expressed a similar sentiment, pointing to the example of academics working with activists on Black Lives Matter and with indigenous activists associated with Idle No More. For Bhambra and Holmwood, getting their skin in the game has meant reluctantly moving outside of the university to create spaces for community-based research in inner-city areas with limited higher education provision, setting up the New Centre for Contemporary Cultural Studies (NCCCS) in Birmingham, and the online publication *Discover Society*. Bhambra argued this provides '*a powerful online platform to promote social science to a general audience as a different form of collegiality*'. For Power, this meant becoming a student again, undertaking a law degree to be able to support students prosecuted by the criminal courts following the student protests in England in 2010.

Leadership

At the heart of my enquiry lay a question about the current state of leadership in Higher Education. Peter Scott expressed the positive view that '*in a purely technical sort of professional way universities are pretty well led*' and Mary Evans had some '*sympathy for Vice-Chancellors with Boards of Governors on their backs*'. However, there were much more critical responses, including Scott, who felt that '*in terms of intellectual leadership the record is not so good*', and from Stefan Collini who complained that there has been no attempt by Vice-Chancellors '*to represent the interests of the higher education system as a whole*'. Collini felt that academics had become '*disconnected and disenfranchised*' with no-one in senior management to speak up for them. Marina Warner spoke of the bullying she and others had experienced: '*Deans are brought in as the henchmen for VCs... humiliating people and shouting at them.*'

Thomas Docherty argued that as Vice-Chancellors had become more powerful within their institutions the University appears to have lost its place as a social institution of any real significance as '*a maker of social values*'. He felt that Vice-Chancellors were adopting a model of leadership '*that isolates the leader from everyone else, it is a heroic tragic version of the leader, the leader as a charismatic figure*'. Gurminder Bhambra said that Vice-Chancellors only speak out '*when there is a threat to their income stream... so there has been complicity at the highest level, gambling on being part of an elite top 40... destroying a system of HE that worked effectively*'. John Holmwood agreed '*hardly any Vice-Chancellors have spoken out... going with the government agenda, mouthing the language of human capital and economic growth. The Russell Group is almost entirely self-interested*'. Toni Pearce, during her time as President of the National Union of Students, made a speech to Vice-Chancellors where she castigated them for not speaking out in public: '*not saying what they believe in and why, and that they have an academic basis for making that judgement*'. Marina Warner felt it was not only about Vice-Chancellors and senior managers, but that complicity extended to academics who in an effort to avoid time-consuming administrative tasks had allowed a vacuum to develop and be filled by colleagues '*who have gone over to the other side... throwing in their lot with the commercialisation of higher education and rewarding themselves with high salaries*'. Patrick Ainley felt the outcome was that '*management has supplanted leadership*'.

This was reflected from experiences in the United States where Chris Newfield felt academic leadership was based on corporate models, very adversarial and short term in a situation where '*I don't see faculty being empowered or supported, rather put down for their oppositional politics and demonised*'. Steve Fuller argued that what has been most lacking is leadership that promotes higher education on its own terms: '*the university is doomed without academic leaders who defend the university as a distinctive institution*' even if, for Fuller, '*the only people with the knowledge, authority and power to defend this ideal are not rank-and-file academics but the university senior administrators*'. I was reminded by Michael Bailey of a previous generation of Vice-Chancellors, for example, Richard Hoggart and Asa Briggs, who '*saw themselves first and foremost as scholarly academics, not afraid to rock the Establishment boat*'. Yet despite the dominance of neoliberal managerialism, Des Freedman made the point that the university has not been completely overtaken by a marketized bureaucratic system so there is still the space for an alternative model to emerge out of a '*reluctant leadership... who are still committed to a more social democratic model of making a difference... I think there is still a way to go. This is by no means the end*'. Marina Warner expressed a similar view '*there is a sense of revolt in the ranks, but people haven't risen up*'.

Conformity

There was a general agreement about the culture of conformity among academics. Thomas Docherty said '*lots of people are very critical and disconnected with how things are going in higher education but are not disposed to say anything about it publically or do anything about it*'. Gurminder Bhambra felt that one reason was the privileged employment position of senior academics, who are among the top 10 per cent of earners in the country. John Holmwood said: '*the problem with academics is that they have had their mouths stuffed with gold*', pointing out similarities to the ways in which medical doctors had been encouraged to support the formation of the National Health Service in the UK. Peter Scott felt that another reason for conformity was university bureaucratic systems, for example, quality assurance protocols '*although it is not their intention they do have a policing function … alongside other negative unintended consequences*'. Mary Evans felt conformity was induced by '*very subtle shifts in terms of the kind of questions being asked when applying for funding and the kinds of investigations that are not encouraged*'.

Thomas Docherty argued that conformity was the result of fear about the consequences of speaking out: '*It is horrifying that people who are paid to think are now put into a position where they are afraid to think, so the culture of conformity has a deep political and institutional correlate … the polemical statement would be that thinking has been criminalised.*' Max Haiven said that Graduate Schools in North America engage in a form of '*systematic oppression*' where activist students are '*weeded out as dissidents and radicals*'. He also spoke of '*faculty who have tried for years to fight the neoliberal agenda are now exhausted*'. Steve Fuller argued that all this leads '*to a radical disengagement with the university as an institution*'. Thomas Docherty pointed out that alongside this conformity exists '*the clandestine university where academics do their real work that avoids the fantasy "official" university*'. There are others who feel that the issue is not conformity, but the lack of an alternative campaign which disenfranchised academics could support with the trade unions. This campaign could be organized around student fees, the price of student accommodation, university governance and the so-called anti-terrorism Prevent legislation and academic freedom. Des Freedman wants academics to see the connections between the challenges that are facing them '*from the point of view of struggle rather than just moaning about academics being complicit*'. Chris Newfield, on similar lines, argues, '*There isn't a platform, it is still in the realm of discontent and criticism … so I am very much more focussed on platform development to force myself to think concretely about where to go and how we can get there with specific steps.*'

Students and the student movement

There was not much sense of having anything to learn from the student movement, although students were by no means to blame for the current predicament and were to be admired for their capacity to struggle. Steve Fuller felt that there was '*no unified class consciousness, which one might have associated with the student movements of the 1960s*'. For Max Haiven, the student movement was '*very fractured*', and for Gurminder Bhambra, it was divided by sections of the student population and had become 'too sporadic and piecemeal'. Peter Scott felt that in a society awash with credit, students regard fees as 'the new normal', as well as 'careerist NUS Sabbaticals and SUs who see themselves as protectors of the student as consumer'. Nina Power argued students overburdened by debt and anxiety exhibit a sort of *'heaviness about the way in which they study'* reinforced through *'a symmetrical continuum of violence'* by the police against students, protestors and people of colour. All of this is compounded by lack of student identity because of the compartmentalization of people's lives and the modularization of courses.

Des Freedman argued that students are strongest when they break out of set-piece occupations to win arguments to improve campus conditions alongside academics as part of wider community struggles with the local community and other workers. Mary Evans gave examples where students campaigned on behalf of university support staff and cleaners: *'I think they were fabulous campaigns involving what a lot of people would rather not hear about'.* There was a strong sense of how teaching can be a form of public intellectuality, testing out ideas on students and of the need for academics to engage with more collaborative forms of active learning. Chris Newfield said:

> I see students as a public, so what works and what doesn't work on them I pay very close attention when I am lecturing. I would really like to set up closer collaborative relations with students than is possible in the big state schools that I teach in ... we are missing a huge opportunity to do active learning development of the kind they realise they need and want.

For Steve Fuller, teaching should be seen as a way of *'remastering elite, esoteric forms of knowledge as vehicles of mass empowerment'.* Patrick Ainley wants to develop what he called *'thick HE'* as a sort of *'general intelligence that is theoretically informed and practically based'.*

There was a strong view, expressed by Thomas Docherty, that students should be regarded as producers of knowledge through their *'contribution to teaching and learning as a dialectical process, teaching us by their responses to our teaching, letting us know that they have important things to say'.* This is supported by Mary Evans who pointed out *'the extraordinary richness and vitality of the work that is produced in British universities by students, the undergraduate dissertations and end of year shows. This is something that Vice-Chancellors should be talking about, not transferrable skills but commitment and creativity. We should nurture it and praise it to the skies...'* There is a sense that the tide may be turning with a new leadership of the Labour Party. Michael Bailey felt that *'younger students, postgraduates, and academics feel a bit more empowered by the fact that Labour has started to take an active interest in higher education issues, e.g. supporting academic freedom, the idea of the university as a public good, and the abolishment of tuition fees'.*

Courage to be critical

While not all those interviewed see themselves as public intellectuals, they all have the courage to be a critical voice against the assault on the public university, sometimes as the disinterested scholar but at other times with a sense of common, organic, collective and democratic purpose. There is some support for the notion that universities have been managed effectively as businesses, but this is part of a critique about the failure of intellectual leadership by Vice-Chancellors, along with a fearful culture of bullying and intimidation that has emerged as part of the pressures of financialization. While the focus of the critique is on senior managers, there is a willingness to accept that academics have been complicit in this process out of their own self-interest. Yet, there is a sense that the public university has not been completely overwhelmed by the law of money, and that critical academics should work towards building a campaign against financialization alongside trade unions and the students, making links with other matters of public concern. In the UK, this was seen as being as part of an emerging political project within the Labour Party to restore people power to public services. There was strong commitment to the importance of teaching and collaborating with students on learning and research as a way of consolidating the power of the academic voice.

In the final section, I want to reflect on my experience of being a senior manager at an English University and the way in which I attempted to develop my own academic voice as a way of building and appropriating the general intellect against the assault on public higher education.

General intellect

I went over to 'the other side' in 2007 when I became the Dean of Teaching and Learning at University of Lincoln, having previously taught Sociology at Warwick. While at Warwick I had been director of the Reinvention Centre for Undergraduate Research, a project that sought to democratize the production of knowledge through collaborative work between academics and students so that undergraduates become part of the academic-intellectual project of the university (Neary and Winn 2009). I went to Lincoln to work with others to make the democratic production of knowledge the organizing principle for the whole institution, and in a way that sought to remake the institution as a radical political project so that knowledge becomes a new form of common wealth against the increasing financialization of higher education (Neary and Winn 2012). This meant getting close to what Docherty refers to as 'the clandestine university', making contact with the disenfranchised and the disconnected faculty and students so as to abolish the financialised university and establish a new form of dissident institution (Neary and Saunders 2016).

I had a strong sense of intellectualizing the practice of teaching and learning based on an attachment to critical theory, influenced in this context by Marx's notion of the 'general intellect' (Marx 1993: 706). Marx uses the concept of the general intellect as a way of capturing the possibility for human emancipation through the social power of the knowledge of humanity. This idea undermines the charismatic scholar-hero who populates the literature on public intellectuals while adding substance to the idea of knowledge production as a democratic, collective process. The general intellect means knowledge not as a capitalist value for 'the knowledge economy' but that 'real wealth is the developed productive power of all individuals' (708), for 'every individual and the whole society' (706). In a passage that is particularly relevant for those of us who work in universities, Marx recognizes the extent to which the general power of science, knowledge and technology, which has been used to increase capitalist productivity, can now be reappropriated as knowledge at the level of society. This forms a new type of 'social intellect' (709), 'for society generally and each of its members ... the development of the individual's full productive forces, hence those of society also' (708). It is this revolutionary potential for 'general social knowledge' (706) that lies at the core of my own pedagogic practice.

The concept of the democratic production of knowledge became the organizing principle for a teaching strategy adopted at Lincoln, with the title Student as Producer. This regards students as researchers and part of the institutional culture of academic inquiry, by including undergraduate research as a core aspect of the undergraduate curriculum. Student as Producer does not start from an affirmation of the capitalist university but focuses on the dysfunctionality of the core activities of higher education: research and teaching. It challenges and invites academics to consider ways in which this negative arrangement might be re-engineered as part of a democratic and collective production of knowledge, meaning and social value. This is not so that they become revolutionary Marxists, but as part of a dissensual culture in which everybody has something to learn (Readings 1997).

The slogan Student as Producer is ripped off from Walter Benjamin's paper 'Author as Producer' (1934). At the core, Benjamin's paper lay the question how do radical intellectuals act in a moment of crisis, 'making it one of the most important attempts to theorize the role and efficacy of the intelligentsia in revolution' (Gough 2005: 1). Benjamin argues against bourgeois thinkers who distinguish themselves by their commitment to the working class 'only *in the mind* and not as a producer' (91), in favour of 'an intelligentsia interested in liberating the means of production and hence active in class struggle' (93). The Marxist title of the University of Lincoln's teaching and learning strategy felt like a small victory in an environment dominated by 'managementese' (Docherty 2015: 54).

During my time as Dean of Teaching and Learning, I became the embodiment of the neoliberal university, but expressed myself as a 'reluctant leader' finding every opportunity to democratize decision-making processes as well as involving students in the production of the whole institution. I continued to publish and give public lectures that developed the negative critique of higher education on which Student as Producer is based. Student as Producer gained a reputation as a pioneering approach to teaching and learning, as well as formal recognition for teaching quality in the mainstream Quality Assurance Association and Higher Education Academy evaluations. The University of Lincoln continued to be committed to a progressive student engagement agenda, but, along with other higher education providers, remained locked into a model of financialization where the production of knowledge and science is based on economic growth, industrial productivity and debt, as if the economic collapse of 2008 had never happened, or had even begun to be resolved (Williams 2006).

I withdrew from the role of Dean of Teaching and Learning in 2014, reverting to the position of Professor of Sociology at Lincoln, but continued to work on the concept of Student as Producer as part of another experiment outside of the university. This experiment became the Social Science Centre, established in 2011 to create another form of public intellectuality based on the model of co-operative higher education with no formal connection to any higher education institution. The Centre is run by forty students and academics as members working together consensually, based on a model of critical pedagogy, in a more radicalized version of Student as Producer, where members have much to learn from each other. Courses include: the Sociological Imagination; Co-operative History of Education; and Do It Ourselves Higher Education.

Administrative roles are shared out among members in a non-hierarchical way. There are no fees, only subscriptions based on what people can afford, as well as donations in kind. Costs are kept to a minimum by using members' free-time and making use of public facilities. The Centre does not award degrees, but offers credentials at the level of higher education qualifications, validated by the scholars and associate members who are not directly involved in its day-to-day running. The day-to-day running involves the preparation of courses and publications, but also the mundane, banal activities that form the lifeblood of any social institution. They also include time for critical practical reflection through which the work of the Centre can be considered. At the Social Science Centre, these activities are seen equivalent, dissolving the distinction between intellectual and manual labour. At the heart of everything we do is a research project to create new forms of social value, based on a sustainable relationship between humanity and nature. Members of the Centre are currently exploring ways in which the model can be amplified and sustained, recognizing that at the core of this problem lies the recasting of a concept of publicness itself as the basis for a viable life-enhancing form of social institution (Social Science Centre 2013).

This work challenges the fundamental assumptions about higher education and seeks to articulate in a critical, practical way the concerns expressed by public intellectuals who have given their voice to this chapter: the relationship between academics and students; the nature of knowledge and science; hierarchical models of leadership; as well as the dominance of objectivist methodologies and financialized priorities. The intention is not to establish an alternative provision based on a contrarian ideology or social theory, but to work in collaboration with others to create a new form of higher learning out of the negative dysfunctionality of the capitalist university. The assumptions on which this revolutionary work is based are grounded in the real practice of academic–intellectual life.

Inventing the future

At the core of this chapter lies the related questions of professionalization and whether it is possible to be a critical intellectual inside an English university? With regard to professionalization it would appear that academics have allowed themselves to be overwhelmed by a culture that is not based on a self-regulating code of ethics, integrity and expertise as in other professions (Saks 2003). Rather this emerges within a culture of continual professional development where professionalism is based on a set of management imposed performance metrics, which are seen to be an anathema to the academic project (Deem et al. 2007; Shattock 2013). In terms of being a critical academic voice, writing about the Undercommons, an idea that comes close to the concept of the 'clandestine university', Harney and Moten (2013) deny the significance of critical academics, who are now tolerated as harmless creatures in the business-university as a front to maintain the illusion of academic freedom. In this situation Harney and Moten maintain the only response is 'to steal from the university' (2013: 26). Newfield disagrees, he admires Harney and Moten's work but says: '*I don't think they really earned their conclusion in that book… We don't do enough, we are not critical enough… but you can essentialise that in a way that is disabling*.'

The interviews reveal a high level of critical activity, with academics raising their heads above the parapet, putting their careers on the line, organizing campaigns to express dissent, making strong links with students in occupations and marches and through their teaching, even becoming a student to support students victimized by the law. The interviews provide real, critical-practical examples of how to reclaim the vernacular, not simply as the voice of people but as a way to 'become fully human' and take responsibility for our own critical intellectuality as a form of 'historical consciousness'. In my own work with others, I have attempted to avoid stultification and exhaustion by attempting to dissolve the dichotomy between the conceptual abstractions and concrete action by which we work through critical practical activities, with examples of how this might be done: Student as Producer and the Social Science Centre. Marina Warner provides another way of doing this that speaks to the interview method used for this inquiry. She argues that we should write through abstractions as if they were real life, as a form of political narrative that she calls 'fairy stories'; not a careful fiction (Osborne 1996) but as a way of inventing the future; so 'the story becomes the weapon of the weaponless' (Warner 1995: 412). In this way, to 'live as if the freedoms you desire were yours already. Only by refusing the constraints that are imposed can they be broken – this is also true of imagining another life, making a new world' (415), as a sort of 'wishful thinking' (418).

So we might ask ourselves as academics the question: 'What do we wish for?' and can we find ways of bringing it to life.

5

Openness, Politics and Power

Martin Paul Eve

Among many changes to research practices in higher education (HE) with which those in leadership roles are having to contend, open access is one of the most globally transformative but also most contentious phenomena. The term 'open access' refers to the removal of price and permission barriers to scholarly research by open dissemination on the Internet (Suber 2012: 8). Such an idea, whereby the fruits of HE's research are extended to anybody with access to the Internet, free of charge, obviously sits in harmony with many of the goals of mass intellectuality and particularly those with an emphasis on 'sharing' as a stage in a move towards an integrated and productive general intellect (University of Utopia n.d.; see also Stallman 2010; Virno 2003: 38).

As simple as this fundamental concept might be, though, it is also, as I will demonstrate, highly politicized and situated within frameworks that complicate a relationship to mass intellectuality. For one thing, our set of 'open' practices is defined in specific ways with a myriad of contentions around who controls the space of 'open' (Hall 2016a; Weller 2014). For another, as Nigel Vincent and Chris Wickham noted in the foreword to a British Academy volume on the topic, open access 'has a current force, however, which is not only moral but now political, with Conservative politicians in effect lined up with unequivocal egalitarians' (Vincent and Wickham 2013: 6). This has been seconded by Cameron Neylon, a prominent figure in the OA world of the sciences, who recently likewise pointed out on Twitter that to work on open access projects is to find oneself accused one day of being a neoliberal sell-out and the next of being an anti-corporatist Marxist (Neylon 2013). It is also the case, though, that critical thinking in the academy tends to turn its gaze away from its own practices where they seem self-evident. Academic publishing is one of these areas, where intra-disciplinary practices become normalized and absolved from scrutiny by its routinized form.

In this chapter, to address these topics, I will consider the range of political interpretations that have been placed upon 'open access' to academic research. This stretches from those, like Jeffrey Beall, who condemn the phenomenon as a mode of 'collectivizing production and denying the freedom of the press from those who prefer the subscription model of scholarly publishing', to those, such as John Holmwood, who see a danger in OA of neoliberal appropriation and re-enclosure (Beall 2013; Holmwood 2013a,b). I will also examine the ways in which open access to reading can facilitate a co-productive mode of open access to writing; a mass intellectuality.[1] Indeed, it strikes me that open access may be a fundamental historical prerequisite for a mass intellectuality, in which a society-wide and disciplinarily ambiguous co-production and mutual harnessing of intellectual labour – wheresoever it may be found – can become possible.

Beginning from a description of the forms of open access, I will note that there are intrinsic power motivations at play in the enforcement of OA mandates, often linked to corporate finance, and that, at this particular historical moment, it is possible to effect apolitical interpretations, socialist interpretations and capitalist interpretations of the movement. Like many social changes engendered by the Internet – and while eschewing technological fetishism (Sayre 2005) – I will also argue that it is very difficult to predict the outcomes, even if one group's intentions are clear.

From this diagnosis, I will next move to suggest the ways in which those with a democratic outlook on mass intellectuality can take a role of intellectual leadership – through innovative experimentation – to act to decouple the potentially dangerous side effects of OA from its liberating potential: an upending of traditional hierarchies of research universities based purely on extant accumulated capital. Finally, I will note that OA on its own is not enough, amid radical projects, to rethink the hierarchies and divisions of labour, but that it can be a useful tool along that road, so long as proponents are vigilant for the dangers of recuperation and co-option.

What is open access and why is it relevant?

For a piece of academic research to be deemed 'open access', it must be available digitally for anybody to read at no financial cost beyond those intrinsic to using the Internet. This demands the removal of price barriers.[2] This is similar to most of the material on the world wide web but it is not the way in which scholarly publication has traditionally been offered. Indeed, comparatively few websites charge readers to view their content, yet most academic publications are paid for by university libraries through purchases or subscriptions. Open access means reconfiguring how we publish academic work so that peer-reviewed scholarly research is available freely to the reader on the world wide web (relying on digital technology to allow instant, near-free copying). In the original declarations on OA from around 2002, the term was also defined to mean that people should be permitted to re-use this scholarly material more liberally than is allowed by the fair use/fair dealing provisions of copyright law, so long as the author is given credit (Brown et al 2003). This is the removal of permission barriers that advocates claim brings a host of advantages, such as the creation of a teaching/course pack of lengthy extracts. When these two 'barriers' are removed, this is called open access and it modifies the current model for scholarly communications quite dramatically. It also causes substantial economic reconfigurations because in order to implement some forms of open access we must formulate new economic models to support the labour inherent in publishing.

Many advocates of open access believe that the greatest mass exposure to research will be achieved by making research free to read. The benefits of this economic reconfiguration include academics whose university libraries cannot meet the price of subscriptions and a set of heterogeneous publics for whom much research material remains unaffordable. As George Veletsianos and Royce Kimmons put it, '[m]any scholars hope and anticipate that open practices will broaden access to education and knowledge, reduce costs, enhance the impact and reach of scholarship and education, and foster the development of more equitable, effective, efficient, and transparent scholarly and educational processes' (Veletsianos and Kimmons 2012: 167). In other words, through a democratization of access, the *hope* is that a type of mass intellectuality – in which any member of society can also contribute to the production of knowledge, from spaces far removed from the traditional academy – might emerge. As shall be seen, this is not a universally held belief, though, and many have objected to open access for both of its elements (price and permission), while others, of course, object to the extension of open access to a co-productive mode featuring different types of expertise. That said the levels of objection are tiered according to the ways in which OA is implemented. Models of OA that place the economic burden directly upon researchers are far less popular with those researchers than those models that seem to co-exist peacefully with the existing subscription ecosystem.

To understand the preceding statements, it is necessary to know that there are a variety of ways in which open access can be achieved. These are usually referred to through the jargonistic matrix of terms: *gold*, *green*, *gratis* and *libre*. Gold OA refers to research that is made available openly *by the publisher*. Gold open-access journals are usually either entirely open access or 'hybrid' (in which subscription publications carry a subset of open-access articles). Gold OA has implications for the business models of publishers. If publishers cannot sell the work (because they are giving it away for free), then they need a different model to remunerate their labour. One way of achieving this in a gold open-access mode is to require that authors or their institutions pay a fee to the publisher, thereby inverting the current subscription model. This is known as an 'article processing charge' (APC) or a 'book processing charge' (BPC). Many publishers are adopting this model for gold open access. The logic is that publishing here becomes a service for which academics and/or their institutions pay. Gold OA is not the same as 'author pays', though. Indeed, this was not integral to the term as it was coined by Stevan Harnad. At the time of writing in late-2015, the majority of gold OA journals in the Directory of Open Access Journals do not charge a fee (Directory of Open Access Journals n.d.), although as David Crotty points out, there are complications with this calculation; it actually depends on how you define 'majority' and whether this pertains to articles or journals (Crotty 2015).

The other term that is used to describe a way of achieving OA is *green*. Green open access refers to the delivery of OA by an *institutional* or *subject repository*. An institutional repository is a database-driven website, usually housed within a university library, that holds copies of affiliated authors' works along with the associated metadata. Whenever an academic has published work (even in a subscription journal), he or she is encouraged to add it to the repository in accordance with publisher policies. This work is then made publicly available, green open access.

Many publishers allow authors to do this and there are several tools to allow authors to check publisher policies, such as SHERPA/RoMEO (Jisc n.d.).

However, green open access can be a poor and downgraded substitute when compared to gold. Unlike gold open access, the version uploaded to a repository is not always the 'version of record'. Furthermore, there is frequently (but not by necessity) an embargo period that delays the public availability of a green OA version. This is claimed to protect publisher revenues. In disciplines with strict normative citation standards to the version of record, green open access can also be problematic; it will not function as a substitute if the pagination/content differs in the green OA version. Lengthy embargoes can also devalue green open access in some fields of contemporary study where the most current research is needed quickly.

Green and gold are the routes to remove price barriers to research. On its own, this is called 'gratis' OA. The material is free to read but has standard copyright provisions. If permission barriers are also removed, this is termed 'libre' OA, an aspect usually achieved through a form of open licensing. Traditionally, academic authors sign their copyright over to publishers, who then hold the exclusive dissemination rights to the research material for the duration of the copyright term. However, all the early declarations on open access also specify the lowering of permission barriers as a crucial part of OA (Anon 2003; Chan et al. 2002; Suber et al. 2003). Open licenses are legal texts founded upon copyright that an author can use explicitly to allow others to redistribute and, in some cases, modify the work legally. The demand for attribution remains in the vast majority of cases. The most frequently used and best known libre licenses are the Creative Commons Attribution licenses.

For reasons of space, I will now move on from the basic terminology. Those who would like more on this should consult one of the many excellent guides on the subject, but most importantly, Peter Suber's *Open Access* or my own *Open Access and the Humanities* (both freely available online). What should, I hope, be clear is that in its most positive forms open access potentially takes a step towards a socialized model of research through the removal of payment to access work (even if it does not lower the barriers to collective production of that work). As I will show throughout the rest of this chapter, though, that promise is somewhat utopian (in a pejorative sense) and often compromised in various ways. I remain convinced that OA is a move in the right direction; it is just not the final end destination.

Competing interests and powers in the academic publishing space

While I have thus far detailed the background to open access, the variety of political factions involved in the emergent dominance of open-access publishing should give cause for concern. Clearly, when major corporations and economically right-wing governments (which intrinsically depend upon inequality and competition; Davies 2014) also want open access, it is unlikely to be purely for the sake of social equity. Such arguments are particularly applicable to the permissive licensing provisions of open access. For instance, it has been prominently argued, most notably by John

Holmwood, that 'Open Access under CC BY [one of the most liberal of the open licenses] is one of the measures designed to speed up commercialization, by making scientific innovations more immediately accessible, especially to small and medium-sized enterprises' (Holmwood 2013b). Others have argued that there is implicitly a moral violation in the reuse of academic material (Allington et al. 2015: n.4).

This desire for the extraction of research's use-value at sites distant from the university (what is called, in contemporary parlance in the UK: impact) acts as the catalyst for two other distinct mechanisms. First, because the economic protections of copyright in academic publishing are exercised by the publisher, a resistance to open access on corporate financial grounds is triggered. Second, the commodity form of research material within the contemporary university is more thoroughly unmasked, as demonstrated by corporate-financial resistance and through corporate value extraction.

The first of these aspects is the easiest to place. Indeed, one of the oft-touted arguments by left-spectrum OA advocates is that commercial publishers extort their captive library clients.[3] At the parliamentary hearings in the UK in 2013, this was most clear in the evidence of Alicia Wise, representing Reed Elsevier. Elsevier is well known for its vocal opposition to, and legal lobbying against, OA in the States (Grant 2012) and Wise confirmed that Elsevier reported a 37 per cent profit with 'a revenue stream of £2.06 billion and a profit level of £780 million' in 2012 (Wise 2013: Ev3). In the face of such astonishing profit margins, it is hard to fault the argument that at least some resistance from such corporations must come from a desire to protect the conventional economics of subscription publications, which have served them very well. Advocates point out that the corresponding margins of major oil companies are around 6.5 per cent or that Big Pharma usually manages about 16 per cent (Bradley 2011).

Another large-scale operation is Taylor & Francis/Routledge. In terms of turnover, Informa Group, who own Taylor & Francis and Routledge, posted an operating margin of 28.4 per cent in 2012 with a £349.7m adjusted operating profit (Informa 2012: 1). Thirty eight per cent of this was derived from Informa's publishing operations, which were 'dominated by subscription assets with high renewal rates, where customers generally pay us twelve months in advance. This provides strong visibility on revenue and allows the businesses to essentially fund themselves, with minimal external capital required' (Informa 2012: 9). For publishers thriving on subscription economics, regardless of whether this system limits those who can read research work, to use their own words: '[i]t is a uniquely attractive mode' (Informa 2012: 9). It is not unreasonable to deduce that corporate entities may be wary of open access when the subscription model has yielded a year-on-year 10 per cent increase of dividends to shareholders (Informa 2012: 1).

The list goes on. Bloomsbury Academic, the publisher of this volume, although a smaller player, is a humanities and social science publisher that is notable for a series of mergers and acquisitions. In recent years Bloomsbury has bought up entities such as Continuum, an organization that had itself previously acquired Cassell, T&T Clark, Berg Publishers, Methuen Drama, Arden Shakespeare, Bristol Classical Press, Fairchild Books and AVA. This forms a continuation of a worldwide trend of concentrating corporate power within fewer entities. In its 2012 financial report, Bloomsbury posted an adjusted continuing profit of £12.1 million on a continuing margin of 12.4 per cent. Of Blomsbury's activities, '[t]he Academic & Professional division grew the most year on year with a £2.9 million increase in continuing adjusted operating profit, due to both the acquisition of Continuum [a solely humanities-orientated publisher] and a significant increase in income from content licensing deals' (Bloomsbury Group 2012: 7). Interestingly, the Bloomsbury Academic imprint, when it was originally launched in 1998 under the stewardship of Frances Pinter, was OA by design: '[t]he new publishing model [would consist] of releasing works for free online through a Creative Commons or other open license, and then offering print-on-demand (POD) copies at reasonable prices' (Park 2008). This did not move to mass scale, possibly because of fears for ongoing revenue, but Bloomsbury does continue to publish some books in an open-access form.

It is worth saying, in the face of this critique, that 'publishers' is not a homogeneous term. Some publishers are commercial and do very well out of the system for their shareholders. Others are mission driven but run a surplus. Still others, like many precarious university presses, are very close to bankruptcy (although not Cambridge UP or Oxford UP, which post very healthy profits back to their parent institutions). In other words, academic publishing is itself an industry that is designed to extract surplus value from the labour of academics and the research university. When this industry operates through a paywall model, however, other sectors that would like unencumbered access to research material for their own purposes of value extraction will join forces with egalitarians (who hope for equal access to HE research material and a co-option of a shift towards mass intellectuality) to change the system. In this way, even when industries are in broadly different fields (such as pharmaceuticals) and they want open access to research, they can find themselves *in competition* with academic publishers who operate on a sales/subscription model. This is one reason why strange political alignments have developed in the emergence of open access.

If it is clear why corporate bodies might wish to recuperate a narrative of liberation, why are enthusiastic socially orientated academics less willing to see how their co-option by such entities unfurls? I would suggest that the core reason for this is that it can *superficially appear* that the research work of the academy is different in its terms of production to other manufactured commodities. After all, in the ideal situation, academics are paid a salary in order to give their work away; a rare situation of patronage in contemporary economics. This can lead the more optimistic opponents of marketized HE to deduce that open access might present a point of resistance to the commodification of knowledge. In fact, such an argument would run, what could better resist this process than work that is, in two senses, priceless? Sadly, such a conclusion is flawed. Open-access research is not radically anti-corporate, despite what detractors such as Jeffrey Beall might claim (Beall 2013). Indeed, OA articles have both exchange and use value, even if they are disseminated freely. On top of this, it is also clear that the production of research/scholarship is not simply an esoteric activity undertaken for its own, pure sake. In fact, research is, instead, one of the instruments that transforms academic labour is into productive labour, especially when aligned with the historical provision of land grants (nineteenth century), research patenting (early twentieth century), mid-century war funding and late-twentieth-century venture capital (Winn 2013b). As with open-source software, what emerges around open access to scholarly research is the university as a service industry, providing training in methods of reading, understanding and (re-)producing such material. When considering the role, function and exceptionality of scholarship, then, it is important not to simply fetishize a return to a form without value. Instead, as Winn puts it, one must remember that 'the trajectory of higher education and its conceived role and purpose in public life over the last century can only be fully understood through a critique of capitalism as the historical mode of production which (re-)produces the university' (Winn 2013b).

From this thinking, however, gold OA highlights the strangeness of ascribing a monetary value for the purchase of a research article or book: the primary audience for its purchase is the same as its genesis (academics write, universities buy). That said, eliminating this demand-side price and instead thinking of an OA article or book as 'free' (and labour-free) can lead to the fallacy that a gold open-access work could resist the commodity form. If something is given away for free, such logic would run, is it a commodity? This originates from a simple oversight of the fact that cost does not equal value.

Open-access articles and books still have an exchange value because universities will pay for the transformation of labour time into published articles, which also hold a use-value since they are of use to people other than the creator, regardless of whether the object is purchased for a monetary sum. As Joss Winn frames this, comparing Marx's examples in *Capital* of linen coats to open-access journal articles,

> there is a common qualitative substance shared by both the linen and the OA article, one common to both the labour of an academic and the labour of a weaver: human abstract labour. Thus, the labour of the academic who writes the OA article cannot be conceived in isolation from all other products of labour being exchanged in the social world of capitalism. (Winn 2015c: 6)

This dissemination presents the opportunity for the extraction of surplus value from the labour of academics, which explains, at least in part, why centre-right governments are so keen on OA (Holmwood 2013a). That said, even those who do not share that agenda can find themselves desiring open access, purely because it may engender a broader, mass spectrum of access to research. Sceptics might counter, though, that this egalitarian spectrum is only one in which academics are more freely exploited and that supply-side payment models for gold will lead only to a less-equal community where researchers without funds cannot publish.

Within a framework of mass intellectuality – understood as a transformation in the social relations of knowledge production so that knowledge produced for the 'valorization of value' (the M-C-M form that Marx describes in *Capital* whereby accumulation only ever spirals upwards) becomes, instead, knowledge produced for humanity, harnessing an unalienated and co-productive 'general intellect' that obliterates the traditional notion that '[t]hinkers must live estranged from their community' (Virno 2003: 38) – we should consider the logical flow for knowledge production and where open access can be situated. Open access, as it is theorized, seems to become a first step for the co-production of knowledge for humanity. It is a mode, potentially, where the fruits of existing production (the commodities) are open to anybody even when they cannot pay (although they must have access to the Internet). In truth, this is perhaps the great leveler given to us by the Internet; the non-rivalrous object form that can be disseminated at a near infinitesimal cost has caused many intermediaries to wither away across a distributed network. In theory, a neutral peer network validates the intellectual soundness (and, by extension, normativity) of material that is disseminated within it, and where production and consumption are open to anyone. In practice, of course, things do not work out so well as open access unfolds within capital.

Leadership, mass intellectuality and open access

Indeed, open access is prone to co-option and recuperation. It is situated within a discursive field where its positive rhetoric of sharing and liberation is often outflanked by commercial constraints. Commercial publishers will only move to open access when they are sure that they are no longer in competition with the other entities seeking to extract surplus value from academic labour. It is worth noting, though, that several commercial publishers look to be enacting a twenty-year plan to control other sites of value extraction in the academy (such as research data management) to militate against the collapse of the subscription market. However, for those who would like to align OA with the goals of mass intellectuality, outside of these extant frameworks, then, the question becomes one of realignment. How is it possible to conceive of OA within a 'common ability to do, based on our needs and capacities and what needs to be done'? How can OA be made to intersect with 'what needs to be done [...] at the level of society' (University of Utopia n.d.)?

Alongside its grim culture of audit and assessment, scholarly publishing has evolved to fulfil the need for communication of ideas and facts that have been found to accord with current epistemological systems. The end-goals that this communication serve vary by area of study, even if such 'disciplinarity' is of dubious construction. If there is a societal need for medicine, then there is a foundational need for a system to communicate the latest research on disease. If there is a societal need for an understanding of aesthetics, then there is a foundational need for a system to communicate the latest research on art. The current division of labour, however, perceives that the 'need' for such understandings should be isolated to specific factions of society: 'academics', those who labour within the increasingly marketized and financialized academy, the university. This is what can make possible an author-pays model, since it is supposed that a limited subset of knowledge producers will have recourse to institutional funding in order to remunerate publisher labour.

In other words at present, scholarly communication is predicated upon the division of labour, of technical specialization and of expertise founded on competition. Such a system purports to serve societal needs but does so by incentivizing individual gain. After all, the medical advances in the twentieth century were astonishing and they were predicated upon intense specialization. However, the advantages conferred by these new understandings were denied to vast swathes of the world's population on the basis of capital and legacies of colonialism. This is not to say that democratization of information dissemination would, on its own, rectify the problems of the concentration of the means of production. This is the fallacy that draws a parallel between the rhetoric of information liberation and social liberation. It is instead to note that such a process is a step in the right direction. Such a division of labour also accounts for the problems of library leadership in spurring the open-access movement. While many in the academic library world have seen the potential advantages of open access, they have often been unable to persuade academic colleagues which is at least in part due to the hierarchy of power within universities that would deem librarians to be 'support staff'.

While, then, open access presents a way of giving access to research that is vastly better suited to the mass consumption of information produced by the academy, the political overtones of the situation can be traced back to Karl Kautsky's orthodox Marxist writings at the turn of the twentieth century. Kautsky identified, in his essay 'The Intellectuals and the Workers', a set of antagonisms between the intelligentsia and the proletariat. While Kautsky noted that 'An intellectual is not a capitalist' and that, therefore, 'the intellectual does not stand in any economic antagonism to the proletariat' (a statement some may, now, find hard to swallow), a more general problem lies in the fact that 'The intellectual, armed with the general education of our time, conceives himself [sic] as very superior to the proletarian'. In other words, according to Kautsky, the intellectual perceives, in the proletariat, a 'low level of intellectual development, which it is the intellectual's task to raise. He sees in the worker not a comrade but a pupil'. Kautsky concludes that:

> The alliance of science with labour and its goal of saving humanity, must therefore be understood not in the sense which the academicians transmit to the people the knowledge which they gain in the bourgeois classroom, but rather in this sense that every one of our co-fighters, academicians and proletarians alike, who are capable of participating in proletarian activity, utilise the common struggle or at least investigate it, in order to draw new scientific knowledge which can in turn be fruitful for further proletarian activity. Since that is how the matter stands, it is impossible to conceive of science being handed down to the proletariat or of an alliance between them as two independent powers. That science, which can contribute to the emancipation of the proletariat, can be developed only by the proletariat and through it. What the liberals bring over from the bourgeois scientific circles cannot serve to expedite the struggle for emancipation, but often only to retard it. (Kautsky 1946)

Although Kautsky's thinking is clearly more broadly applicable to the role of the academy, rather than specifically concerned with publication, in the contemporary era it applies equally within this sphere. If the goal of revolutionary projects remains to abolish the hierarchy of labour – an aspect that becomes ever more difficult and distant – then collective dissemination alone is insufficient. Open access does little at present to achieve a longer-term goal of co-production. It is, though, a necessary prerequisite to that project. Whether or not OA will be integrated within such an agenda will depend upon how hard its advocates are willing to fight against the co-option and recuperation of open dissemination by big business. It will also depend upon a thorough assessment of the populist/specialist divide. To demonstrate this final assertion, I will only finally turn to the symbolic economy of research dissemination.

If research publication takes place within an economically predetermined field, it is one that is stratified because of the aforementioned patronage basis on which research in the university is produced. Researchers do not need to sell the product of their work to earn their salaries, although they do sell their labour power. This frees academics from the need to produce popular work (which comes with commensurate downsides for mass intellectuality and co-production). However, researchers' salaries are directly determined by the need to place their research material in specific venues. Particular journals and publisher brands are used to stand in as proxy measures for the quality of the work within when it comes to stretched hiring and tenure panels. That is, we know that researchers could technically publish wheresoever they might like. However, in a time-short economy, many researchers want filtering systems to determine whether work is of a good standard. They tend to turn to publisher and journal brands as a shorthand, even if we know that prestige of these venues and the quality within cannot be direct correlates of each other. (Every academic, e.g., can think of the poor article or book that was nonetheless published by a 'top' press.) Various systems of managerial pressure and configurations of leadership also tend here to take on a coercive function within a complex and interdependent ecosystem of motivations for the placement of articles and books.

This system of proxy measures acts, once more, to conservatively concentrate power into the hands of existing entities who may oppose broader dissemination or more collaborative production. It furthermore isolates the Anglo-American world from the rest of the global research community as academics grow used to expecting to find 'quality' research only in specific venues that they have pre-canonized with authority. It also flags, though, the financialized nature of research production, mediated by a symbolic economy of prestige, even in a world where it looks as though researchers are free from market imperatives. The gross misalignment of personal incentives for researchers with mass-intellectual co-production makes the task of bringing research publication to this debate one that is far from easy. It is, though, a task that is extremely important. I would suggest that engaging with the OA agenda as pre-compromised but as a nonetheless positive step towards the goals of mass intellectuality is a serious area to which scholars of co-production and the future of the university should devote themselves. I also suggest, for further reading, that examples of such leadership might be taken from Eileen Joy, at Punctum Books; from Rupert Gatti, at Open Book Publishers; from Gary Hall, at Open Humanities Press; and perhaps from the organization that I founded, the Open Library of Humanities.

Notes

1 I understand co-production, in this context, to mean a mode in which intellectual research outputs are created by a variety of actors from across a variety of spaces, not confined to an academy isolated from other spheres of production. This is more than the 'independent scholar' phenomenon and instead refers to those from all walks of life co-contributing to the development of intellectual outputs. I will return to a definition of mass intellectuality shortly.

2 Much of the material in this chapter is reworked from my book on open access. This work is available itself under a CC BY-SA license (Eve 2014).

3 I use the term 'left-spectrum' here for those OA advocates who wish to eradicate the profit motive from scholarly communications.

Part Two

Potentialities

6

The (Im)possibility of Mass Intellectuality: Viewing Mass Intellectuality Through the Lens of the Brazilian Landless Movement

Joyce E. Canaan

Introduction

Is it possible to make the university a place where the productive labour of academics does *not* serve the interests of the globalized, marketized elite? Over the past forty years, as numerous Northern academics have noted (primarily in the last decade), there has been a profound restructuring of Northern universities and of academics within them, so that now both are increasingly conceptualized and realized as profit-making and income-generating. Academic knowledge production has become highly quantified and monitored, and has been reconfigured to serve transnational capitalist interests. Indicative of this restructuring of universities and of its consequences for academics are two articles, written ten years apart, which speak of the '(im) possibility'[1] of being 'an intellectual worker in the neoliberal university' (Banfield et al. forthcoming; Davies 2005). The usage of the bracketed '(im)' in the word '(im) possibility' in both authors speaks to academics' acknowledgement of significantly changed material conditions of academic labour, making this production an even more alienating processes than previously. If these are the current conditions of academic knowledge production, what hope is there that these conditions can be made not just tolerable, but be radically transformed?

This chapter seeks to address this question in two stages. The first builds on Banfield et al. (forthcoming) and others and provides a Marxist conceptualization of present conditions of knowledge production in the university, as a means of reweaving and reconfiguring it. I use the concept of mass intellectuality to do so, given its view of knowledge production as a potentially 'communal process of production', which requires the negation and overcoming of current knowledge production strategies that 'damages the sociality and solidarity of the academic's wider communities with whom she is now in competition' (Hall 2014; University of Utopia n.d.). I suggest that the concept of mass intellectuality provides a much more powerful analytical tool than does the concept of 'leadership' to understand what is happening in the

UK university today, and to develop strategies to redress rather than accommodate oneself to current conditions (see, e.g., Bolden et al. 2014).

The second stage scrutinizes the concept of mass intellectuality in order to expand it. It does so by using the pedagogy of the Brazilian Landless Workers' Movement (hereafter the MST – the **M**ovimento dos Trabahladores Rurais **S**em **T**erra). The MST are rural workers who have sought over the past thirty years to overcome their oppression as landless, often illiterate, agrarian workers. At the core of their struggle as a social movement is a dialogical concept of popular education through which these workers aim to overcome the contradictory positions of being landless agrarian workers whose agency is potentially further sapped by illiteracy that seems to inhibit thinking and doing otherwise.

The pedagogy of the MST arguably offers a way to move beyond landlessness, illiteracy and other 'fences' (Stedile 2003) that block participants' agency, and capacity to move from the negation of their humanity towards a fuller humanization. As the concluding section indicates, the MST project offers insights with which to move away from the Northern, neoliberal university towards more revolutionary alternatives.[2]

The (im)possibility of intellectual workers in the neoliberal university?

The title of Davies's (2005) article on (im)possibility, indicates the author's focus on the conditions of contemporary 'intellectual work' which she views as producing academics discursively as affectless beings for whom there is no possibility of 'human emotions' such as 'happiness, sympathy, greed, envy, love or lust' (Watson, in Davies 2005: 1). This article, like many others (see, e.g., Ball 2013; Canaan 2010, 2012; Gill 2009), explores how neoliberal managerialism discursively produces what Gill calls, 'affectless, embodied experiences ... [of] exhaustion, stress, overload, insomnia, anxiety, shame, aggression, hurt, guilt ... fraudulence and fear of exposure' (2009: 2). What emerges from this work is an understanding of how the financialized, marketized conditions now structuring higher education (HE) impact academics subjectively, damaging them in embodied ways.

However, these analyses do not go far enough. Taking steps towards creating discourses 'on different grounds' (Davies 2005: 13) does not overcome these conditions, rather they offer strategies for self-accommodation to these conditions. To do so, I turn to Marxist analyses of wider determining contexts in which such toxic processes (Berardi 2009) are produced.

Banfield et al. note that the university has never been a space free from elite interests. It has 'drawn its life breath from oxygen formed in the tension ridden mix of human freedom and accommodation to powers of church, state and capital' (1–2). The third element, Capital, is now dominant; and it more fully contains those within it than did the church or the state. Banfield et al. remind us that the antagonism between labour and Capital has been 'the source of historical change' since capitalism began (4). Thus, Neary and Winn point out that capitalist social relations began with the enclosure of land that was formerly owned commonly. Enclosure forced workers off the land leaving them thereafter with only their labour to sell, and thereby enabled the 'fabrication of human labour as waged work, forming the basis for capitalist relations of production' (2012: 415). However, De Angelis (2004: 3) reminds us that enclosure acts today as 'a *force* with totalizing drives that exists together with other forces that act as limit to it'. This process is 'not just about taking resources away from people, but [is] the first step towards attempting to define new subjects' in 'the capitalist market' (2002: 19). Arguably what is happening to intellectual workers as knowledge producers is another step in the process of defining the subject in the capitalist market.

Enclosure ensures that workers produce commodities from whose production they are estranged or alienated (Marx 2004). Marx's notion of 'the two-fold character of labor' (Marx 1867) helps us to understand the commodities produced by labour as simultaneously having use value – 'the form of the commodity's body itself, iron, linen, etc., the tangible, sensible form of existence' (Marx 1867) – and exchange value – the 'theoretical category for articulating a real, active, social process that normally goes unspoken' (Winn 2014: 8). Capital's power over labour gives it the capacity to extract as much labour for as little pay as possible to ensure as much *surplus value* monetized as profit as possible (Winn 2014: 8). As a result, commodities produced have greater importance to capitalists than the pay and conditions of the workers employed (Marx 2004).

Capital's control over labour has intensified during the past forty years when there has been a shift from 'small, entrepreneurial' to 'large [transnational] corporate businesses' of monopoly capital'. The university has been remade 'in the image of' … 'a monopoly capitalist corporation' (Banfield et al. forthcoming: 2). Banfield et al. argue that this has been possible through a threefold attack by Capital on workers' labour. First, new technology allows Capital to extract more labour from fewer workers and to worsen remaining workers' pay and conditions through scientific management of the labour process, including monitoring workers' productivity. Second, these technologies help build knowledge production infrastructures that reify academics' knowledge. These infrastructures generate capacity for profit-making processes by producing intellectual property that is increasingly owned, controlled and sold by global corporate interests. Third, emboldened after the economic crisis of the late 1960s and early 1970s, these interests now have the power to pressurize and lobby governments to deregulate the Keynesian State. As Harvey (2005) states, in the early post-war years Capital was embedded, or contained, by a state that needed healthy and somewhat educated workers to ensure the most efficient extraction of surplus value in massive, highly profitable, Fordist factories. Through automation, fewer workers were needed to produce such goods and this has allowed capital to be dis-embedded from the State.

It seems that Capital has now more fully enclosed knowledge production than previously. As Winn (2014: 9) put it, there is now an:

> absence of collective agency among academics, one that is grounded in the common production process of the university as a social cooperative endeavour … [This has led academics to be] preoccupied with our individual

> position in the 'marketplace of ideas' ... over and above the ways we reproduce ourselves through an active dependence on other workers and students.

The current emphasis on competition between students, academics, departments and universities are currently hegemonic:

> [transnational networks of] academics and think-tanks, policy makers and administrators, finance capital and venture capital and private equity, education publishers and philanthropists [seek] to regulate the State and the institutions that are structured by it, like universities, for the market, for enterprise, and for-profit. (Hall 2014: 824)

Some academics seeking a world beyond wage labour argue first that the current remaking of the university 'for the market, for enterprise and for profit' (Hall 2014: 824) *ignores* how capitalist interests have actively harnessed the collaborative, collective processes that academic work requires. Academic work rests on the *social* relations of knowledge production (Moten and Harney 1999), at whose core lies 'an active dependence on other workers and students' (Winn 2014: 9). To build fuller and richer processes of interdependence requires that academics look beyond their *concrete* conditions of work, which is being structured by Capital so as to increasingly separate academic workers from that which they produce and from each other (Winn 2014: 7–8).

To move beyond contemporary working conditions requires putting control of academic knowledge process lies in the hands of its producers (Postone 1993). If the university is shaped communally, if 'sharing becomes a social force ... of action against a transnational corporate capitalism' (University of Utopia n.d.) and, importantly, if this productive process utilizes a pedagogy that is elaborated in the lessons learned from class struggle, from ... 'doing', then a revolutionary university can be realized. In such a university, 'our common capacity to do' (University of Utopia n.d.) can help create *'mass intellectuality'*. Mass intellectuality aims to develop 'the more generic attitudes of the mind[,] ... [its] productive resources [which include] ... the faculty of language, the disposition to learn, memory, the power of abstraction and relation and the tendency towards self-reflexivity' (Virno 2001). Mass intellectuality as a concept assumes that it is possible to reflect upon and move beyond one's immediate, concrete conditions of academic labour.

Those who seek, for example, to widen the concept of academic leadership singularly focus on formal leaders such as Heads of Department. They argue that *all academics* could exercise *individual* responsibilities and rights to take steps towards addressing the markedly limited collegiality now operating in the university (Bolden et al. 2013). Their perspective remains at the level of the concrete, failing to consider the wider causes of this lack of collegiality. Mass intellectuality is not like the process that Marx calls 'general intellect'; the latter is a process through which Capital congeals workers' skills and labour into fixed, industrial machinery. Mass intellectuality aims to develop an abstract collective, co-operative, collaborative alternative that starts from the immediacy of the toxic material and social relations that contribute to the absence of collegiality. Mass intellectuality aims to develop an *abstract* strategy to overcome the concrete conditions producing the university as a financialized, marketized entity and academics as subjects with this logic and structure (Neary and Winn 2012; Winn 2014: 6). To take steps towards overcoming this restructuring of the university requires dissolving 'the barriers between work and life' and 'enabl[ing] ... the teacher and student to form a pedagogical alliance for the collective, socially negotiated overcoming of capital's power-over learning, teaching and [research]' (Hall 2015b: 12).

To move outside and beyond the neoliberal, financialized, marketized, university controlled by Capital seems hard to imagine, never mind realize. However, concrete steps are being created in the UK as elsewhere. A significant example is the Social Science Centre (SSC), Lincoln that, like many other alternatives, began in response to the 2010 UK Coalition Government's HE reforms. These included the intention to treble student tuition fees, and to open-up HE to private providers. The SSC is created in response as a co-operative, operates in collectively owned space positioned by and for its members, outside government control; and considers all members, 'scholars' – a term that contests 'the traditional relation of power between academics and student' (Social Science Centre 2013). The SSC also aims to 'reconnect research and teaching' with the concept of 'student-as-producer' (Social Science Centre 2013), to negate the government policy reform idea of students as consumers.

Indeed, the SSC arguably offers a very different notion of leadership: collective, collaborative governance concretely negates the assumption that leadership refers singularly to those who hold formally determined leadership positions. All members of the SSC can potentially and collectively lead on any issue to be discussed and explored by scholars (Bryman 2007; Macfarlane 2013). In developing this point, the next section considers the pedagogy of the MST through the lens of mass intellectuality. I do so in order to consider how ideas of mass intellectuality might be expanded.

The (im)possibility of mass intellectuality: The pedagogy of the MST

I now critique the (im)possibility of mass intellectuality with the pedagogy of the MST. This analysis rests on discussions, first with Brazilian popular educators and critical pedagogues in Brazil in September 2015 and December 2015–January 2016, and second with Brazilian and English critical pedagogues/popular educators in October 2015. The analysis also relies on an engagement with the literature produced by and about the MST. The analysis is grouped around critiquing three key concepts related to mass intellectuality: the role of contexts; the idea of the mind as a fundamentally generative human capacity; and the development of collective agency.

1. *Mass intellectuality as a concept is located in the widest determining context – it seeks to understand how Capital shapes the material conditions within which Northern academics and students live and work.*

I start with this assertion to highlight the radically different conditions in which the MST work compared to those of the predominantly urban, middle-class Northern academics working in, against and beyond the neoliberal university. It is from this basis that we can consider how to use the lens of the MST to expand our understanding of mass intellectuality. Mass intellectuality as a concept negates the 'assumption of individual craft' that has long-guided Northern academic knowledge production, an assumption encouraged by elite effort to persuade rather than coerce academics' compliance with elite interests (Moten and Harney 1999: 26). It also negates the leadership tropes that how individual academics can exercise leadership under current difficult conditions (Bolden et al. 2012).

Mass intellectuality's collective basis provides grounds for the creation of an alliance of alternative social relations that acknowledges, and seeks to work against, the current context in which there is an 'absence of collective agency among academics' (Winn 2014: 9). It is also from this basis that mass intellectuality is defined to enable students to negate the idea that students act as customers buying a service that academics 'deliver' in order for students to obtain a product at the end: a degree (Hall 2015; McGettigan 2013). Those developing mass intellectuality acknowledge that what its realization requires is a pedagogy of and for class struggle aiming to engage in acts of 'doing' so that steps towards a revolutionary university can be taken (University of Utopia n.d.). For the university to become a site of struggle against the reproduction of knowledge that serves transnational capital's interests, knowledge production must start with struggle, by co-operatively doing and being.

A crucial step that requires development is what class struggle means for mass intellectuality. This can be more concretely addressed by considering the MST's pedagogical response to class struggle. The MST aims to overcome the social relations of material production that landless, rural Brazilian workers face. This starting point is the basis for a pedagogy of collective agency aimed at moving beyond current class-based, colonizing material and social conditions. As in other Latin American social movements, the MST aims to build 'organic link[s] between popular education and "popular movements"' (Tarlau 2013: 5) – that is, education is at its core a social movement (Kane 2001).

The pedagogy of the MST seeks to develop explicit transformative strategies with which landless rural workers fighting against the neoliberal capitalist order can contribute to 'the formation of a new social subject that calls itself "*Sem Terra*" (people without land)' (Caldart and the MST 2011: 171) which seeks, and sometimes achieves, collective 'control of their own destiny' (71–72). The MST members in occupation aim, with the help of MST (and sometimes supportive external educators),[3] is to occupy land owned by the elite, and to try to make this land arable and productive. Their goal is to collectively overcome their material condition of landlessness by gaining the legal right to own the land they have occupied. Their action starts with the concrete manifestation of its abstract aim of overcoming current conditions.

My colleague Paolo Vittoria works with the MST and other social movements as a popular educator who co-created the Popular Education Social Forum in Rio de Janeiro. He is also a critical pedagogue at the Federal University of Rio de Janeiro and collaborates with Northern academics seeking to understand the material conditions of being a landless worker and the consciousness that this produces.

> To be a peasant, an agrarian worker, without land, is a contradiction. It speaks to the wider system of oppression, where the *Latifundio* [landowners] exploit the system and whose presence is not just on the land; they make themselves into the consciousness of the people. (Vittoria 2015a, in conversation with Canaan and Neary, 10 October 2015)

Vittoria immediately links landlessness to the material and social conditions that produce it. What are these conditions?

Brazilian rural workers' landlessness, like landlessness in other parts of Latin America, was created in the context of colonialism. This entailed both the extraction of natural resources from the land, the enslavement of African people for capitalist production in the Caribbean and Latin America, and the forced removal of peasants on land they had long inhabited (Santos, 2014). As Leher and Vittoria (2015: 145) note, when Brazil became a nation in 1888, the rural elite had already expanded their land ownership by 'freeing' rural slaves in the 1830s. Capitalist extraction of surplus value and natural resources grew during the twentieth century. Whilst around 30 per cent of the population lived in urban contexts in the 1940s, government 'national development' programmes amplified urbanization by governments from mid-century. During the 1964–1985 dictatorship, this urbanization was further amplified so that by 1991, 75 per cent of Brazilians lived in urban areas. This process continues (Leher and Vittoria 2015; Tarlau 2013: 11), and it is from this context of growing landlessness among remaining agrarian workers that the MST formally emerged in 1984, building on mid-century, reformist and revolutionary programmes (Leher and Vittoria 2015).

The literacy programme that Freire famously created, and that has profoundly informed Latin American (and other) popular educators and critical pedagogues, emerged in the aftermath of the Cuban revolution of 1959. It was one of several attempts to overcome the infrastructure that European and the US colonizing forces imposed on Latin American countries as producers of agricultural goods and sources for mineral-based wealth. Freire's popular education, a key influence on the pedagogy of the MST, sought to counter the US government efforts to prevent any post-1959 'contagion' of revolutionary zeal. Popular education provided a pedagogy that encouraged people collectively to build 'critical consciousness with a view to turning the undifferentiated mass of rural workers into conscious people aware of their legal [and] social rights' (Leher and Vitttoria 2015: 149). The MST pedagogy entailed an ongoing spiral process of dialectical, dialogical action, followed by collective dialogue/reflection, followed by re-forming collective agency. This leads then to further action, in order to regain land, survive and thrive as a dignified, replenished collective subject continuing to struggle for its fuller collective agency and to support nearby communities that are starting down this road.[4]

The underpinning trajectory of this pedagogy could help those developing mass intellectuality, through reflections on how to reconstitute, for example, the student–lecturer dyad so that it could help create collective agency. This would require not just collectively learning, teaching and reflecting on these acts but, crucially, collectively engaging in political struggle in which education serves the wider purpose of building a sustainable, egalitarian, spiral-like process of transformation in the community lives.

2. *Mass intellectuality fuses predominantly urban Northern middle-class knowledge workers with that which they produce. It views the mind as a fundamentally generative human capacity.*

The starting point of the MST's pedagogy is radically different to that of mass intellectuality. Again, Vittoria helps Northern academics appreciate the challenges that rural landless workers face so that we can think with these ideas to build appropriate projects for our own contexts:

> To be illiterate is to not know one's rights, to not be able to read the bible,[5] to not know how to get on a bus. Illiteracy is a form of profound dependency. When you are learning to read and write you are creating autonomy… Dependence [of the oppressed] is a very comfortable and crucial state-of-being for the elite. Creating literacy in popular education entails the strategy of working with generative words… Workers learning literacy are learning [for example] about the right to understand the law that the elite are using to oppress them. (2015b)

As illiteracy levels are so low at present in the North, our common-sense understanding often fails to recognize the amplified sense of disempowerment that illiteracy may produce. Conversations I had with MST members of a settlement I visited (January 2016) indicated that illiteracy was partly caused by landlessness. Landlessness limited family income and often required all family members, including children, to participate in agricultural work, when it was available, for their survival. Thus, material constraints led to children being made illiterate. Vittoria, like Stedile (2002), speaks of the multiple 'fences' of disempowerment that landlessness, illiteracy and other factors create.

Importantly, the MST pedagogy seeks to reconfigure powerlessness as 'profound indignation' (Tarlau 2013: 21).[6] How can we in the North understand this? We can think about this strategy concretely with Vittoria's example of how illiteracy prevents peasants from gaining knowledge of the history of land ownership that has led to a legal system shaped from and for the benefit of elite landowners. Rather than continuing to feel powerless, a popular education-guided literacy programme that Freire and others created looks beneath the seemingly innocent neutrality of the legal system. That is, beneath words like 'laws' and 'land ownership' lie the abstract ways that the legal system works to benefit the already elite at the expense of landless peasants. For the MST, guided in part by Freire, a word learnt in literacy classes is 'more than just an instrument which makes dialogue possible; accordingly… its constitutive elements… [are] reflection and action' (Freire 1970).

The MST pedagogy rests on the assumption that learning to read words is linked to learning to read the world. Its pedagogy 'is preoccupied with the questions of our time, and that helps to strengthen social struggles and create solutions to the concrete problems of each community in the country' (Tarlau 2013: 21). This pedagogy shapes how concrete problems are faced and how strategies for their overcoming are collectively created. With such strategies, a possible sense of disempowerment or immobility is re-fashioned and can fuel a fire of indignation. Addressing the concrete questions that, for example, landless people have about their landlessness provides steps in a process of nurturing 'a minimum general critical spirit, a universal citizenship and a collective desire for radical change in order to achieve the utopia of constructing a new society' (Fernandes 1996, in Tarlau 2013: 3).

This critical spirit that is being nurtured requires, on the part of the popular educator, engagement in acts of 'love', of 'commitment to others' and 'to their cause, the cause of liberation' (Freire 1970), which aim to abolish the oppressive conditions under which they live and work. Emotions and intellect are fused in this process. This point was clearly brought home to me when a Brazilian popular educator, critical pedagogue, comrade and friend said, in response to my initial inability to understand the fullness of MST pedagogy: 'For you in the North, the process of understanding stops here (gesturing down from the top of his head to his neck). For us in the South, it goes further' (pointing to his heart and body more generally). The Manifesto of MST educators confirms this powerful point with their defence of 'a pedagogy that is concerned with all the dimension of the human being' (MST, in Tarlau 2013: 2).

Heart, soul and spirit, as well as mind, are integral to the MST pedagogy. Why? Crucially, a pedagogy that includes all aspects of people makes it possible to 'awaken… the dreams' (MST, in Tarlau 2013: 21) that motivate MST participants to engage in the dangerous process of occupying land held by landowners, often with people they have not known previously.

For the MST, and other social movements in Latin America more generally, the process of building a social movement fuses mind, body and emotions – as well as spirit for some. This goes beyond the assumptions of those developing mass intellectuality who view academic knowledge production as a 'communal process of production' (University of Utopia n.d.) that seeks to negate and overcome current knowledge production strategies of the corporate financialized university today, which are creating a sense of 'dissociated sociality' (Virno 2001). Is it enough to utilize language conceptualized as a 'reflexive process' through which 'the power of abstraction' serves liberating purposes (Winn 2015b: 9)? What if 'the power of abstraction' was fused with feelings of hope and possibility that are stirred by thinking and doing differently? What kinds of strategies might this entail? What kind of 'pedagogy' can be elaborated if those involved in creating mass intellectuality together engage in concrete strategies of 'class struggle' to link doing, thinking and being against the ways that these are encouraged in the neoliberal university (University of Utopia n.d.)?

3. *Mass intellectuality aims to build and deepen a sense of collective agency; it is literally a co-labour collaboration, which aims to engender a sense of capaciousness that enriches and supersedes the possibilities of and for individual agency.*

How can mass intellectuality entail co-labouring? I would suggest that here those engaged in this endeavour learn with the MST. Caldart and the MST (2011: 73) discuss what is 'educative' about the MST. Interestingly, here they refer to E.P. Thompson's work, as have other Brazilians linked to the MST with whom I have spoken:[7]

> We can see the MST as a space of formation, in the sense of 'making yourself', as in E. P. Thompson's *The Making of the English Working Class* (1963). As in nineteenth century England, uprooted workers in modern Brazil are transformed

> into a collective struggle ... The landless are making themselves a new social *subject* ... a collective whose daily actions, connected to a concrete social struggle, are producing elements of a type of culture quite different from the hegemonic social and cultural patterns in present-day capitalist society. An example of this is the decision, taken at local levels in each settlement and often after much debate, to opt for collective rather than individual farming. (Caldart and the MST 2011: 73, italics in original text)

In this quote, Caldart and the MST elaborate several points, some of which have resonances with mass intellectuality. First, both are engaged in counter-hegemonic struggle for an anti-capitalist society. The MST aims to make (as E.P. Thompson suggests rural workers in England previously did) a space of collective 'social formation' that moves them from dependency on and powerlessness towards an elite. Their aim is to make themselves anew as a collective subject engaged in collectively organized, concrete struggle against Capital on a daily basis. Of course strategies *cannot* be those of mass intellectuality. The former live and work together in rural areas and rely on one another so much more profoundly than do intellectual workers who come together primarily to work and who live scattered around a wide area.

Like the MST, Hall suggests that mass intellectuality must respond to 'crises that emerge from the contradictions of capitalism' by engaging in counter-hegemonic class struggle such as 'refusal of academic labour in formal educational institutions, the development of the academic commons, the use of free and open source software and copyfarleft licenses, the realization of peer-to peer-networks' (Hall 2015: 10). All of these examples require collective action. The first one potentially occurs within the university today whilst the rest can occur in spaces within or outside the university. All of these actions entail collective action.

It is hardly surprising that there is no mention in mass intellectuality of creating a new social subject given that its participants live their daily in urban, dispersed spaces that do not entail collective support and reliance on one another. This difference is highlighted by the narratives of those in the MST who are living, working and struggling to survive together in the countryside, in camps or settlements. Clearly, the MST articulates a profound sense of collectivity. Knowledge production alone is the designated task of mass intellectuality. Could or should it entail more than acts of work-related knowledge production alone? Could it not, as I have argued, expand beyond mind to body and emotion, if not spirit?

Conclusion

Mass intellectuality, as the following points indicate, has the following components.

- The concept is located in the widest, determining context – that of the ways that capital shapes the material conditions within which Northern academics and students live and work.

- It fuses predominantly urban Northern middle-class knowledge workers with that which they produce. It recognizes that the mind offers a fundamentally generative human capacity.
- Its aim is to build and deepen a sense of collective agency; it is literally a co-labour and collaboration. Co-labouring produces a sense of collective agency, a capaciousness that enriches and supersedes the possibilities of and for individual agency.
- Collective agency is built through acting and reflecting that aim to overcome the alienating conditions of university knowledge production today. Its aim is to build a palpable sense of the shared possibilities and responsibilities that knowledge-making can offer.
- Knowledge-making as a process dissolves the barriers that create teachers and students as separated beings, with teachers having power over students.
- To overcome the teacher/student dyad requires the dissolution of the current knowledge production process in which teaching, learning and researching are separate and separating acts.
- Dissolving as a process of metamorphoses what has been,[8] which itself enables the making of what could be.

This chapter suggests that mass intellectuality offers a powerful analytical tool with which to critique the contemporary university that is now so deeply imbricated in and imbued with a commercialized, commodified, quantifiable neoliberal capitalist logic, structure and processes. By looking at mass intellectuality through the lens of the pedagogy of the MST, I am suggesting that mass intellectuality could do much more. It could include more aspects of individual and collective subjectivity. It could more fully elaborate how it is guided by critical pedagogy, which its authors mention in passing but do not explore its usage with one another and with students. Those writing about mass intellectuality could also expand beyond mind to, body and emotions, especially as the poststructuralist literature explores the ways that the neoliberal university creates a toxic environment for academic workers today (and which ignores the wider, abstract social relations which cause this toxicity).

As I have listed above, much more can be written about what mass intellectuality entails. I suggest that by looking at this global Northern concept through the lens of global Southern movements of social transformation such as the MST, anti-capitalist Marxist concepts can be revised and, potentially, expanded so that they can more fully and effectively enable the movement away from the enclosure of knowledge production that now occurs in corporate, financialized social relations.

Acknowledgements

Thanks to Richard Hall for his insightful and encouraging editing of the first draft of this chapter that helped me pull out my argument.

Notes

1 According to Banfield (personal communication), he and his colleagues did not know about Davies' article or its title when they wrote their piece.
2 Space limits prevent me from discussing the current threats that the MST and wider progressive struggles in Brazil face due to the ongoing right-wing parliamentary coup now occurring.
3 Supportive agrarian experts initially research the fitness of land for a proposed occupation before the occupation begins.
4 An MST *settlement* (that had successfully gained collective ownership of their community) that I visited in January 2016, was supporting a nearby *camp* (occupying land and fighting to gain the right to own it collectively).
5 As Frei Betto (2001a: 2) explains 'Calling on people to be the agents of their liberation, "the Kingdom of God is not up there, but here in front of you"' in Issa (2014: 89).
6 Dinerstein (2015) similarly speaks not of fences but of the literal and metaphorical 'wires' that separate landless peasants from the land they seek to occupy and then own.
7 Several Brazilian education activists I spoke with referred to these works (and others) as guiding their pedagogy and praxis because they were analyzing the wresting of rural English peasants from the land on which they had lived and worked for generations.
8 Thanks to Sarah Amsler for this phrase, this insight.

7

Still Spaces in the Academy? The Dialectic of University Social Movement Pedagogy

Eurig Scandrett

Introduction

Education is a core function of the university. It is hard to conceive of any future for higher education (HE) in which education does not feature. The struggle for the future of academic work is therefore a struggle over education: its meaning, purpose, practice and opportunity. Education is always a social process in which conflicting interests seek to select, transmit, distribute, construct and critique knowledge. In a knowledge society, knowledge increasingly takes a commodity form, is privatized and partially replaces other means of production as drivers of capital accumulation. But education is also a social relation, an interaction between human subjectivities and therefore always contains the capacity for agency.

Capitalist production increasingly relies on the dead labour of the collective human brain, excluding the worker from the creative generation of knowledge in the economy. However, knowledge continues to be created *both* in collectively challenging these social relations *and* in experimenting with alternatives. Autonomous Marxists have proposed that mass intellect emerges from the struggle over general intellect in the context of mass communication and participative management – mass intellectuality is made possible by the necessity of capital in a communication age, to devolve production to the initiative of workers. Here, it is argued that mass intellect emerges also through resistance – not only to techno-capital but also to other forms of exploitation and oppression. Moreover, this process of liberating the general intellect through the specificities of resistance is educational, and therefore offers possibilities in university praxis even as social relations of education are infected by capital. No matter how much of the general intellect is converted into capital in the life of the university, education retains the possibility for engaging with knowledge-generating processes that are excluded from this, where mass intellect is liberated through resistance.

Johnson (1993) noted that working-class and subaltern educational movements have historically demanded 'Really Useful Knowledge' which is evaluated on the basis of a critical epistemological contribution to collective interests and emancipatory struggle.

The struggle over education and its practice – pedagogy – is therefore a conflict over whose interests knowledge serves, and at the centre of the struggle over the future of the university. So long as university work involves education – the education of social human beings – there remain spaces in the academy for emancipation of mass intellectuality. One of the key theorists of education as a site of contested interests in knowledge was Ettore Gelpi (Griffin 1983).

Gelpi (1979, 1985) developed the concept of lifelong education when he was head of UNESCO during the 1970s and 1980s, a period of intense social conflicts: post-colonial, racial, gendered and class struggles. For Gelpi, such conflicts are fertile grounds for understanding the structural contradictions of society and building collective ways forward politically. Conflicts are knowledge-producing and therefore centrally relevant to education. Crises, which we are currently experiencing in HE, are pedagogical opportunities. For Gelpi, the role of the educator therefore is to identify and respond pedagogically to social conflicts. There is a leadership role for educators here, but only in relation to those engaged in struggles around such contradictions – leadership emerges from such critical encounters between educators and social movement actors. In contrast to some trends in autonomous Marxism and post-Marxism (Hardt and Negri 2000: 127–129; Laclau 2015), Gelpi's analysis of the relationship between knowledge and political economy is unequivocally dialectical. This chapter draws on this analysis in demonstrating how dialectical contradictions can be a fertile source for the liberation of mass intellectuality. I also draw on the insights from Marxist social movement theory developed by Laurence Cox and Alf Gunvald Nilsen concerning the role of knowledge and intellectual production in a process that develops from the achievement of concessions, through militant particularism and campaigns, to the development of social movements from below which challenge hegemonic control of the 'social structures of human needs and capacities' (Nilsen and Cox 2013: 64. See also Cox and Nilsen 2014).

This chapter discusses a number of case studies of educational responses to social conflicts which have involved the institution of HE where I am employed: Queen Margaret University, Edinburgh. This selection of case studies is largely personal – I have been involved in some way or another with all of them. They are not necessarily particularly remarkable, and do not involve iconic examples of subverting the latest technology for emancipatory purposes. The purpose of this selection is not to make a special case for these initiatives, beset with failures as well as some achievements, but rather to scrutinize ordinary attempts to engage with the constraints of the university in a particular historical context and to assess how and where leadership has emerged at the interfaces. They hopefully serve to demonstrate and critically analyze spaces within the academy where 'there is some degree of autonomy for educational action, some possibility of political confrontation, and at the same time an interrelation between the two' (Gelpi 1979: 11).

For the autonomous Marxists, mass intellectuality is liberated through the peculiarity of information technology as it tends towards labourless production. However, it is argued here that the general social condition of resistance to oppression in multiple locations within and out with the labour process and in relation to the violations of technology, has the potential for liberation of mass intellectuality. In none of the case studies presented here, is information and communication technology dominant. All involve contributions to the liberation of mass intellectuality through critical engagement with contradictions in social relations. Many involve conflicts in relation to technologies, largely chemical-based, multinational 'toxic capital' (Mac Sheoin and Pearce 2014). Although not primarily a theoretical argument, the case studies provide a counter-balance to any tendency to reify information technologies which can lead to a teleological reading of history, and vanguardism of a technological proletariat (Dyer-Witheford 1999: 503). Some have made use of information technologies, others responded to or generated different technologies, and the agents of mass intellect range from academic specialists to non-literate Indian urban poor.

I argue that there are still spaces in the academy for emancipatory education, despite – or even because of – the neoliberal crisis of the university. Universities have never been privileged places for scholarly reflection independent of the conflicts of the political economy of the world outside (although they have certainly been places for the privileged). The current crisis potentially makes universities privileged places for the realization of mass intellectuality, because they are educational spaces in which the structural contradictions of neoliberal capital are so explicitly being played out.

The chapter initially sets the context in which the case studies have occurred: the historical development of HE in Scotland and the particular origins and political economy of Queen Margaret University. Three areas of work are then described, in which educational leadership has emerged from the interaction of academics with sites of social struggle. First, educational work which has been developed through dialogical engagement with NGOs rooted in popular social movements. Second, research which has developed as knowledge exchange through dialogue with groups in social conflict. Third, the conflicting roles of employees in the university, it is argued, provide pedagogical opportunities through campus trade unions.

The case study of NGO-mediated conflicts focuses on environmental justice and gender-based violence. The first set of conflicts is around the environmental impact of economic development on communities: of new and old technologies; of local action groups; the NGO Friends of the Earth and the University. The second set of conflicts relate to the crisis of women's resistance to domestic abuse; the development of political responses to gendered violence through Women's Aid and the wider feminist movement; and the collaboration with the Scottish State and with Queen Margaret University. The ongoing struggles and many failures in attempts to build on these projects to embed lifelong education within the institution are explored.

Second, the relationship between research, knowledge exchange and lifelong education is explored through case studies of action research in India with social movements interfacing chemical technologies: the Bhopal survivors' movement and Community Environmental Monitors in Tamil Nadu. The research draws explicitly on the pedagogical praxis of Paulo Freire to seek to generate knowledge useful to social movements. At the same time, the author's engagement with the movements has brought educational and institutional contradictions and opportunities within the university. The ongoing development of a knowledge exchange centre aims at a synthesis of action research and critical pedagogy under the cover of 'public engagement'.

Finally, a trade union case study will explore the educational opportunities arising from conflicts over university governance, local action against bullying, performance management and new managerialism. These are ongoing struggles with many defeats, but a close analysis serves to explore the opportunities for liberating the general intellect of academics as workers, through industrial relations.

These case studies cover three core areas of academic work: pedagogy; research and employment relations. They illustrate emergent mass intellectuality through educational responses to social contradictions, in which leadership has emerged through the interface between the agency of the educator and the praxis of social struggle.

Author's position

The presentation of context, case study and analysis needs to be foregrounded with a reflexive positioning of the author, who has been involved, directly or indirectly, and in some cases in leadership positions, within each of these case studies. As an academic biologist in the 1980s, I completed a PhD in Plant Science and postdoctoral research, at a time when the neoliberal policies of Margaret Thatcher were generating new conflicts over the role of scientific research. Since the 1970s, the radical science movement had been providing a critique of social interests in scientific knowledge, and turning this into practical political challenges to elite natural sciences, Big Science, and the use of scientific knowledge production by financial and military interests. The movement moreover was experimenting with alternative forms of 'people's science', ranging from industrial democracy to science shops to popular planning in socialist states. By the 1980s, when I was in the early stages of a scientific career, the movement was in retreat from an alternative critique from the New Right.

The direction of travel was obvious: Scientific knowledge was to serve the interests of capital. In 1984, the industrial disaster at Union Carbide, Bhopal, made the destructive implications of that process clear. I made the decision to leave my early career choice as a scientific researcher and moved into community education and environmental campaigning for fifteen years, ultimately returning to academia as a social scientist.

Background

During its 300-year union with England in the UK, Scotland retained a separate education system, albeit one which converged in the centralized multinational state. George Davie (1961) famously critiqued the loss of what he called the 'democratic intellect' in Scottish Universities as they became closer to the professional specialisms of England. Davie's democratic intellect owed more to philosophic generalism which Scottish students of all disciplines studied, than to any popular access to this philosophy. However, the idea of the democratic intellect has in more recent times linked university education to the wider (and somewhat mythical) traditions of the educational generalist: the 'lad o' pairts', autodidactism, the relationship of education to class empowerment and a culture of scepticism towards the use of education for individual advancement and social mobility epitomized in the Scots expression '*ah kent yer faither*' (I knew your father. i.e., I know where you come from and you're no better than the rest of us).

Scottish civic nationalism has developed considerable strength in the past few decades in a complex relationship with neoliberalism (Scott and Mooney 2009). The union with England in 1707 left some key Scottish institutions under the control of a Scottish educated elite – education, the law, the church, aspects of the arts and media – whose autonomy from England was contested but largely outside of any democratic control within Scotland.

As with its educational generalism, Scotland's tradition of political radicalism has been overstated (Gall 2005). Nonetheless, during the 1980s, while elections returned ever increasing majorities of Labour politicians from Scotland to a UK parliament with a Conservative majority government which was systematically privatizing public assets and dismantling the welfare state, this democratic deficit was converted into a form of radical civic nationalism. By the time the Tory government had been toppled in 1997, the demand for political devolution in Scotland was unavoidable and the Scottish Parliament was instituted in 1999.

HE policy has since been devolved to Scotland. Tuition fees, introduced by the Labour government in Westminster, became a political football in Scotland between Labour, Liberal Democrat (coalition partners in government from 1999 to 2007) and the Scottish National Party, which abolished tuition fees when it formed the government in 2007. In 2010, the government published a Green Paper on the future of HE (Scottish Government 2010) and in 2011 established a five-member commission on HE governance representing university management, students and staff unions, and chaired by Professor Ferdinand von Prondzynski (von Prondzynski et al. 2012). The commission's report recommended some significant proposals for making university governance more democratic, accountable, diverse and transparent. Some of these principles have been endorsed by the Scottish government and enshrined in the HE Governance (Scotland) Act 2016. However, throughout this process, the Principals and Chairs of Court – those with a vested interest in the status quo – have been manoeuvring to avoid these recommendations being implemented (see Smith 2013).

Queen Margaret University

The origins of Queen Margaret University lie in the nineteenth-century women's movement's campaign for access to education for working-class women. In Edinburgh, where domestic service was a significant source of employment for working-class women, feminist activists Christian Guthrie Wright and Louisa Stevenson established the Edinburgh School of Cookery in 1875. Through a series of iterations, the Edinburgh School of Cookery and Domestic Economy became Queen Margaret College in 1972 and achieved university status as Queen Margaret University in 2007 (Begg 1994).

The current university is small, with 4,000 campus-based students and a staff of around 500, half of whom are academics. Three quarters of students and two-thirds of staff are female. In 2006, the university moved from its prime site locations in Edinburgh to a purpose-built campus on green belt land outside the city. This land was purchased prior to 2007, while the old buildings were sold after the economic crash and the plummet in land prices. QMU now has the largest debt to turnover ratio of any UK university by a large margin.

Case study 1: Education: Environmental justice, gendered violence and public sociology

The first case study originated with the NGO Friends of the Earth (FoE) Scotland in which I was employed from 1997 to 2005. FoE Scotland is an independent NGO and the Scottish member of FoE International confederation, which Doherty and Doyle (2013) categorize as a Social Movement Organisation. With the formation of a Scottish Parliament, FoE Scotland launched a campaign for environmental justice, emphasizing the connections between social justice, environmental damage and resource limits at a local and global level: 'no less than a decent environment for all, no more than our fair share of the earth's resources' (Dunion and Scandrett 2003). Central to this strategy was building the capacity of communities to identify and challenge local environmental problems while making the connections with structural causes of global environmental damage. To this end, an educational project was devised in conjunction with QMU (Scandrett 2007).

The pedagogical starting point was the experience of communities struggling for environmental justice. The participants – subsequently referred to as 'agents' – were selected on the basis that the knowledge which they took from the structured learning, and that which they brought to it, was the collective property of their community engaged in struggle. The issues which the agents were contesting ranged from the introduction of new technologies (offshore fish farming; microelectronics) to the impact of long-standing industries (opencast coal; waste incineration) and post-industrial aftermath (land contamination; dilapidated public housing).

The course was based around the knowledge and experience of struggle shared by agents in dialogue with the knowledge and experience of the professional campaigners in FoE Scotland and of the academics in QMU. Thereby, each source of knowledge was subject to interrogation and challenge and, over the course of the programme, selected from and validated on the basis of its usefulness to the agents (see Scandrett 2014). The programme was accredited by the university as a Higher Education Certificate in Environmental Justice. The intellectual leadership emerged from both FoE Scotland and, through dialogue, with communities of struggle: academics, professional campaigners and grass-roots activists brought different expertise to a Freirean pedagogical process which critically interrogated each other (Agents for Environmental Justice and Scandrett 2003). Ultimately, there was an attempt to incorporate the course into the university degree programme, which would have attracted state funding of fees. This would have enabled activists from communities of struggle to replace more traditional students on existing courses, thereby challenging some vested interests in the university. This was blocked by risk-averse senior management who supported the work as a fringe experiment but resisted acknowledging its intellectual leadership within the university.

Several of the struggles revolved around the introduction of new technologies, although there were no cases where the use of information technology was central. One community constituted women formerly employed in microelectronics production in Greenock, South West of Glasgow. While information technology was central to this struggle, it was not in its use, but rather the exposure to toxic chemicals in its production, by material labour. The collective knowledge employed included an analysis of the political economy of the microelectronics on which information commodities rely (Crowther et al. 2009). Another struggle involved the introduction of fish farms to the coastal waters of North West Scotland, which was made possible in large scale by developments in agrochemicals. Conflicts here often centred around disputed interpretations of ecological knowledge between the companies, regulators and local communities that are dependent on agriculture and fishing (Crowther et al. 2012) – of accumulation by dispossession (Harvey 2006). Locating the conflicts over knowledge in the context of global political ecology was an important component of the education programme. This is not based on information technology (which, as Crowther et al. 2009 describe, was somewhat peripheral) and its achievements were modest and ultimately concessionary. Nonetheless, the role of the university in analyzing the limitations of these achievements is an important component of what Nilsen and Cox (2013) call the 'social movement process' – the collapsing of hegemony through a praxis of confronting capital and realizing the limitations of the militant particularism of a local struggle, and raising the conflict to a more systemic level.

Although the environmental justice course with FoE Scotland was not fully incorporated into the university's programme, a partnership with Scottish Women's Aid was better established in the institution from the beginning. The struggle against violence against women has been a core component of feminist activism, especially since the second wave movement in the 1960s and 1970s focused attention on the politics of personal lives and intimate relationships. Refuges for women fleeing domestic violence were an important site of praxis for the movement which not only provided protection from violence and practical welfare support but also became a source of feminist knowledge generation (Dobash and Dobash 1992).

In the UK, Women's Aid emerged as the organizational leader of the refuge movement and of feminist politics, a social movement organization with roots in the lived experience of women escaping domestic violence and other forms of abuse. In Scotland, local Women's Aid groups established Scottish Women's Aid (SWA) to support local action and to take forward the campaigning priorities and other emergent policy issues of the movement. Along with other parts of the feminist movement in Scotland, SWA succeeded in ensuring that a gendered understanding of domestic violence, and the connection between tackling domestic abuse, violence against women and structured gender inequality, was reflected in Scottish Government policy. One aspect of this policy was the provision of training and education, which led to a collaboration between SWA and QMU.

Gender Justice, Masculinities and Violence was developed as a module for activists, volunteers and professionals working in the field of gender and violence, as well as an option for honours year full-time students of psychology and sociology. The module is taught by educators from SWA and QMU staff. The style of pedagogy facilitated a dialogical curriculum based on the experience of SWA and others working in the field; the academic literature; and the personal gendered experience of patriarchal social relations of both those active in the field and full-time students (Orr et al. 2013).

Intellectual leadership emerged from the women's movement, and especially through its successful incorporation into Scottish Government policy, with the potential contradictions that that brings. The curriculum is explicitly framed as a 'war of position', a contribution to shifting meanings in the performance of gender in both private and public space. It therefore aims for a shift in the control over Nilsen and Cox's 'social structures of human needs and capacities' (2013). Outcomes have included changes to midwifery practices in relation to Female Genital Mutilation and the provision of materials at Edinburgh clubs to combat sexual harassment. As a contribution to counter-hegemonic education within an established curriculum the course provides some space for liberation of the general intellect in tension with its incorporation into mainstream policy and educational provision. Moreover, the curriculum also provides an opportunity to explore the political economy of gendered violence, by focusing on the massive increase in global capital investment in prostitution, trafficking, pornography, the beauty industry and other forms of commercial sexual exploitation.

Having achieved a Higher Education Certificate and an Honours module in collaboration with Social Movement Organisations, based on curricula derived from social conflict, an attempt was made to develop an undergraduate degree. The proposed BSc in Social Justice was initiated with a range of community action and campaign groups. It was designed to carve out a space within the mainstream, state-funded university provision for liberating education, and within capped student numbers this would have replaced, rather than supplemented elements of the university curriculum. This threatened vested interests and so the institution withdrew support, offering instead a Master's programme: an addition to mainstream provision as a new commodity, rather than a modest transformation. While this attempt failed, the battle to implement a shift in the provision of education at QMU has recently achieved institutional backing with the validation of an undergraduate programme in Public Sociology.

This case study demonstrates that it remains possible to liberate spaces within the university curriculum for emancipatory education in dialogue with social movement organizations which have emerged from, and engage in, specific areas of social conflict. Limitations have been met, both through university structures and the relatively limited objectives of the SMOs. However, such limitations are themselves a source of curriculum as they expose contradictions within which struggle takes place, providing the potential to raise collective knowledge-generation to a higher level in a small contribution to the development of alternative hegemony. Universities cannot of course undermine the hegemonic knowledge on which they depend, but can create spaces where such activity can be facilitated.

Academic knowledge – the dead knowledge of the collective human brain – is liberated through its dialogue with knowledge generated in struggle as 'really useful knowledge' and de-commodified, mass intellectuality is produced. Intellectual leadership is found not in the structures of university management but in the interface with emancipatory movements where dialogue occurs. The following case studies explore this process in the practice of research and knowledge exchange.

Case study 2: Research and knowledge exchange: The Bhopal survivors' movement study, Community Environmental Monitors and the Centre for Dialogue

One of the key areas in which (public) sociology has reflected on its political role has been in the research and theoretical developments associated with social movement studies. Bevington and Dixon's (2005) seminal paper challenged researchers to conduct movement-relevant research including a serious treatment of theory generated by movement activists in social media outwith academic literature. There have been a number of important initiatives which have worked at that interface between movement activism and academic analysis, including the international Popular Education Network (Crowther 2013) and *Interface: a journal about and for social movements*. Research in these areas often draws on dialogical pedagogical methodologies to seek to synthesize knowledge generation in social movement praxis and in academic activism.

One of the critiques of autonomous Marxism's development of the concept of 'general intellect' is the apparent presumption that liberation of the general intellect is dependent on the high-technology skills of a largely western-educated vanguard (Dyer-Witheford 1999). This is also a concern in social movement studies of the 'movement-relevant' variety, in which only those social movement activists who are literate in western languages and skilled users of social media are included in the endeavour of generating emancipatory knowledge. These concerns about selective bias in movement-relevant studies led me to a research interest in the role of non-literate social movement activists in generating knowledge and analysis outwith formal literacy.

An important example of this is the survivors of the Bhopal gas disaster, most of whom are impoverished women with little education and many of whom are not literate. These survivors have developed a range of sustained movement activities demanding justice (as well as innovative healthcare, epidemiological and governance structures, see e.g., Sarangi 2009) since the disaster in December 1984. The disaster – a leak of toxic methyl isocyanate gas from the Union Carbide insecticide factory – is founded on the deadly contradiction of the political economy of technological development in the Green Revolution: the introduction of privately patented, high-yielding varieties of crops, dependent on technological and agrochemical inputs – essentially making the provision of food in the global South an extension of the accumulation of capital. Located on the poor, northern periphery of the city, close to the railway station, the factory attracted informal settlements from migrant labour, several thousand of whom perished from exposure to the gas, with tens of thousands being injured. Union Carbide, and its owner since 2001 Dow Chemical, have to date avoided any liability. Hundreds of the survivors and a small handful of educated activists, drawing on popular ingenuity, oral narrative and dialogue with committed experts, have developed innovative services and continue to mount campaigns for justice.

In 2006, I participated in a Bhopal survivors' movement study which used dialogical methodology based on Freire's *Pedagogy of the Oppressed* (activist ethnography, video-dialogue, movement participant observation, reflexive activism), to seek to generate a theoretical analysis of the role of non-literate knowledge, out of the interaction between the praxis of the movement and the critique brought by activist–academic researchers (the author, an Indian academic, and two Indian activists employed as research associates). Discussion of some of the methodologies and outcomes of this research is documented elsewhere (Mukherjee et al. 2011; Scandrett and Mukherjee 2011). The key issue here is the way in which this research legitimized within the university a form of academic practice alongside a movement mobilizing against the oppression of the technological development of global capital. In doing so, it contributed to the process of liberation of mass intellectuality of non-literate people.

Provisional results of the research in the form of generative themes were presented to groups of survivor-activists using visuals as well as verbal feedback, and collective discussion facilitated further to contribute to the analysis. The first publication constituted an English translation of excerpts from nineteen interviews with survivors/activists, which was launched during the twenty-fifth anniversary of the disaster (Bhopal Survivors' Movement Study 2009).

Ongoing and continuing solidarity in scholarly activity – raising awareness, solidarity campaigns, fundraising – ensures that university work retains some accountability to the survivors' movement. One of the intellectuals active in the movement, Satinath Sarangi, who abandoned a PhD in 1984 to work with the survivors in Bhopal, was awarded an honorary doctorate from the university. Bhopalis, both gas-exposed survivors and their affected children, have visited the UK at the invitation of the university and given presentations to students and public lectures. This is of course marginal to the principal work of the university, which is able to accommodate individual academics' partisan political activity without disruption to its more managerial and commodifying agenda. Without a department of chemical engineering or anything similar, there is no risk of conflict with the Bhopalis' adversaries in Dow Chemical. However, the opportunity for critical, emancipating knowledge to be generated by a collective movement made up largely of non-literate activists is significant.

A similar dialogical methodology was used to research a literate group of activists in Cuddalore, Tamil Nadu, who are employing lay-science techniques to identify and challenge industrial pollution. Living, working, farming and fishing beside the chemical manufacturing plants in the SIPCOT industrial estate, these Community Environmental Monitors have devised systematic mechanisms to identify chemical emissions through smell, sight, touch and impacts on fish and crops. These correspond closely to the results of monitoring by scientific techniques, but are in the hands of the community and are used in investigations by the pollution control board to hold the chemical companies to account (Narayan and Scandrett 2014). In this case, the methods were adapted in discussion with the monitors who retained control of the data in the form of video-recorded interviews for their own use - any subsequent analysis of these data will require researchers to request access from the activists.

These constitute ordinary examples requiring minimal external funding, of legitimizing within the university, research and scholarly activity for dialogical engagement with social movements engaged in liberating mass intellectuality. What is perhaps more significant is where such spaces, carved out of university practice, coalesce with other activities by academics and start to build a counter-narrative to the dominant neoliberal university. Other projects at the margins of the university led by academics in dialogue with community-based, sectoral and campaigning organizations have coalesced in the Centre for Dialogue and Public Engagement. The principle of the Centre is that lifelong education, critical pedagogy, action research, knowledge exchange and community engagement constitute a continuous body of practice founded on the principles of dialogue. By establishing dialogue with key publics - in our cases: communities challenging environmental pollution; women fighting gendered violence; people organizing against the diagnostic power of a psychiatric establishment; young people establishing an independent voice against the dominant discourses on alcohol use - leadership emerges from outwith the university. In the contradictions of social relations and spaces, the role of academics at the margins of the institution can play a role in the liberation of the general intellect. This intellectual leadership provides a locus for undermining the neoliberal direction of travel of the university sector.

Case study 3: Managerialism, bullying and campus trade unionism

The examples provided so far have explored spaces for emancipatory praxis within the work of education and research which is part of the normal employment contract of an academic. Leadership has come from activist academics and social movement organizations, and is fostered in publics whose leadership capacities have been deliberately repressed, whether as women, poor, mad, illiterate or young. The next case study focuses on the contradiction of the university employment contract which, on the one hand requires professional independence to provide specialist education and academic freedom in research, and on the other, specifies the role of academics and their colleagues as employees of the university, in a political economy which conspires to exploit their intellectual labour for the purposes of productivity. This contradiction, responded to collectively, provides a further set of opportunities for educational action and political confrontation.

The introduction of the tools of managerialism in universities has stimulated a search for alternative models which avoid the pitfalls of New Public Management while meeting the perceived needs of both managers and staff in a twenty-first century institution. Some of this literature advocates new forms of collegiality (Burnes et al. 2014), or 'neo-collegiality' (Bacon 2014). One of the contributors to this literature, Professor Petra Wend, became Principal and Vice-Chancellor of Queen Margaret University in 2009. Aspects of her co-authored publication on English universities give some insights into her management of this Scottish university.

> the enormous increase in student numbers, which began with the Robbins Report (1963), led to successive governments cutting universities' funding and compelling them to act more like business enterprises than educational institutions. In turn, ... vice-chancellors have become more like powerful chief executives, collegial forms of control have decreased and academic staff are increasingly told what to teach, how to teach, what research to conduct and where to publish. However, we argue that this can be dysfunctional not only for staff, but also for senior managers. The latter may now have a freehand to make decisions, but without the willing co-operation of staff, the implementation of these decisions becomes much more difficult. The paper ... [advocates] ... a new form of collegiality in universities, one which is compatible with rapid decision-making at the university centre and effective execution of change at the local/departmental level. As such, it provides universities and their staff with a win-win situation; senior managers can implement their decisions more effectively and staff are once again meaningfully involved in the running and development of their departments and universities. (Burnes et al. 2014: 905)

In this model of university governance, strategic direction is led from the top with the 'invited participation' (Cornwall 2002; Miraftab 2004) of all staff, in institutional public spaces (workshops, 'speed dating' sessions, etc.) where all staff are encouraged to give their views. Once devised, this strategic plan is treated as institutionally owned, incorporating the contributions of the staff, who are therefore expected to co-operate willingly in its implementation. Below the level of senior management, staff operate 'a new form of collegiality', motivated to deliver against a strategic direction to which they have contributed. Dissent is viewed as disloyalty or collegial dysfunction. Middle managers have the role of implementing the strategic plan trickling down from above, and at the same time facilitate the new form of limited collegiality from below. In this model, there is no space for the 'invented participation' (Miraftab 2004) of collective staff interests independently of management, through trade union organization.

Associated with this form of 'participative management' for the university, is disproportionate power given to middle managers who are not structurally accountable to the staff; and a growth in the problems of managerialism, including bureaucratization of normal academic work, micromanagement, surveillance, productivity requirements, performance management, deprofessionalization, intimidation, creeping managerial powers in unaccountable non-management positions, divisiveness and outright bullying.

The author is an elected branch officer of University and College Union (UCU) at QMU, was branch president from 2010 to 2015 and was involved in raising evidence of some of these practices and associated ill health of employees, through collective bargaining and industrial challenge. Through a process of dialogue, both individually and collectively with union members, as well as with sister unions on campus, the strategy was developed of using a collective grievance against a 'structure and culture' which tolerates bullying to the detriment of the health of members.

The focus on structure and culture provided an opportunity to address systemic issues rather than the individuals who exploit them and to focus on the distinction between management and leadership in terms of power and accountability. It succeeded in bringing senior management to the table to negotiate with the unions on these issues. A working group was established consisting of equal representation from unions and management, which conducted some evidence-gathering research. At the time of writing, more than three years after the grievance was taken out, structural and cultural issues related to managerialism, bullying and accountability, as well as interpretations of collegiality, remain on the collective bargaining agenda.

UCU membership is made up of a range of highly educated academics whose collective intellectual labour is employed by the University to maximize productivity. Responses to workload pressures, management interference, deprofessionalization and bullying are often interpreted as defective behaviour by individual managers or colleagues, rather than a systemic outcome of a logic of labour exploitation. Regular discussions about a collective grievance on structure and culture, and reflections on trade union strategy, serve to raise the collective knowledge of the underlying contradiction, from a 'local rationality' to militant particularism, and to analyze the strategies of management to concretize conflicting social relations in their interests.

The masking of social relations of exploitation through invited participation has been variously described as a 'new tyranny' (Cooke and Kathari 2001), or 'dispossession through participation' (Collins 2006). The damaging impact on staff is experienced in the 'voluntary' commitment to increasing workload, mistrust of colleagues, excessive stress and mental illness. However, by focusing on key points of contradiction, the trade union organization on campus can serve to expose the purpose of the strategy in the defence of staff interests. While much of this takes the form of winning small concessions through negotiation and tactics, the ongoing confrontation takes a strongly pedagogical form as members progressively understand the contradictions of our own situation through a social movement process.

The trade union then becomes a vehicle for the expression of dissent, not merely around terms and conditions but also within the expression of academic scholarship. The unions can adopt a function which has been abandoned by the public university by exposing the weaknesses of the governance model and creating new spaces for educational action and political confrontation within the academy. The collective grievance over structure and culture which tolerates bullying therefore becomes a key site of struggle which exposes the contradictions of attempting a form of university governance which seeks to incorporate staff into their own exploitation.

This is not just a local issue at QMU. At a Scottish level, the struggle over HE governance between the conflicting interests of, on the one hand staff and students, and on the other, principals and governing bodies, has had a similar impact. Union-led campaigns and conferences on 'Reclaiming the Democratic Intellect' and the 'Future of Scottish Higher Education' have generated more widespread critical debate. This case study does not recount any heroic industrial action, nonetheless the increase in managerialism which emerged through the contradiction between professionalism and productivity has increased the confidence of members to participate in the more everyday work of collective action and the educational role of exposing such conflicts.

The leadership of a trade union representative comes from their contradictory location of demanding concessions on behalf of a collective membership/worker base, from a neoliberal university which demands ever-increasing productivity and commodification of knowledge generation from these workers. Such leadership only sustains for as long as consent is granted by the social movement, the community, the sector, the workers. It is always contingent – leaders may come and go while leadership remains in that contradiction.

Conclusions

There was never a time when HE reflected the needs, capacities and long-term interests of society. Universities, colleges and institutions of education have always reflected the struggles over the generation, selection and distribution of knowledge among competing interests. The origin of Queen Margaret University in the Edinburgh School of Cookery was borne of the women's movement's campaign for access to education for working-class women and for public health and nutrition. George Davie's lament for the loss of the Democratic Intellect in Scottish Universities reflected a struggle over the control of the curriculum between interest groups. The Robbins Report (1963) and the rise of mass, liberal HE was similarly a response to the post-war class compromise of social democracy. The people's science movement and the emergence of the Science Shops in the 1970s, their subsequent decline and transformation into networks of participatory researchers, similarly reflect an ongoing and constant struggle over the ownership, democratization and purpose of knowledge generation. Margaret Thatcher's battles over 'near market' research, and the trend for science parks for university spinoff companies, generated new fields of conflict.

The current neoliberal crisis is similarly a location for pedagogical and political contestation. Democratic learning and knowledge production is not a fixed institutional state but is always contingent and borne of struggle. There was no utopian past that is being dismantled by neoliberalism, nor is there a new utopian space for HE in the near future, but there are spaces of possibility for mass intellectuality in the struggle. This generates many failures from which learning occurs but there are also achievements and spaces for production of emancipating knowledge in the contradictions of the university in crisis. Academic activists are working both *in* and *against* the university in new contradictions and new spaces (London Edinburgh

Weekend Return Group 1980). There is no pure market relation anywhere and especially not in the production of knowledge.

Ettore Gelpi's conception of lifelong education remains a source for intellectual leadership from the margins. This

> is characterised by struggles in social life and educational institutions in such areas as: the type of relationship between formal and non-formal education i.e. dialectical or dependent; the contribution of such non-teaching educators as cultural, social and political movements to education activities; ... the extent to which self-directed learning is encouraged, especially that of a collective nature. (Gelpi 1985: 8–9)

The reproduction of liberating praxis in the university comes from spaces carved out from the contradictory location of the educator/researcher/worker/activist/intellectual. These contradictory spaces perpetually challenge the commodifying mainstream. The reappropriation of the means of knowledge production in the labour process occurs through constantly returning to its contradictory nature. Traditional intellectuals in the universities can also be organic intellectuals engaging in dialogical work in the spaces of contradiction. Leadership comes from that contradiction. Academic leadership comes from dialogue with social movements and community action groups who are engaged in fighting social conflicts.

Acknowledgements

In addition to time liberated from within university employment and some in-kind support, the projects described here were funded by the following sources. The Agents for Environmental Justice project was funded by the National Lottery Charities Board and follow-up work funded by the European Union. The Bhopal Survivors Study received small grants from the Nuffield Foundation, British Academy, Carnegie Trust for the Universities of Scotland, Barry Amiel and Norman Melburn Trust and Lipman-Miliband Trust. The SIPCOT Community Environmental Monitors work was funded by the Carnegie Trust for the Universities of Scotland.

8

Bradford's Community University: From 'Constellations of Knowledge' to Liberating the 'General Intellect'?

Jenny Pearce

Introduction

This chapter reflects on an experiment around exchanging knowledges between academics and communities ('knowledge constellations'). It is also about the practical challenges of enabling the intellectuality of society ('general intellect') to flourish autonomously and critically in a context of market-driven and value-differentiating knowledge institutions. Bradford's 'Community University' was set up by university academics and community activists to explore issues of power and participation in the locality and beyond. 'CommUNIty' as it was named by a community participant, was guided by varied theoretical influences as well as the knowledge and experience of participants. However, it was primarily an exploration of the application and democratic potentialities of new approaches to learning and knowledge production in the context of national shifts in the meaning and purpose of higher education (HE). Progressive intellectuals often appear to imagine that the intellectual life of the mass of the population, which has been so fragmented by interventions of the market and the state, is merely waiting to be 'liberated'. This chapter highlights the obstacles as well as rewards involved in attempts to build a democratic platform for knowledge exchange, which could challenge the selective recognition of whose knowledge matters.

As an experiment which purported to build a process of mutual learning between academics and community activists, there were numerous tensions around the multiple motivations, expectations and backgrounds which individuals brought to the process. These partly reflected the empowering and disempowering subjective effects of the prevailing knowledge production system. CommUNIty participants were driven by a range of goals, which were not necessarily incompatible, but which required co-recognition and co-management. Some academic and non-academic participants articulated more easily, or were more aware of, their reasons for participating than others. Some participants wanted more structure and clarity on the purpose from the beginning, others liked the openness as it would enable them to shape processes themselves. Some hoped to nurture activism while others did not see themselves as activists. In general, non-academic participants were motivated less by abstract ideas than by the prospect of practical help with future study or employment, for instance, or by a new space for sociability or particular goals of building community participation in their neighbourhoods. CommUNIty was about the big political issues for some and for others about smaller-scale, local problems.

This chapter explores how an attempt to question conventional understandings of knowledge and the role of the 'University' as a knowledge producing institution, translates into practice. In particular, what are the challenges that arise in a complex, socially and culturally plural urban environment such as Bradford. It asks, can knowledge be exchanged horizontally in such contexts? In other words, can all knowledges be recognized for their worth, thus enabling experiential and academic knowledge, for example, to generate new questions and insights on our world? How far could or should the idea of a 'University' focus on building cultures of change making and activism rather than structured study *about* activism? Or can both goals be fruitfully combined? The big issue which links this chapter to the themes of this volume is the extent to which a process aspiring to generate democratic exchange between the academy and the community, might be a step toward the liberation and reappropriation of society's intellect in general, what Virno (2004: 108) calls 'the most generic aptitudes of the mind', such as 'the faculty of language, the inclinations to learn, memory, the ability to abstract and to correlate, the inclination towards self-reflection' (2004). It is the faculty of thought that capital has harnessed, argues Virno. CommUNIty implicitly explored whether knowledge exchange might liberate the general intellect from such capture, in the way it recognized and revalorized the multiple constellations of knowledge that society can draw upon. This in turn, aspired to stimulate a wider, deeper and more plural exercise of citizenship, participation and leadership.

The chapter will begin with the origins of CommUNIty before critically assessing its achievements and limitations. A final section will link CommUNIty to the general themes of this volume. It will conclude with a reflection on what this experiment teaches us about the difficulties of rethinking the theory and practice of knowledge production at a time when mainstream HE is distancing itself ever more from sources of intellectual life outside those selected to serve the market economy.

From constellations of knowledge…

The idea behind the Community University was that there is real energy in the knowledge and experience within communities and also different understandings of power, which have grown out of many local struggles. We are not talking here about communities where school to university is an automatic step, although many individuals end up in Further and Higher Education. These are communities, from poor to lower and middle income, who struggle to make their voice heard and become increasingly disillusioned with the world of formal education and politics. At times, this takes them into isolationism and potential vulnerability to right-wing appeals or into a local world of achievable small-scale goals and/or occasionally towards activism for causes associated with the left.

The realization that among such communities ideas of power and participation have nevertheless emerged which can make a real contribution to rethinking politics and change was the conclusion of a research and social action review paper on Power in Community (Pearce 2012). This revealed that within varied communities of the North of England, not only was there a wish to act and make change but there was also a rejection of 'power', or the kind of 'dominating power' that one group described as 'like a hot potato you have to quickly pass it on'. Another argued 'I want to be listened to. I don't want to be dominating. On an estate, someone who is dominating, you back off. That's what estates are like' (Pearce 2013: 657). Most participants did not want positions of power or to 'represent' others, and they saw power rather as about 'cooperating, listening, sharing and enabling others' (645). The groups involved ranged from: an action campaign against dangerous waste dumping in Queensbury, Bradford, an area of lower middle residents where the British National Party (BNP) had once gained support; a group of groups in a poor and ethnically diverse part of Sheffield; a group trying to democratize their Mosque in Manningham, Bradford; a tenants group on Braithwaite and Guardhouse, a mostly white estate in Keighley; and young inner-city lads, also in Manningham, who had set up a football coaching group to keep local boys off the streets (Pearce 2012).

The Community University idea was borne out of this study and the relationships with the community activists who participated in it. Its roots go back even further, to the history of efforts to build engagement between the university and communities of the District on a new basis. The Programme for a Peaceful City (PPC) set up by Bradford academics just before the Bradford riot of 2001, played a critical role in forging these new relationships. A number of research projects had experimented with various methodologies for co-producing knowledge (Blakey et al. 2006; Pearce 2008; Pearce and Milne 2010). Other intellectual influences on the Community University came from the world of activism and social movements (Chesters and Welsh 2006) and in particular from Latin America's history of radical educational ideas and creative social activism (Pearce et al. 2010).

Latin Americans have been less subject to historic strategies of 'governmentality'. Internally absorbed social discipline as outlined by Foucault (2008), for instance, with respect to European history, do not describe the Latin American case. Indeed, sociologist of the Latin American state, Miguel Angel Centeno, writes that the 'symbol of authority in Latin America is not necessarily an internal Freudian policeman but a riot policeman with dogs' (Centeno 2001: 300). Neighbourhood organizing and social movement activism has been particularly persistent and creative in the region, despite the violent responses from the state and other actors. Intellectuals have been drawn to this activism and many have contributed frameworks around knowledge, research and learning which have had global resonance, such as Colombian Orlando Fals Borda's work connecting subaltern knowledge with committed academic/intellectuals and Paulo Freire's literacy and conscientization work in Brazil.

Despite being a highly urbanized part of the world, and with many significant urban community and social movements, it is from rural and indigenous Latin America that some of the most creative ideas on knowledge have emerged in recent decades. These are spaces and territories where dissent from the knowledge assumptions behind neoliberalism has clashed most intensely with peasant and indigenous knowledge and attachment to land and culture. Rural Latin America has long been a site of contestation over a peasant farmer and agro export model of development, and over land reform and land concentration. Under neoliberalism, free trade agreements, mining and oil concessions have all led to heightened tensions between market-driven developmental modernization and indigenous and peasant communities. The latter have not only mobilized to defend their communities, they have begun to place their knowledge before society and invited it to listen to alternative ways of imagining development, as well as justice, autonomy, nature and social organization.

In this way, social struggles become what Icaza and Vazquez call 'epistemic struggles' (2013: 683). Boaventura de Sousa has called these knowledges born out of struggle: 'Epistemologies of the South', where 'South' 'is a metaphor for the life experiences of those that have suffered the systematic injustices caused by capitalism, colonialism and sexism and for the validation of the kinds of knowledge they resort to in order to resist such injustices' (Ziai 2013: 730). This includes new foundations for living together, such as *Buen Vivir* (Living Well), which grew among Bolivian and Ecuadorian indigenous organizations. In Mexico, Subcomandante Marcos of the Zapatistas, the movement born of an insurgency against the North American Free Trade Agreement (NAFTA) in 1994, has referred to the need to build 'constellations of knowledge' between academic and non-academic knowledge (Ziai 2013: 730). Many of these movements have gone on to develop ways of sharing their knowledge. The Brazilian Landless Workers Movement, the MST (Movimento dos Trabalhadores Sem Terra) set up its own University in 2005, the Universidad Florestan Flores, in Sao Paulo. In Colombia, the rural peace communities living in the midst of civil war in Uraba, set up the Universidad Campesina, or Peasant University in 2011. Finally, in Mexico in 2013, the Zapatistas organized an *Escuelita* or Little School, and invited Mexican students to come and learn about indigenous understandings of the world using a horizontal pedagogy, Raul Zibechi described it thus:

> The Little Zapatista School, for which more than a thousand students went into autonomous communities, was a different way of learning and teaching, without classrooms or blackboards, without teachers or professors, without curriculum or qualifications. Real teaching begins with the creation of a climate of fellowship (*hermanamiento*) among a plurality of subjects, previously with division between an educator with power and knowledge, and ignorant students in whom knowledge must be inculcated. (Zibechi 2013)

These efforts by Latin American social movements to call upon academics to learn from their knowledges while recognizing that academics also have knowledge to offer movements, was a background inspiration for some in the setting up of CommUNIty.

However, they highlight the complexities of trying to upturn the 'higher-horizontal' approaches to knowledge in a context where activism is not driving the process, but where it is emerging from within institutions which are part of the hierarchical approach to knowledge. There has been a history, of course, in the UK of efforts to develop alternative educational pathways for working people and those deprived of the opportunity for further education. The Workers Educational Association founded in the 1920s is still going strong. There were experiments with a Communist University in the 1960s, and Northern College was founded in the 1970s to offer education for those with limited qualifications. Some of these may be influenced by alternative horizontal pedagogies, but not necessarily. More recently, there have been experiments emerging directly from activism, such as Tent City University, set up through Occupy London. Such activist movements emphasize more the need to rethink knowledge production itself, as the Tent City University website put it under the heading 'anyone can teach, everyone can learn', and: 'we remain committed to promoting collective wisdom and looking at how we use knowledge together' (Tent City University 2012).

...to building CommUNIty

There is a strong difference between experiments which begin from movements and those that are launched from mainstream institutions, like our own, albeit with participation from community activists. The foundational impetus is very important for the way an experiment evolves. CommUNIty won funding from the Economic and Social Science Research Council (ESRC) and the Joseph Rowntree Foundation (JRF) for the co-produced bid. This was enormously important to getting university buy in to the experiment as well as to the practicalities of implementing the CommUNIty programme. It meant that we could fund meaningful activities which had been agreed with participants and which could be scheduled for times and days when participants felt they were most likely to be available. Thus, we were able to organize a residential weekend, two field trips, and sessions in the evening with food and drinks. We had the funding to invite the University creative arts director to enable us to use drama and other forms for expressing ideas than traditional academic ones. It also enabled us to organize a final event for over one hundred people, when participants could both present through an 'act of communication' what the Community University had been about for them and be presented with what we called 'CommUNIty Honours' (CommHons) in recognition of their participation. At the same time, we reached out to other organizations who were working at the community level. We brought together, among others: Trade Unions who were widening their movement to focus on community as well as workplace organizing; Citizens UK who were building a new form of organizing around low wages and other demands; and, the Community Organizing Programme, funded by the government through which efforts were being made to facilitate grassroots community building, as well as community activists from the North and elsewhere.

However, the time between putting in the bid and notification of funding success was too long for the lives of some of the individual participants. They were dependent on opportunities as they arose, sometimes had difficult events in their personal lives, including health issues, and we lost some of the momentum we had when the process began. As we began recruiting for new participants rather than relying on the networks of our original participants, so the complexities of building a Community University opened up. It became apparent that without an 'articulating movement', there are many disarticulated constituencies from which CommUNIty could draw. We organized a pop-up shop in one of the many empty shops in Bradford city centre, where we offered debate on food banks, drugs, violence and peace. We discussed the idea of CommUNIty with the homeless in an inner-city shelter and with community organizers on estates. The discussion with the homeless was sobering. A part of the group was vociferously cynical towards any initiative that came from a powerful institution, such as a university. Another part recognized the integrity of the initiative, but nevertheless, no one signed up. In the end, we more than reached the numbers we could cater for (around sixteen), through the founder participants' networks and the PPC network. A Community University Council was set up, which included members of the founder participant networks, academics, two community 'facilitators' and an Impact Adviser whose job was to keep feeding back on progress and help us all reflect on what we were doing.

We launched CommUNIty, therefore, with a fairly random mix of people from very varied backgrounds, academic histories and cultures, all of them with extraordinary stories to bring to CommUNIty. In her Act of Communication to the Final Event, one participant gave an introductory speech referring to the 'Motley Crew' that gathered in CommUNIty, a few lines of it are:

> Community workers, a professor, an Imam, an asylum seeker, a theatre director, an ex-prisoner, a diversity Officer, lecturers, paid and unpaid activists. They all had stories to be listened to. Stories of lives lived. I said what joined us together was the love inside each of us and then felt a bit silly. Anyway, we have journeyed together. (Midgely 2014)

Perhaps, one of the enduring aspects of CommUNIty is the way the group built an identity despite the many differences around faith, educational and social background, disability and traumatic pasts/presents, and attitudes towards and experience of activism. However, there are also real challenges in taking on board such mixed needs and backgrounds. The community facilitator roles were particularly important in this respect, thinking in ways academics are not trained to about process and communication. We learnt that the most significant contribution of CommUNIty probably lay in the way individual participants began to rethink their potential and possibilities. This alone made the experiment worthwhile. However, in order to turn this into a more sustainable alternative approach to learning, education, participation and citizenship, it required either more active institutional support and promotion or an upsurge of societal critique and action around power and knowledge.

Arguably, the process highlighted the importance of new kinds of leadership. In HE, managerialism makes some Vice Chancellors today look more like CEOs of enterprises rather than facilitators and innovators around the relationship of universities to society, and in meeting the challenges facing people and planet. At the community level, leadership is required which could encourage Universities to recognize how to work with the wealth of unvalued knowledges within society. CommUNIty was committed to the second, but without committed leadership in universities, it remained an experiment (which continues in more informal form), albeit one that impacted on individual lives and generated much learning about the challenges of working with multiple constellations of knowledge and experience, while turning this into something that might liberate the 'general intellect'.

CommUNIty: Horizontal knowledge and hierarchical expectations

CommUNIty highlighted the possibilities of knowledge exchange and also its limitations without a broader institutional and/or societal commitment to it or a strong enough activist movement to place it on society's agenda. It also exposed the importance of time and process in reconciling the many possibilities in the initiative. Thus, for some CommUNIty was about pathways for recognition of experiential knowledge and non-formal education as part of new forms of lifelong accreditation of skills and learning. CommUNIty would show that community knowledge is an asset which could generate learning for community participants *and* academics. At the same time, it would strengthen the varied individual agendas of change among the former and potentially construct a collective one. It would be a process in which the distance travelled in the course of the year differed for each participant. For others, the equal value of knowledges meant that pedagogy was entirely the wrong approach and what mattered was facilitation of conversations. Pedagogy, it was felt by some, suggests a teacher/learner dynamic rather than a mutual learning between knowledges. Here, the academics tended to fill vacuums with their pre-existing intellectual passions, leaving insufficient space and time for those of participants to shine through. Hierarchical expectations tended not to dissipate in such moments, but to be reinforced by assumptions about knowledge that academics cannot shed very easily despite a commitment to do so. Each of the academic participants recognized that participating in change processes rather than lecturing about them was an ethical stance which gave intellectual coherence to their scholarship.

There was a strong awareness of the distancing capacity of academic language. Specialists can talk and discuss in shorthand and also invent a conceptual language where words fail ideas. Yet despite efforts to be inclusive, some sessions were not accessible for all. As one participant described an evening session: 'it went over my head, the evening sessions didn't relate to me, my mind started to wander' (CP in Blakey 2014).[1] While topics for classes had been broadly developed within the power and participation framework of the original bid, insufficient attention was given to the mix of educational backgrounds and interests. Nor were participants asked to present rather than participate in the more formal sessions. Attention was given to the pedagogic mix of formal (evening sessions), informal (field trips) and non-formal (creative sessions, conversations, visits to community events). However, not enough thought was given to the power dimensions involved in learning and teaching, or that knowledge exchange is a qualitatively different process to both of these. Implicit hierarchies remain present and influence relationships. Some asked, 'What did the academics learn?' One academic suggested that she had indeed learnt:

> Everyday things like gardens stand out – intellectual ideas get humbled and made real – the modesty of most processes of change – I have learned from people on the ground all my life, people who might not have qualifications but who have wisdom. (AP in Blakey 2014)

Participants felt these tensions differently. A number who had problems with the educational world came to feel more comfortable: 'I didn't really go to school, the teaching model scares me; this is bringing people together to learn in a different way' (CP in Blakey 2014). Community participants were encouraged to write field diaries or find ways of recording feelings and experience during the year programme.[2] One participant wrote a detailed field diary and after the first evening session held in a local community centre, he wrote:

> It was good to see so many people turn up to the first evening meeting. Tonight's session did what was intended and made us all consider what we really hope to achieve as community activists. (Bradshaw 2014)

This participant was one of several who were involved in inner-city community gardens. They came in order to see what they could learn about encouraging more people from their communities to participate. Bradshaw (2014) records how, through knowledge exchange and learning what others were doing, he found valuable prompts to thinking, such as 'recognising hidden needs within our own community and… demystification of what it means to go to university and encourage engagement by people who think university is not for people like them'.

Participation and activism were key themes of the programme, but were understood in different ways and were not the primary goals of everyone. Some did not want to highlight their personal goals in attending, but did so more in private conversations. These ranged from pathways to qualifications and entry to Further and Higher Education, to self-empowerment and an understanding of the 'bigger picture'. Some were very reluctant to use the word 'activist' to describe what they did and even uncomfortable: 'It's about my community and what's happening there, and there is another level for me to go, but I don't want people judging' (CP in Blakey 2014). Nevertheless, in the course of CommUNIty, a number of participants felt more comfortable with the idea that their local focus on change mattered. A number of participants emphasized the personal growth that took place through their involvement:

> It's given me a lot of confidence. It's surprising and delightful to feel I do have the confidence to say what I want to say – I stood up and spoke at a national conference for the first time ever. I was incensed – it's about having the passion – you can do anything. The course said 'you can do lots of things, you can have an impact'. (CP in Blakey 2014)

All participants, academics and non-academics shared some commitment to 'making a difference'. This formed a solid basis for the process and mutual respect in its integrity, despite questions about its implementation. The field trips to visit innovative community projects – Marsh Farm in Luton, Incredible Edible in Todmorden, and Offshoots in Burnley – were particularly useful *both* for being shared learning experiences among the academic and community participants, *and* for opening up the range of possibilities and practical ideas for action and change for the latter.

The tension between process and structure and between loose goals and clear goals was there throughout the process. Bradshaw wrote in his diary after the residential which began the year's activities: 'It is obvious that CommUNIty is still finding out what it actually is, but this is no longer a concern. In fact it is a bonus as it makes me realize that we all can play a key role in determining its direction and content' (Bradshaw 2014). Others, including some in the academic organizing team, wanted more clarity and planning. There is no doubt that there was a great deal of learning by doing, which generated real challenges, particularly for the stated goal of knowledge exchange.

CommUNIty never really worked through the different characters of the knowledges to be exchanged. Academic participants perhaps felt that they were bringing a more conceptual knowledge and theories of change from a wide reading of literatures and field research in multiple contexts. But academics are by no means alone in conceptual knowledge – community participants can be very schooled in theories and capacity for abstract thinking. A number of participants also had wide experience of change processes in varied contexts. However, conceptual knowledge, which seeks to interpret realities from outside them, is more difficult for those with limited access to HE. Capacity to think conceptually and analytically is what such education purports to nurture, although not always successfully. As such knowledge has become more distanced from experiential knowledge, the importance of the link between the two has been lost. One outcome is that academic knowledge has gained status on the one hand, but is paradoxically deeply rejected on the other, gaining a reputation for 'abstraction' with limited relevance and application to the real world. Academics under multiple pressures from the new management of knowledge production (see final section) do not easily adapt to the accountability demands of communicating to non-academics and recognizing what they learn from them.

At the same time, many academics are encouraged to extract knowledge without returning their analysis to those who provided it. Many academics, particularly but not only those under temporary contracts, are under individualizing pressure to perform and compete. They are not required or encouraged to engage outside their specialist areas, let alone outside their institutions. The broader intellectuality in wider society is diminished and devalued as academic knowledge becomes more specialized, institutionalized and valued, including in monetary terms. In turn, many in the wider society reject their own broader intellectuality as academic knowledge gains dominance over all other forms and excludes them. The possibility is lost that knowledge from experience is also a source of intellectuality and vital for the search for solutions to real world problems and in ways that academic knowledge alone is often not. At the same time, the relevance and importance of academic knowledge is also lost to people who sense that it ignores at best, belittles at worst, their own ways of knowing. The importance of testing opinion against evidence as well as against the opinions of others, which academic knowledge can offer, becomes more difficult to develop without mutual respect between knowledges. The encounter between knowledges works when it evokes curiosity and mutual respect for the learning of the 'other'. All forms of knowledge need to be actively recognized and have space for expression if knowledge exchange is to be a real process.

The Community University thus served to emphasize the difficulties involved in releasing the 'general intellect' from the constraints of the knowledge producing system. Virno's 'general aptitudes of the mind' exist in a capitalist political economy which pursues the 'best' brains for its knowledge economy, but which has little interest in mass intellectuality as such. Rather, it creams off the intellect it needs through HE institutions, which concentrate resources and status in its opposite – the intellectuality (and leadership) of elites. Yet, it can be argued, that only through experiments such as CommUNIty is it possible to see those constraints for what they are and to imagine new ways of addressing them. This final section, therefore, focuses on these constraints, beginning with the effects of hierarchies of knowledge and leadership on the internalized self-perceptions of individuals as 'knowing' persons. Such effects were ever present in the efforts of the Community University to seek a horizontal exchange of knowledges. They are being deepened by the neoliberal valorization of knowledges in market terms. This is making it ever more difficult to recover the 'general intellect' and enable it to serve society rather than capital.

'Higher' and 'horizontal' knowledge production

The juxtaposition of an institution of 'Higher' Education with a 'Community University' immediately highlights the boundary-building hierarchies around knowledge and the limitations to the emergence of new leaders and forms of leadership that these construct among those whose knowledge is discarded. Such hierarchies are deeply internalized by individuals in capitalist societies. People learn to devalue their knowledge and experience, making horizontal experiments based on recognizing the worth of different knowledges especially difficult. Michel Foucault describes this well when he writes: '…The disciplines characterize, classify, specialize; they distribute along a scale, around a norm, hierarchize individuals in relation to one another and, if necessary, disqualify and invalidate' (Foucault [1975] 1991: 223). The very experience of trying to inject a note of horizontalism is to live the varied effects of such stratification processes on individuals who have ended up feeling deeply lacking in their knowledge and/or deeply resentful about the way knowledge hierarchies strip their experience of value. Such is the status around skills of the mind, for instance, that no amount of manual capacity can quite compensate for the sense of intellectual inadequacy among those whose thinking skills are used with their hands. 'Higher' can, of course, be about the pursuit of ever better quality of knowledge, something potentially compatible with varied organizational forms and something most would see as vital to all intellectual and practical endeavour. However, this volume suggests that while this is the stated aim of changes in HE, rather it is a new configuration of capitalist knowledge extraction that is taking place.

The Italian philosopher, Paolo Virno (2004), sought to trace the shift from the general intellect to the intellectuality of the masses alongside the shift from Fordist to post-Fordist production. Whereas Marx coined the term 'general intellect' to express how general and social knowledge was extracted and translated into fixed capital, that is, the machine, the 1980s and 1990s saw capital use the general intellect in a totally new way. Marx had posited some important points about knowledge in the *Grundrisse* and the way capital has successfully absorbed the general productive forces of the 'social brain', or the accumulated knowledge and skill in society (Marx 1993: 694). He also imagined the future shift from the role of labour in the generation of surpluses to that of technological expertise and organization. Virno argues that it was the 'defeated revolutions' of the 1960s and 1970s which enabled capital to reinvent and restructure itself because it knew how to draw on the strong principles of individuation in those revolutionary moments. Post-Fordist capital has literally capitalized (but not mechanized) what Virno calls the intellect in general.

Even if Virno's post-operaist reflections do not convince all, he does remind us that 'Higher Education' is in the process of transformation alongside wider economic changes. Indeed, the logic is to serve the latter, rather than enable the general intellect to develop according to a spontaneous and social logic. With the market focus on the apparently individual source of knowledge and skills, it negates the way knowledge is constructed socially, and at the same time, selectively recognizes the knowledges which matter and whose production must be privileged. All of this appears to be about natural, organic processes of objective selection of the 'best' knowledge, but in reality the University is moving closer to a regulatory cum coercive power behind the organization and validation of knowledge production. Individuals are discouraged from engaging with 'other knowledges', and from recognizing the limits of their own knowledge (Wainwright 1994). The University is constructed as at the heart of the *production* of knowledge as well as its *consumption*, and governments have incentivized its adaptation to those processes with almost no debate among even its own knowledge workers. In the process, it has opened its 'ivory tower' to markets in ways that are likely to widen social and economic distances, and generate new forms of hierarchy around the meanings and purpose of knowledge and intellectual life.

In recent years, a number of scholars have drawn attention to the marketization trends in UK HE (Brown and Carasso 2013; Collini 2013; McGettigan 2013). From charities at least discursively dedicated to the pursuit of public good, universities are being encouraged to see charitable status as a hindrance to their capacity to access expanding 'global HE markets' (McGettigan 2014). The 2010 introduction of student fees opened the door to new private providers in the University system on the basis of a minimum provision of students on degree programmes. This is an incipient but nevertheless noteworthy process of introducing competition into the sector. Second, it encouraged the remaking of universities 'in the image of consumer-oriented retailers' (Collini 2013: 8). Increasingly universities have come to resemble corporations with highly remunerated CEOs or Vice Chancellors, as they seek new private income streams. And third, it enabled the so-called 'elite' universities in the sector to recruit as many students with high A-level scores as they can, while the non-elite universities would compete 'at the bottom' by even reducing their fees if necessary, thus mirroring the supply–demand operations of the market. By not reducing fees, universities signalled that they were still aspiring to be in the 'top' echelons of the university system, but they risked the financial penalties of failing to recruit, particularly among higher grade students. The lifting of the cap on student places in 2015 eroded the 'non-elite' universities' capacity to recruit higher grade students even further. It also generated more potentially market-driven disturbance in the system, given that the lifting of the cap was to be funded by selling off a student loan book that was widely deemed to be worth much less than predicted given so many former students failed for some years at least, to reach the salary threshold that triggered repayments. By 2015, competition for the high-grade students, threatened further fall outs in the HE system. The possibility that some universities might one day 'go bust' with no expectation of public sector bailout, is not to be ruled out. Thus, the knowledge economy begins to generate new understandings of knowledge and excellence, while apparently opening up to all prepared to pay or pay back. In reality, it creates further boundaries between what is constructed as excellence and non-excellence and valued and unvalued knowledge.

The link between these shifts in the context in which Universities are operating and the Community University, is that even before they were underway, there was a wide gap between Universities and the societies they served. There was always a distancing logic in the public university, but at least some space for critical thinking underpinned by public funding. Student radicalism of the 1960s and 1970s is part evidence of this, enabling a social and generational challenge to power and authority as well as renewed experimentation in democratic form. However, social mobility through access to HE in a context of lively debates on theories of state and society as well as street protest on big issues of the day, slowed down greatly over the decades that followed. During the last decade, the very ideal of the public university has been challenged.

The importance of *access* to HE has remained, however. The widening participation agenda of the New Labour governments 1997–2010, aimed both to open up HE to non-traditional applicants and promote its social outreach. The Dearing Report of 1997, as well as recommending changes to tuition fees, also promoted interest in the broader social purposes of HE. 'Community engagement' became a fundable item through the Higher Education Innovation Fund (HEIF) and under HEIF, the University of Bradford won an award to promote such engagement. In 2005, it embarked on a systematic effort to engage with its communities. There was particular resonance with such activities in Bradford, which in July 2001 witnessed the worst disturbances on the UK mainland for twenty years just a few miles from the University campus. Mostly Asian young men fought the police on White Abbey Road (Bujra and Pearce 2011).

University recruitment fell 25 per cent in the year following the riots. Colleagues in Bradford's Peace Studies Department had been part of the Ouseley Commission set up by the local authority to explore community relations in the District and set up the PPC just prior to the riot. The PPC went on to create safe spaces for dialogue and discussion about the challenges facing Bradford District. Through the HEIF bid, Bradford academics developed a measurement tool for this work, and at the same time, tried to steer 'measurement' towards a qualitative self-evaluation tool for working *with* rather than delivering *to* Bradford's communities (Pearce et al. 2007). However, the tension between using community engagement as another form of recruitment and/or to display University expertise made it difficult to build a new kind of relationship between Universities and their communities. This was not so much about the willingness of individuals, but about the logics and incentive structures built into the system.

Nevertheless, the institutional embrace of 'community', demonstrated that there were originally two faces to the neoliberal reconfigurations of Universities between Dearing 1997 and Browne 2010: 'Community engagement' opened up the social remit of the University to ways it might serve the communities around it. However, the other 'face' was that of 'creeping marketization' in response to the funding crisis facing UK universities highlighted originally by Dearing. He had found that public funding per student for HE had declined from a value of 100 in 1976, to 79 in 1989 and to 60 in 1994, while between 1979 and 2011 student numbers increased by 320 per cent (Collini 2013: 9). Recognition of a funding crisis paved the way for the search for solutions outside the public purse. Dearing's recommendations were for a mixed approach, with some component of low interest student loans. However, over the New Labour years, it became clear that the post-Cold War emphasis on less state more market, was to continue. This greatly accelerated after the 2008 economic crisis and the 2010 and, in particular, 2015 elections.

The other face of the neoliberal reconfiguration, around 'community', reflected the implications of the emphasis on the retreat of the state. The self-regulating role of societal bonds was increasingly highlighted. This idea had emerged originally with the rise of liberalism in its first eighteenth century iteration and which generated the idea of 'civil society'. 'Civil society' conceptually articulated a concern with reconciling the tension between the individual pursuit of self-interest and the need for minimum social cohesion (Howell and Pearce 2001). It is no coincidence that 'civil society' was born again at the end of the Cold War with the neoliberal resurgence. Bauman (2001) captures well the significance of 'community' in this resurgence. Whereas 'civil society' referred to the associational life which generates new bonds, such associational life also generates contestation, as the Italian Marxist, Gramsci, had emphasized. Community, on the other hand, rests on more familiar bonds, bonds of proximity rather than self-determined interests.

The wave of interest in 'community' coincided, argued Bauman, with the 'times of disengagement', and paradoxically with a renewal of emphasis also on the 'individual'. However, unlike the individualizing process which accompanied the rise of the interventionist power of the state from the fifteenth and sixteenth centuries, and which Foucault famously analyzed, the last few decades have seen the disengagement of the state from its previous regulatory and socially interventionist guise. Bauman argued that today:

> domination does not rest primarily on engagement-and-commitment; on the capacity of rulers to watch closely the movements of the ruled and to coerce them into obedience. It has acquired a new, much less troublesome and less costly – since requiring little servicing – foundation: in the uncertainty of the rules as to what move, if any, their rulers may make next. (2001: 41)

Thus, the strengthening of community and the micro-organizing of society coheres with the dynamic of an individualizing model, and ultimately aspires to prevent social disintegration while promoting individual aspiration. A number of scholars have traced the impact of this on HE (Hill 2008).

For those who reject the 'neoliberal turn', the effort to compensate for it through an enhanced emphasis on civil society and community and on its short-lived guise under British Prime Minister David Cameron, of the 'big society', is hard to stomach. The left has both a state-oriented and anti-state-oriented wing, without the latter being pro-market. The former has emphasized big organized actors, such as trade unions, capable of taking on the state and big enterprises. As the economy has transformed, and trade unions weakened outside the public sector, it has been harder to maintain a state-centred vision. The anti-state wing, on the other hand, has emphasized creative associationalism outside the state, but appears to lack a project for society as a whole, a hegemonic political bloc, for example (Mouffe 2013). Defending the idea of the 'public' is not, however, the same as defending the state *per se*. It is possible that reactivating participation outside the state could both defend this notion of shared and co-operative 'public' space and provision, while making clear that the world outside the state is not equivalent to the market, but a knowledge producing and opinion forming arena in between. The 'times of disengagement' could stimulate new thinking about state society relationships. This is precisely what CommUNIty sought to nurture.

Conclusion

The transformation of state–society relationships requires a reappropriation and qualitative growth of the 'general intellect' before the intellectuality of the masses is fully captured for the new phase of market liberalism. This in turn, implies experimentation with 'horizontal' rather than 'higher' education. Distinct forms of knowledge can then be *exchanged* in order to grow new knowledges. These could encourage participation and critical citizenship as well as foster new forms of leadership and more diverse leaders, capable of generating convincing alternatives to the orders emerging from market logics and which rapidly become unquestioned norms and conventions. This was a driving force for some behind the Community University. However, CommUNIty was also embedded in the pre-existing logics behind the construction of the 'University' and the 'Community'.

CommUNIty cannot claim to have perfected a process of knowledge exchange and still less to have liberated the general intellect. However, it built connections between an interesting and creative mix of individuals and knowledges while exposing all the challenges involved in the tasks of knowledge exchange and liberation. In practice, connections between intellects need to be reforged through new instruments. These instruments need to overcome not only the capture of the general intellect, but the discarding of knowledges which do not serve capital and the market. As the account of CommUNIty indicates, the task is not easy. Academics need to question how their role increasingly serves the 'disqualifying and invalidating' nature of disciplined knowledge production. Recognizing the value of the knowledge outside the institutions of knowledge production could co-generate engaged citizens and activists with good and independent judgement, able to imagine their contribution to societal change and leadership. Experiments such as CommUNIty open up new ways of articulating the rich constellations of knowledges available in the world. The outcomes for the individual participants were many, but one of the most poignant was the participant (Austin Bradshaw) who said: 'I wanted to write from it, I hadn't anticipated that, it made me want to write songs, it made me want to sing.' His Act of Communication to the Final Event was his song: 'This Town is Falling Down,' and the last verse captures the sense of what drove CommUNIty:

> There are leaders at bus stops, thinkers in the store,
> Builders and teachers, lions that roar.
> There are those with the power to have so much more.
> We must build it up, we must act before it falls down, down, this town is falling down.

Acknowledgements

The author acknowledges and appreciates the input of all participants in CommUNIty in the ideas which inform this chapter.

Notes

1 All quotes from now on are from CommUNIty participants interviewed for the Impact Adviser's Final (unpublished) Report, (Blakey 2014). Here, I have distinguished between Community Participant (CP) and Academic Participant (AP).
2 The academics wrote up notes and formal records of each session which were circulated.

9

Aesthetic Education, Critical Pedagogy and Specialist Institutions

Jonathan Owen Clark and Louise H. Jackson

I

Hierarchical structures within the higher education (HE) sector are reflected in the current debates regarding the status and social construction of the idea of 'The University'. However, these same debates do not sufficiently take into consideration the way in which different sites within HE may participate in the defence of this same idea, and in the different ways in which they may do so. By focusing on the small, specialist HE art institution, this chapter seeks to do two things. First, it aims to position these institutions firmly within the debate about the politics of contemporary HE, a task that will occupy Section II of this chapter, which also provides some historical, contextual and background information on the definition and nature of the 'art school'. Second, it aims to critique the currently posited role for these institutions as sites for the production of the 'cultural entrepreneur' or 'artistic leader', and other terminology derived from corporatist ideology, which has become commonplace in discourses surrounding the value of an arts education.

This second critique, we suggest, derives from the unique idiomatic nature of art itself; a nature that is rooted in the perceptive and sensory capabilities of the experiencer, but which extends to the manner in which the perceptual transformations enacted by art can cause disturbances, perturbations and 'irritations' into more general networks of communication in contemporary society.[1] This connects the arts, and arts education in particular, not only with a central theme of this volume – the concept derived from Marx's General Intellect, namely, 'mass intellectuality' – but also certain key ideas from contemporary writing on globalization within postcolonial theory. This allows us to introduce the idea of a suitable 'aesthetic education' which, due to the posited autonomy of the communicative power of art itself, acquires an important ethical status.

Deriving a suitable definition of this latter concept, which we take from a recent collection of essays by Gayatri Spivak, will be a central idea that frames what follows. Introducing this volume, Spivak begins with the following provocative statement: 'Globalization takes place only in capital and data. Everything else is damage control.'

We are interested in examining what role the small specialist arts institution, through the provision of a suitable 'aesthetic education', may play in countering the cultural damage Spivak describes. We will argue that rather than reduce themselves simply to sites providing solely vocational and technical training serving the economic demands of the entertainment industry, art schools have a vital, perhaps unique or autonomous role to play in what Henry Giroux has termed a 'utopian pedagogy' that can provide possibilities for both societal critique and enhanced democratic engagement.[2] The autonomy allocated to arts practice is justified in Section III through a constellation of interconnecting ideas, which will take us on a journey first away from Marx, and then back to him again. We conclude in Section IV with some remarks on ethics.

II

We henceforth use the term 'art school' to refer to institutions specializing in disciplines more broadly defined as music, dance, drama and the fine arts. A renewed study of the mechanisms of training for these disciplines within the higher education landscape allows a similarly renewed focus on the dogma that predicates intellectualism as part of a knowledge economy, a process that has resulted in HE institutions becoming increasingly little more than 'adjuncts to what is called international civil society' (Spivak 2012: 1). This is clearly a motivating factor behind the predilection for science subjects within the current context of the increasing neoliberalization of HE, which has positioned arts-based disciplines at risk by requiring them to justify their existence through largely instrumental frameworks such as graduate employment destination, the earnings of graduated students and the economic exchange value of the vocational aspects of arts training. This further reduces the arts to a mode of consumerism, and necessitates an analogous reduction of a suitable 'aesthetic education' to the training of individuals merely to satisfy this consumer demand. This is most recently exemplified in the UK in the Institute for Fiscal Studies paper (Britton et al. 2016) where a 'disappointment' is highlighted that the graduate premium is not apparent within the Creative Arts, with disciplines in this area producing graduates who earn typically 'non-graduate incomes'.

But, let us recall first the key points of this debate surrounding universities and public HE (see, e.g., Maskell and Robinson 2002; Molesworth et al. 2010; Docherty 2011; Holmwood 2011; Collini 2012; Williams 2013; Rolfe 2013). We can summarize the main points perhaps as follows – in recent years, the above authors' argue, HE has seen: increasing marketization through the introduction of student fees, resulting in the ubiquity of the notion of consumer satisfaction; an increasing accountability framework that similarly promotes consumerism through the guise of the protection of public money; a fundamental change in the relationship between institution, teacher and learner; and reductions in teaching grants and the promotion of 'best practice' themes within learning and teaching, and a focus on recruitment and income generation from research activity. These factors have all contributed to the construction of the now dominant idea held both within and about HE that the university subscribes to a capitalist mode of production that exists to contribute to a knowledge economy, coupled with a political emphasis on the essential utility of knowledge.

Many of these trends have crossed over from the large cross-faculty HE institution to the art school. In amongst this debate however, Stefan Collini makes a passing reference to a subsection of publicly funded institutions that have as their main function the conservation of the past:

> A third function [for the justification of universities] is the preservation, cultivation, and transmission of a cultural tradition, [which] cuts some ice if it is understood to be confined to a small number of outstanding institutions, somewhat analogous to the case for national galleries and museums. (Collini 2012: 91 [our addition])

We suggest that this idea is fruitful in connecting the above more general debates about the purpose of HE to the more restricted setting of the art school, which we can now define more fully. These are specialist arts-based HE institutions, which are: usually small in terms of student numbers; largely associated with the artistic or performance disciplines; and, exemplified by the Conservatoire, Drama School and Fine Art School models. These institutions will usually focus on instruction in one or two disciplines only. In addition, students follow more practical or vocationally orientated training than would be found in universities delivering similar programmes in the arts. Many of the specialist institutions have a long-standing place in leading and preserving the artistic traditions of the country, but alongside these are newer, privately funded specialist centres that generally focus on commercial artistic practices, particularly in the field of popular music. Many specialist institutions are now focused on producing the 'artistic leaders' of the future and embed notions of 'creative entrepreneurship' within their programmes.

After the reform of UK Higher Education in the 1990s, all of these specialist institutions were expected to provide standard HE qualifications that functioned according to a common framework. Although some had previously awarded university-validated degrees, and in the case of the art schools, degree equivalent Diplomas, there was and remains a tension between the pure vocational training traditionally pursued in the specialist institution and the type of learning that takes place within a university. This tension is founded in the practice/theory dichotomy and exemplified in the common perception that artistic practice is technical skill divorced somewhat from its historical, social and political contexts. In the field of Art and Design, some of the tensions relating to this were highlighted in the 'Coldstream reports' from the Department of Education and Science National Advisory Council on Art Education between 1960 and 1970, respectively. These reports were the impetus to connect history and theory in studio-based learning that had until this point always been taught separately. This integration was described in The Structure of Art and Design in the Further Education Sector (1970) as enabling 'the student to understand relationships between his own activities and the culture within which he lives as it has evolved. Such studies should therefore offer him different ways of looking at art and design, and begin to build up a background against which he can view the experience of the studio' (11).

The impact of these reports on Fine Art Education has been substantial. However, more generally and certainly within the Performing Arts, how theory relates to practice continues to underpin not only tensions between the types of knowledge reproduced within these educational contexts but also how these institutions position themselves within the HE sector more generally. These institutions were explicitly established to focus mainly on vocational training, a notion that became important within the broader discussions relating to the development of HE as a way of equalizing opportunities for social mobility. Vocational training is an attractive concept for advocates of social justice within and through education because it is perceived to empower those who would not ordinarily gain a HE to do so. However, after the 1992 Higher Education Act, the distinction between providers of vocationally orientated education and more traditional institutions was, at least on paper, removed. In the case of music conservatoires, until the Act of 1992, these institutions did not traditionally award degrees, focusing on training for diploma awards that had as their function the mastery of technique on a particular musical instrument, that has its roots in a conservation of historical models, often passed on through aural traditions. Thus we arrive at the notion of a specialist institution that is directly linked to excellence, elite training and generally a 'conserving' of the artistic past (see e.g., Thistlewood 1992 or Ford 2010).

This allows a return to what, as we saw earlier, Stefan Collini critically introduces as the third function of The University (after creating an employable workforce and providing economically beneficially research), namely 'the preservation, cultivation, and transmission of a cultural tradition' that is 'confined to a small number of outstanding institutions' (Collini 2012: 19). Collini describes the rationale for supporting such institutions as 'analogous to the case for national galleries and museums' (2012). Our essay takes this suggestion as a key point of reference, but with some important modifications. If the notion of cultural preservation is a guiding principle for specialist institutions to exist, then they become little more than production lines for the training of the next generation of musicians, dancers and actors in certain prescribed traditions. This already negates the need for a specialist institution of having any responsibility as a site that contributes to the intellectual development of society, but is merely responsible for the preservation of an approved and franchised culture.

Cultural preservation also negates, as previously mentioned, the potential ubiquity present in art that we can call, after Adorno, its inherent 'negativity', and which we can define in three ways: 'aesthetic negativity is the enactment of the determinate refusal of predication on the part of artworks' (Durao 2008: 12); '"Aesthetic" designates the suspension of every determinate relation correlating the production of art forms and a specific social function' (Rancière 2010: 138); 'What art actually is, is contradiction, rejection, negation – its essence is its aesthetic negativity' (Menke 1999: 3). It is precisely this 'negativity' wherein the true subversive potential of the arts resides, and the unique way that art communicates through perceptual media can give the arts a particularly important, arguably autonomous role in mounting suitable societal critique, through the 'materials, processes, pedagogies [of the art school], that disrupt and question forms of cultural dominance' (Hickey Moody and Page 2015: 5). In Section II, we sketch a theory, following Spivak, of a suitable 'aesthetic education' that not only trains artists in the techniques of art production, but informs them in addition of its multiple receptive possibilities, or of the potentiality for art to enact social and political change, a mechanism whereby: 'the provocative otherness of the aesthetic sign drops like a probe into the all-too-familiar, to make it in this way into something genuinely familiar for the first time' (Menke 1999: 93). Therefore, an aesthetic education is something more than arts training; it requires the art school to couple the teaching of technique with both critical thinking and sociocultural awareness, to refuse to disconnect the procedures and processes of art-making from the transformative possibilities of its reception.[3]

The purpose therefore is not to justify the existence of the art school within normative accountability frameworks, but rather to suggest ways to mobilize the particular position and autonomous aspects of the arts and arts education. In order to do this, our approach necessitates working through what Henry Giroux suggests is something critical to the countering of social injustice, something that he terms the 'mobilization of utopian imagination' (Giroux 2007).[4] Our approach, then, will conflate the idea of 'aesthetic education' with a type of utopian pedagogy, one that invokes new vocabularies that engage with both social and ethical concerns, while at the same time engaging the role of perception and perceptual imagination to promote such a new apparatus. As Giroux describes the wider project of concern here:

> Defending higher education as a vital public sphere is necessary if we are to develop and nourish the proper mediation between civil society and corporate power, between identities founded on democratic principles and identities steeped in those forms of competitive, self-interested individualism that celebrate selfishness, profit-making, and greed. This view suggests that higher education must be defended through intellectual work that self-consciously recalls the tension between the democratic imperatives or possibilities of public institutions and their everyday realization in a society dominated by market principles. Education is not training; at its best, learning is connected to a culture of curiosity and questioning, the imperatives of social responsibility, and at the same time recognizes that political agency does not reduce the citizen to mere consumer. (Giroux 2007: 35–36)

Also central to our construction of an 'aesthetic education' is the opposition to the increasingly dominant idea within the arts school of the 'creative entrepreneur', defined in one (anonymous) source as: 'an artist able to retain their creative integrity, sustain an independent arts practice and survive in the light of 21st-Century challenges'.

On first glance, this definition may seem unproblematic: It postulates an educational platform that allows a creative individual to engage with ways of establishing and sustaining a career. However, hidden within the definition are several assumptions, including both the reduction of education simply to an investment vehicle, and a similar reduction of education to a simple transaction involving payment in return for the promise of future employment. Harvie (2013) outlines some of these issues pertaining specifically to the artist as entrepreneur or 'artrepreneur' as the risk of 'individualism, creative destruction, and self-interested profit-making' that can accentuate 'the uneven – and unfair – distribution of wealth, opportunity and even survival in contemporary culture' (107). The function of HE in promoting this cultural shift of artistic behaviour becomes clear when we explore how the notion of entrepreneurship in arts education has been adopted.

The Higher Education Academy (the UK-based institution that promotes excellence in learning and teaching) has promoted the notion of entrepreneurship within arts education in a variety of publications. In Burns (2007), the dance conservatoires are described in particular as focusing on 'intensive professional dance training' (15). Burns continues:

> It is apparent from the research that HE dance programmes are increasingly recognizing that working in the dance world requires the student to understand and capitalize on their skills within the context of the wider application of their work within society. When this is done well, the conceptual grasp of the value of dance and its application in social contexts means that the 'dancer' is able to view their work in the round. This allows the graduate to set about creating a sustainable career. When this is absent the student will graduate unaware of what they have to offer the market place. (Burns 2007: 32)

The aim of dance education, according to this view, is to ensure a successful transition of the student into the market place. And the notion of entrepreneurship enables such an artist to successfully navigate economic social structures. Another example of how the notion of the creative entrepreneur has been promoted, this time within music programmes, is explained by Beckmann (2005) in terms of the way that 'entrepreneurship emerges as a philosophy that empowers, rather than limits, individuals. Thus the goal of entrepreneurship, especially in an arts context, becomes the manifestation of ideas through creative means' (14). Beckmann goes on to say that

> arts higher education must also confront the persistent nineteenth century aesthetic that perpetuates the 'art-for-arts-sake' paradigm. This ideology must be re-examined in our pedagogy as it results in net negative effective on music students' professional development. By giving students the opportunity to explore a career in music on their terms and challenging them to see beyond popular myths and outdated aesthetics, they empower themselves and communities as well. (21)

The assumed value in the reduction to economic imperatives is explicit here, but also the notion that this is justified because it meets the expectations of the learners' themselves. Community and social engagement are proven, through Beckmann's model, to benefit from an arts-based pedagogy that promotes full integration with corporatist structures, and without question.[5] This is the very aspect that Giroux describes thus: If, according to a neoliberal perspective, market forces are the only way to improve social inequality, then it 'strips utopianism of its possibilities for social critique and democratic engagement' (Giroux 2007: 32). We will claim later, that one key mechanism for just such a possibility for both critique and engagement is via a participation in the arts, and through the provision of an 'aesthetic education'.

But to return to the notion of the entrepreneur, we can see that inherent here is the claim that entrepreneurship encourages the generation of skills and ideas for the main purpose of providing economic exchange value. As Davies (2014) has previously commented, the creative entrepreneur is understood via 'essential traits of the individual' (47) and within a neoliberal system promotes uncertainty whereby the entrepreneur 'refuses ordinary routines and boundaries' and creates 'new institutional rules' (52). It is then, a short journey to see a connection between how this is theorized economically and then embedded within ideological educational practices: the entrepreneur, as a symbol for a contemporary currency of transferable skills in HE, aims to quantify the exact value of arts-based learning via economic and economically associated outcomes (in terms of employability, salary, benefit to the knowledge economy including social mobility, etc.). It also positions the notion of creativity (as an example of the 'essential traits' Davies alludes to) as an exchangeable, quantifiable commodity that institutions now have to include in order to satisfy the assumed purpose of HE while maintaining an illusion of social justice. Within the sector, there currently exists a mixture of programmes explicitly designed to develop the role of the creative entrepreneur, an assumption that implies that an entrepreneurial approach to creativity allows an individual to successfully engage with the wider economic context, and furthermore that this has added social benefits. But as Collini considers the wider benefits of HE:

> From wholly laudable motives, we constantly fall into the trap of justifying an activity – one initially (and perhaps for long thereafter) undertaken because of its intrinsic interest and worth – as something which we do because it yields incidental benefits which are popular with those not in a position to appreciate the activity's intrinsic interest and worth. If we find ourselves saying that what is valuable about learning to play the violin well is that it helps us develop the manual dexterity that will be useful for typing, then we are stuck in a traffic-jam of carts in front of horses. (Collini 2012: 91)

The types of learning in a specialist institution follow an assumption that what is produced is one simple 'output', namely a competent artistic practitioner conditioned for a readymade and low-paid 'portfolio' career. The instrumental (in this sense meaning non-liberal) didactic or master–apprentice style of teaching is often seen to be the dominant model employed. The implicit rationale for this assumption is that the artistic practitioner produced by the specialist institution does not need to be conversant with the intellectual arguments of their discipline. We reject this rationale and suggest that specialist institutions are sites for intellectual leadership that recognizes the role of the aesthetic in providing spaces for advancing critical thinking, and as such are the idiomatic home of an aesthetic education which is rooted in the perceptual and communicative potentiality inherent in all of the arts, a communicative potentiality that constitutes a type of autonomy for these creative disciplines.

III

In this section, the aim is more fully to describe and to provide a template for the central concept of this essay – the notion of an 'aesthetic education' – which, as we have seen, uniquely connects the idiomatic activity of the art school both to the current debates within the area of utopian pedagogy, and wider debates pertaining to the pernicious effects of internationalization and globalization. Our template for the term 'aesthetic education' will be resourced from three main interconnecting ideas: the concept of 'mass intellectuality' that emerges from Marx's work on the General Intellect, which serves as a central critical theme of the current volume; phenomenological approaches to art and extensions of these into the role of art and art-making within networks of communication in society; how both of these approaches matter *ethically* in an era of globalized education.

Let us start with the first concept. This is defined in Marx as the repository of common human cognitive competencies that are resistant to objectification, commodification and automation, such as the ability to actualize speech from the infinite resources of language.[6] Marx is referring to a type of core human subjectivity that is resistant and irreducible to the machinations of representation and capital. Paul Virno expands on this idea:

> Mass intellectuality is the composite group of Postfordist living labour, not merely of some particularly qualified third sector: it is the depository of cognitive competences that cannot be objectified in machinery. Mass intellectuality is the prominent form in which the general intellect is manifest today. The scientific erudition of the individual labourer is not under question here. Rather, all the more generic attitudes of the mind gain primary status as productive resources; these are the faculty of language, the disposition to learn, memory, the power of abstraction and relation and the tendency towards self-reflexivity. General intellect needs to be understood literally as intellect in general: the faculty and power to think, rather than the works produced by thought – a book, an algebra formula etc. In order to represent the relationship between general intellect and living labour in Postfordism we need to refer to the act through which every speaker draws on the inexhaustible potential of language to execute contingent and unrepeatable statements. Like the intellect and memory, language is the most common and least 'specialised' conceivable given. A good example of mass intellectuality is the speaker, not the scientist. Mass intellectuality has nothing to do with a new 'labour aristocracy'; it is actually its exact opposite. (Virno 2001)

Marx is referring here to the idea of the existence of some kind of common, shared core of human cognitive competencies. But one important part of our argument is that these same cognitive competencies can also extend to perceptual competencies. The human sensory apparatus is involved in highly complex and aggregative processing that, so far at least, has largely remained resistant to attempts at its complete automation. This enables us to introduce immediately the second idea. We can extend, we propose, the original idea of 'mass intellectuality' in Marx to include a common core in human subjectivity of competencies involving 'cognition *in* perception', and in direct relation to the aggregative and often largely tacit nature of human perceptual capability. This incidentally also connects the topic of mass intellectuality immediately to contemporary research in cognitive science, phenomenology and the philosophy of perception. Each of these areas of research aim at elucidating the perceptual *invariants* in the way the 'world shows up for us' that arise as a result of common structures that link the sensory apparatus to our action and movement (see e.g., Gallagher and Zahavi 2008). The elucidation of the structure of these invariants has always been a major goal of the phenomenological project within philosophy. It is not only the cognitive competencies of human subjects that are resistant to objectification and automation, but their *perceptual* capabilities too.

This then immediately links the concept of mass intellectuality to *art*, which, on taking a phenomenological approach, aesthetically exemplifies constant factors in human experience, which are basic to our cognitive perceptual and metaphysical inherence in the world.[7] What are these 'constant factors'? The first thing to say is that they are largely subpersonal (i.e. are present in consciousness but normally hidden to it). These factors are also a learned response from infancy that reflects the reality that the human subject, as a brain-body, is immersed in a physical world which is mind-independent, but which itself determines the conditions for the subject's continued survival. At the same time, the nature of this physical world in perception (what we might call the phenomenal world) is shaped by the subject's innate cognitive and motor abilities, so that: 'The ontological structure of the subject and its objects of experience are thus reciprocally related in key respects. At the experiential level, each is, in effect, part of the full definition of the other' (Crowther 2009: 3). What we will call 'phenomenological' here is the elucidation of the complex nature of this reciprocity, which involves serial differential relations between subject and world on the basis of the subject's modes of perception, knowledge and action (which themselves depend on further differential relations). We also stress, as we have seen, the unconscious nature of many aspects of this reciprocity, which means that some of these differential relations are sensed without us necessarily being aware of them, as a result of their embedding in all kinds of habitual and 'learned' cognitive skills, including sensorimotor skills, that are practical in nature, not linguaform or conceptual, and not based on inferential aspects of the perception itself. These preconscious factors of phenomenological depth include: a tacit *relationality* (hidden orderings of the perceptual field, based on our current positioning, which organize how we are aware of some but not all of the items present to consciousness at once, combined with the move from perception to apperception); *virtual* aspects of perception (how our perception of an object depends, e.g., on the ideational simulation of other perceptions of the same object that are not currently present in experience); and practical knowledge of the *affordances* of objects (or the preconscious awareness of the properties of objects that enable potential ways to enact with them).

The vital point here is that the nature of these underlying features of human perceptive capability, which we linked to the concept of 'mass intellectuality', are intimately bound up with art and aesthetic experience. Moreover, such an approach to aesthetic experience via an appeal to a ground of phenomenological depth factors resists the ubiquity of social or semiotic reductionism: it appeals instead to the intrinsic, or transhistorical significance[8] of the image (or artwork) which is bound up with the conditions of embodied human subjectivity that are described above. Think, for example, of how the themes in visual art history of space-occupancy and implied motion, the generalized ontology of spatial relations achieved through perspective, the depiction of objects via marks on a surface, the 'projection' of a virtual 'elsewhere' from a material base, the disruption of spatial context through framing and so on are all basic to acts of picturing *as such*. These aspects of the embodiment of phenomenological depth in and through a visual medium may change, be recombined or even disrupted in different historically contingent ways pertaining to specific aesthetic *styles*, but they have a significance that is not reducible to history alone. Such intrinsic significance is however not at all 'ahistorical' but is historically revealed and identified through those features that make a work of art a mode of reference *at all*, and thus depends on, 'those transhistorical ontological structures that are basic to individual kinds of cultural phenomena and [which] form conditions which enable their more historically specific transmissions' (Crowther 2009: 22). Such significance, which depends on phenomenological depth factors, is moreover *shown* rather than *spoken*.

What makes art important is not based on formal properties of an image or their *meanings* but how pictures themselves express certain constant factors in human experience. Phenomenology aims at elucidating the *reciprocity* between the subject and object of experience, and a phenomenology *of art* therefore interrogates *how* a picture represents, not just *what* it represents: This explains why art *matters* to us at all, rather than just what it means to us as, for example, a type of semiotic code. We can also extend this immediately to other forms of art. Literature, for example, engages intimately without capacity for perceptual imagination, the way that we can vicariously simulate perceptual scenes in another fictional time and place through the formation of mental imagery. Music seems to us to be bound intimately with the perception of music and gesture, and dance exploits our ability to form 'kinesthetic empathy' with the movements of another body. Art heightens and transforms the phenomenological depth factors that structure our perception and intersubjective awareness and does through utilizing perceptual media themselves.

But if art is idiomatically about perceptual media, how does it enter into, and survive within networks of human communication? If we are going to make an argument that art and arts education has a unique, and arguably autonomous role within what Giroux has called 'utopian pedagogy', and if it is to act in a role of societal critique, this is a vital question. By far the most complete answer to it is contained, in our view, in the work of Niklas Luhmann. For Luhmann, one of the main reasons that art has evolved historically is to act as a kind of bridge between immediate experience and communicative acts that aim at capturing the contents of experience:

'Art uses perceptions and, by doing so, seizes consciousness at the level of its own externalizing activity. The function of art would thus consist in integrating what is in principle incommunicable – namely, perception – into the communication network' (Luhmann 2000: 149). Furthermore, the type of interaction between a work of art and the discursive networks that surround it is one of perturbation and disturbance: 'art *irritates* communication – and forces it to ask – what does this perception mean?' (2000). Art can, and indeed does, function in modernity as a kind of hole that communicative acts of discourse aim to fill in.

Communication in the art system, for Luhmann, is the one form of communication within which purely sensory perception is not only a presupposition but a content carried, together with meaning, by language. From here, it is a small step to perhaps the greatest thinker of art and aesthetics in the twentieth century, Theodor Adorno. It is precisely because of the potentiality inherent in artworks for communicative disruption that they acquire a special, almost autonomous status within the social fabric of the contemporary situation. This, we claim, should be at the heart of what is meant by an 'aesthetic education', which should provide its recipient with precisely the means both to produce and, equally importantly, to analyze the exact nature of this 'communicative disruption', thereby coupling the aesthetic with the political. The subversive artwork drops like a probe into the atrophying conditions of the socially conditioned present, an appearing of unreality into the what is known and is acknowledged to be real: 'In each genuine artwork, something appears that does not exist' (Adorno 1997: 82).[9]

Why is all of this important to the context at hand, namely, the role, within the globalized societies of today, of the specialist art institution? Let us tie up a few threads. The aim of such institutions has become reduced, we have argued, to providing students merely with vocational training in art techniques, coupled with a training in how to situate these skills within a labour market. This is a coupling that has become synonymous with the notion of the student artist as a 'creative entrepreneur'. This reified notion of the entrepreneur, which has become the symbol for a contemporary currency of transferable skills within HE, aims to quantify the exact value to arts-based learning. It also positions the notion of creativity and the individual as a producer of an exchangeable, quantifiable commodity. This leaves the currency of *cultural capital* neglected (at a time when it is most needed). The constructed role of the entrepreneur, who shifts economic resources out of an area of lower and into an area of higher productivity is therefore not the solution to the problem of situating arts practice within a climate of austerity, but part of the problem itself. It results in a situation in which the aesthetic has conceded all ground to the political or at least a narrow sense of political, grounded in neoliberalism.

The problem here is succinct. If, as we have seen, the potentiality for arts training, in terms of critical pedagogy, and in a reclaiming of the possibilities of HE lies in its disruptive potential to networks of habitual communication, then this necessitates a reformed model. This is the idea behind a 'suitable aesthetic education' and of 'artistic leadership' which is something that goes beyond technique, but also requires a whole context of critical thinking as its accompaniment. We need perhaps a return to the model of an art school, in which artistic leadership is coextensive with the provision of a much more holistic intellectual education that includes, and introduces the student to the importance of the interactions between perceptual media and communicative acts. A study then of not just art and works that comprise the trajectory of its history, but a grounding in critical theory, aesthetics, the sociology of art and phenomenology. Artistic leadership then would comprise both the pedagogical approach taken in this holistic sense, but also an attribute that is passed to learners. We suggest therefore that specialist institutions are sites for both *intellectual* leadership and the idiomatic home for a suitable 'aesthetic education' based on artistic leadership, which is rooted in the perceptual and communicative potentiality inherent in all arts. And to conclude the argument that takes us back to Marx again, we can situate the importance of this 'aesthetic education' within contemporary discourses on globalization that have become prevalent within postcolonial theory.

Let us return to Gayatri Spivak, for a moment, who has recently suggested that: 'The most pernicious presupposition today is that globalization has happily happened in every aspect of our lives. Globalization can never happen to the sensory equipment of the experiencing being except insofar as it was always implicit in its vanishing outlines. Only an aesthetic education can continue to prepare us for this' (Spivak 2012: 2). The reach of globalization, despite its ubiquity, is still restricted largely to networks of information and data, coupled to ever increasing flows of internationalized capital. A core of human subjectivity, in fact the exact same core that we can relate mass intellectuality (via the phenomenological extension outlined earlier) remains, even in the midst of globalized societies, resistant to these same networks and flows, and remains despite them, somehow irreducible to their action.

This is what places art, as a form of communication that operates within perceptual media, so important today. In turn, this makes an aesthetic education perhaps uniquely *ethically* important, and thereby gives art a certain autonomy amongst other disciplines in the academy. As John Erikson explains, with a reference to the famous thesis of Marx, in terms of the transformative potentiality of the dramatic arts:

> The presumption of many contemporary political academics is that to interpret the world in the right way is to change it. This may not be so far off, but it depends upon your overestimation of what academic discourse can do (in relation to the level of mass-cultural discourse of the media) [...] On the most mediated level, the world is changed by interpretations that gain mass appeal. Which is why the theatre, taken in its broadest sense, from resistant small performance in oppressive countries, to independent filmmaking to performance actions on the world-wide web, can be seen as a locus for this question. (Erickson 2001: 144)

IV

Let us now offer a few remarks to conclude. We have taken a journey, through art and aesthetic education from Marx outwards, and then back to Marx again, via the interconnected ideas of: mass intellectuality; the phenomenological extension of this same concept of mass intellectuality; phenomenological theories of art and artworks;

the idea of art and aesthetics as rooted in common perceptual systems; the idea that art, as rooted in perceptions, can act as an 'irritant' of communicative systems; the idea of art as the critical negation of society; art, as the barrier, rooted in the sensory, to total globalization; and art and artworks as therefore resistant to systems of commodification and objectification (which brings us straightforwardly back to Marx again).

This leads us to construct ideas of aesthetic education and artistic leadership that are bringing to light, through a diverse and critical pedagogy, all of these interconnected ideas. It suggests a vital role for small specialist institutions in providing an alternative version of leadership in HE, one that reconstructs their position as museums and gatekeepers of a cultural heritage that demarcates an elitist capital, but rather sees them both as guardians of the perceptual and the imaginative, and also as providers of something additional: a thorough education that situates the arts in a globalized context, which is able to not just assimilate, but critique that context. Within the context of HE, this means specialist institutions shifting to situate themselves as an example of what we highlight above: According to Virno (2001), intellect is not contained within the 'product'. As such, utilizing aesthetic experience as distinct to artistic production as a basis for educational conceptualization offers relief and space to become entangled with the potentiality of critique rather than focusing on reproducing knowledges and generating new knowledges according to accepted practices. However, it is important not only to suggest a leadership role for HE, the specialist institution has a role to play more widely than providing the next generation of 'critical producers'. Importantly, by shifting the perception of the specialists as closed communities where only an elite form of production takes place (and access to these centres are controlled by accepted modes of elitist production), the aesthetic experience allows for a communal (but not consensual) mode of critique that can inhabit and invigorate formal and informal spaces of community. Let us offer a final quotation:

> Enter upon this road of abstraction and the time is sure to come when the appropriate object-of-knowledge is stripped of all that is immediate and qualitative, of all that is final, self-sufficient. Then it becomes an anatomized epitome of just and only those aspects which are of indicative and instrumental import. (Dewey 1925: 106)

The above quote from John Dewey's *Experience and Nature* is a useful way of concluding this chapter. As discussed earlier, many current attempts to measure the success and benefit in arts training have arguably focused on just those factors like employability and income generation that could be described as 'instrumental' under Dewey's proposal. The immediate and qualitative nature of arts activity and its reception, which we have attempted to capture in terms of a definition of aesthetic education, are perhaps more what Dewey had in mind. A suitable aesthetic education goes beyond the training of technique and its placement within a marketplace, but must relate to what we might call the *intrinsic* meaning of the arts as well. This meaning, which originates from the roots of art in the perceptual and the embodied, resists generalization and abstraction. In an era when HE funding bodies are increasingly demanding more and more quantifiable mechanisms for the justification of the benefit of arts education, Dewey's words, written now almost a century ago, still resonate.

Notes

1 This emphasis on the perceptual foundation of arts practice and reception allows an appeal to a range of contemporary theoretical and philosophical writing on the arts, including the work of Niklas Luhmann (2000), Jacques Rancière (2006) and Thomas Doherty (2006).
2 This is a theme in a number of other recent studies on arts pedagogy, including Hickey, Moody and Page (2015).
3 Our approach to the term 'aesthetic education' is therefore different that of Spivak, who, while acknowledging that the term can sustain 'no particular global formula' (Spivak 2012: 2) goes on to define it using a modified, or even 'sabotaged' version of Friedrich Schiller's aestheticized account of 'play' coupled to Gregory Bateson's notion of the 'double bind' (Bateson 1972).
4 There is an obvious link here to the work of Niklas Luhmann (2000): his understanding of autonomous art implies that art's main function 'is to assist in the construction of a distinction in social consciousness between "reality" and "imagination"'.
5 There are many other examples of the notion of the creative entrepreneur within the contemporary pedagogical literature on arts training. See for example Casey et al. (2013).
6 For more on the original definition in the *Grundrisse* of Marx, see Hardt and Virno (2006).
7 This is an idea that originally derives from Maurice Merleau-Ponty: 'It is the expressive operation begun in the least perception which amplifies into painting and art' (Merleau-Ponty 1993: 106).
8 See also Crowther (2002).
9 Compare this also to Luhmann: 'the new social system of art communicates the limits of communication; that is, in communicating the breakdown of stable representation systems' (quoted in Harrington 2004: 200).

Part Three

Praxis

10

Six Theses In, Against and Beyond the University

Birmingham Autonomous University

Introduction

Birmingham Autonomous University is a group of ten university students, graduates and workers involved in a variety of networks of struggles on and off campus. We started meeting in 2013 to assess the position and the role of the intellectual labourer in contemporary society. Our contribution is presented as theses so as to express not only the unity of our perspective, but also to demonstrate how homogenizing our expression would have meant speaking in an authoritative and hence contrived voice. Not only would this have been intolerant of the individuations we have attempted to articulate in response to the university. More importantly, it would have masked how a unitary perspective is achieved through our differences rather than in spite of them – something which we have come to believe to be a necessary condition for the emergence of mass intellectuality.

Thesis 1 challenges the myth of a golden age during which universities were not tarnished by capitalism – rendering visible the role they have always fulfilled in the reproduction of labour-power. Against this backdrop, student movements have had to face the inadequacy of reformist responses from universities. Reflecting on these movements, Thesis 2 argues that the power to develop long-term strategies is hampered by the absence of intellectual analyses into the material conditions affecting students. An example of one such condition is the additional burden of emotional labour, which falls on those whom are made to feel undeserving by universities. Thesis 3 descends into universities' hidden abode of production and shows how self-doubt serves universities by fuelling the phenomenon of overwork. An exploration of the structureless form that intellectual leadership must take in order to accommodate this state of affairs then follows. Thus, Thesis 4 argues that without a critique of this sort of leadership it is not possible to devote attention to the non-conceptual conditions affecting the potential emergence of mass intellectuality beyond the university. This inadequacy of the university as we know it to provide a refuge for mass intellectuality is then unpacked accordingly, through an exposition of the vicious circularity of what Thesis 5 calls the 'methodological university'. Consequently, the concepts of practical reflexivity, mutual recognition and good conversation are proposed as guidelines for the foundation of an educational commons. This theme is also taken up by Thesis

6, which reflects on the usefulness of MOOCs for a Marxism that is re-politicized beyond its current status in the academy. Finally, we conclude with a summary of demands that are developed immanently to the conditions we are about to discuss (see Milburn 2015), and which therefore reflect our desire to be in, against and beyond the university.

The university is a factory, burn it down

'The university is a factory' – we hear this cry everywhere, sometimes as a declaration and accusation of contempt. This slogan expresses the commonly held view that this is not how things are meant to be: 'once universities were pure places of learning and research, serving all of society, before neoliberalism and capitalism ruined it all'. Often there is the corollary 'shut it down', for by ceasing its productivity by force we may hold the university to ransom and begin demanding change. Sometimes people shout, 'the university is not a factory!', as if the changes they protest are the turning point of transformation. Never has the university been a place of pure academic and intellectual pursuits, serving and bettering society, unsullied by crass material demands. Rather, it was once a stronghold of the elites, producing the knowledge needed by the upper classes to cement their rule both over the workers in their homeland and in their colonies taken through bloody murder.

Now it produces sites of exploitation – streamlining the process by which exploitation takes place. No knowledge is born that is not enclosed, stolen and turned to poison regardless of the potential it holds to liberate and enrich us all. It produces workers burdened with debt to make them fearful, forcing them to take any work and to be grateful. In this way, dreams become nightmares and purposeful action becomes the shuffle of a zombie. So merely shutting down the university factory as a tactic of struggle is not enough, for the reforms this may bring will merely give us a temporarily more comfortable factory until these too are inevitably eroded. That is not to say reforms would not buy time, nor that temporary relief is worthless – for some it gives the breathing room needed to prevent suffocation – but it will never be enough. So if there is no golden age of the university to return to, what is to be done?

Burn it down! Not in the fire of the phoenix – which brings rebirth and renewal – for we must not strive merely for a renewed and reborn university factory. I would rather burn it in the fire that destroys a structurally unsafe house which has already claimed many lives. Only once the failures of the past have been reduced to ashes can something truly worthwhile be built in its place. Our aim is a form of education which liberates, rather than furthers oppression; where knowledge is not created merely for enclosure or for the engendering of terrified workers ready for the rote of intellectual labour, but for the common learning and benefit of all.

But just as the university factories' life and purpose is inseparable from the function of capitalism, so too is the struggle against it inseparable from the struggle against capitalism. Thus, the struggle of the student and the worker is inseparable. What is study in the capitalist university but labouring to reproduce yourself as a better worker? Even if we were to forget about unpaid academic labour – labour without which the factory could not run – students work regardless. This work takes the form of both waged and unwaged labour, which is therefore unrecognized, for example, social reproduction: Students and workers both have the result of their labour taken from them.

So students must spend their time within the university factory not to remake themselves as the perfect fearful worker grateful for scraps, but rather to learn how to fight. Resources made available to students should be turned against their masters: journals of politics, chemistry, biology, physics and military theory, to name a few examples, should be expropriated (Harney and Moten 2013). Engaging in the struggles within the university will set the ground for the destruction of the interdependent oppressions of which the university factory is a manifestation. Never forget that students are workers, the denial of whose control of the means of production is needed for capitalism to survive, and so must stand as part of the working class against the ruling class. Our aim should not be to reform, but for all to have ownership of the means of material and intellectual production. The university is a factory, burn it down! Society is a factory, burn it down! Let us build a better one in its place.

Student movement strategy

It might seem clear that students would benefit from free education but it is worth bearing in mind that there are most likely other demands of the student whose radical perspectives need to be teased out. It is also important for students to delve deeper into demands like 'more plugs in the library' or 'free printing credits', which appear to us only as student election manifesto points. When these demands are only looked at by those seeking elected positions, analysis of the conditions facing students on their campuses becomes informed exclusively by its reactionary components. In other words, instead of creating arenas for real discussion around recurring issues of need within the education sector, we are left unable to know where to put our resources beyond demanding ambitious reforms. 'Free printing credits' are left by the wayside, unexplored for radical potential, while focus is devoted to national policy work. The attempted workers' inquiry into that movement found students re-evaluating their position within the university. In the UK, we do see some campaigns focussing on specific campus issues, such as the campaign for a week's rest during University of Cambridge term-time (Connell 2015) and against outsourcing of catering services in Sussex (Ratcliffe 2013). However, without systematic attempts at this kind of inquiry forming the basis for campaigns, the student movement in Britain is left without the ability to form a long-term strategy.

Models which build the collective power of the student body from the grassroots, as opposed to a representational basis, are difficult to build because of differences in needs between departments and weakness of ties between postgraduate and undergraduate subjectivities. Typically, the student movement has an inability to tailor its actions and to perceive these differences (Cockburn and Blackburn 1969). Department-level organizing allowing for the articulation of, and organizing around, grassroots concerns, perhaps related to research criteria or syllabuses are a crucial element in achieving this. Therefore, it is important that participants in the student movement actively undertake research and form collectives of the sort that allow us to learn more about these issues. This type of undertaking is one with links to the practice of workers' inquiry. The premise behind 'militant research' is that no distinction is 'made between moments of struggle and moments of investigation' as such it provides tools 'to existing frameworks in radical movements' contributing to research and taking a role in producing knowledge 'which resonates with campaigns and organisations' (Van Meer 2009):

> We did not create elaborate questionnaires or interviews in order to collect information from workers. Rather, we actively participated in the construction of picket lines and blockades; we took part in assemblies and workers' meetings, as well as produced, together with workers, moments of close examination for activist and mainstream media. (Curcio 2014: 377–378)

We can look to the Greek Student Movement from 2007 to 2008 as an example of a strong strain of organizing, not just around the issues of reform – preventing the removal of university asylum (a measure implemented in the 1960s to protect political expression on campuses and restricting the entry of police to university areas), free textbooks, and introduction of a maximum course length – but also around the position of the student within wider society (Angelos and Dimitris 2014).

This type of learning should be developed through the mechanisms of struggle themselves. A departmental assembly would be the best place to begin the inquiry. If there is to be a marked increase in activity, it is likely to be one which comes from a common realization that self-determination can meet the needs of the movement. Workers' inquiry in the form of independently organized departmental assemblies would both provide mechanisms for tactics such as the student strike, while providing a means to determine dynamically the needs to be fought for by the movement.

Self-doubt and overwork

The university has been separated from the public space through its presentation as a selective, 'apolitical' place, isolated from the real world of work and inequality. Its foundation, in a very real sense, negates our experience of everyday life in capitalist society, contradicting our recognition of ourselves and others through experiences and their theorization. There is an implied assumption that those who are part of the academy have to be 'grateful' for being accepted into it, and any failure on their part to 'succeed' is presumed to be due to their own ineptitude to compete. Alienation emerges as a result, leading those referred to by the university as 'non-traditional students' to struggle with self-doubt, feeling as though they do not deserve to be in higher education (HE) (Barcan 2013: 193; Reay et al. 2009: 11–12). They are included within the institution, but they do not belong to it (Van Den Hemel 2008). For instance, one of the participants in a study on working-class students in higher education in the UK stated:

> Academically wise I keep thinking I shouldn't be here; that, you know, I'm not up to the level that I should be. I think it's my own personal, it's in my head. I'm just doubting myself (Barbara, mature, white, working-class history student, Northern). (Reay et al. 2009: 12)

Academia is a place of training where middle class outlooks are presented as the most appropriate, and where being 'critical' entails making arguments within or against established frameworks, without questioning the very exploitation upon which these particular frameworks, and the institutions in which they emerged, depend. The process of 'becoming educated' is therefore conflated with becoming abiding workers, while also 'becoming middle class' (Loveday 2014: 577) by upholding individualistic and materialistic values. Having such responsibilities: as a carer, spouse, parent; of managing money and calculating debt; of deciding whether to prioritize a course, a job or friends; each reflect emotions which are of little concern and relevance to the entitled.

Students have a lack of control over their university work as they are put in a position of constantly reacting to the demands of the institution and its conditions of work, just as workers in any industry have to deal with demands. Central to this is emotional work: planning, worrying, reflecting, hesitating, psychologically preparing for an activity/event; all these involve emotional labour which takes time, energy and efforts that affects us beyond the activity itself. However, the university forcefully makes a separation between the 'time of worry' which is regarded as unproductive, and the '"real" (productive) time of academic work'. Emotional labour is unpaid, unrecognized work which is often private. Indeed,

> despite talk of the post-industrial West, we are still on the production line – only the produce has changed. Instead of cars, toothpaste and toys we produce desire, debt, careers and websites. And for those of us who still insist on being bookish, we produce Academic Excellence. (University for Strategic Optimism 2011: 23)

In an environment where 'speed' and 'efficiency' are deemed part of 'excellence', taking time to manage one's emotions and level of concentration should be thought of in political terms. The overtime spent on academic work can be considered a form of culturally accepted self-harm (Hall and Bowles 2016) and the feeling of fraudulence often leads to overwork. To add a 'positive' take on this situation, universities promote ideas such as 'earn while you learn' and 'lifelong learning' in a manner which presents overwork and speed as desirable signs of a purposeful existence. In doing so, universities can easily move towards short-term and casual contracts by claiming that they offer work 'opportunities' for students. Yet again, we are expected to be thankful for our precarity.

We need to recognize that 'we are *structurally* never good enough' (Barcan 2013: 196; emphasis in original) within the competitive, neoliberal university. By considering emotions as work, the meaning of 'overwork' needs to be re-examined. Overwork does not mean only working productively for too long, but also doing that which may be seen as 'little work', with considerable, time-consuming efforts. Overwork is giving up doing other things which are more socially valuable to the autonomy of the individual. Through our practical–reflexive approach, academic work cannot be separated from life outside the institution; the student is not one-dimensional. Rather, by locating student work and experience as part of the wider logic of societal processes and by identifying the student as a worker-producer of knowledge, we can conclude that the university depends on the overwork of all of its workers and on the isolation between and among students and staff, as well as between them and society more generally. The extra emotional labour of those who do not find themselves 'at home' in HE should be recognized as such. Such genuine acknowledgement of people's experience as the basis for the production of knowledge would mean that the 'accelerated' academy would be slowed down (Moten and Harney 1999).

Mass intellectuality beyond the university

I agree that mass intellectuality has to be situated in a holistic critique of the contradictions of capitalism as they become manifest through the class struggle (Hall 2014: 832). Accordingly, I also strongly believe that under capitalism HE is more socially damaging than it is useful, and that the world as we know it would be a slightly better place without it. That is, HE stands as a barrier in the way of mass intellectuality. Thus, I argue that the emergence of mass intellectuality presupposes more than just the undoing of capitalist expropriation through a dual process of reappropriation and reproduction that moves from universities' intellectual property to the knowledge commons of everyday life. Indeed, I think that this bridging strategy is misguided because it fails to grasp that the complexity of today's world is not something that so-called 'uneducated' people are necessarily unprepared for (Waugh 2009).

I would love to think clearly about mass intellectuality as 'socially useful knowledge that emerges through the definition of an alternative value-form that will work in terms of the social reproduction of society in a different image' (Hall 2014b: 823). Indeed, I would suggest that the real barrier to mass intellectuality is the lack of material, organizational and institutional means for the oppressed – who are society's primary knowledge producers (Hegel 1931: 45) – to explore an autodidactic form of intellectuality. Nevertheless, this seems impossible without a critique of intellectual leadership as we know it. For example, in 2016 the University of Birmingham is set to unveil New Core – a digital administration and 'flat' management system which 'will capture everything' (2015). The purpose of management models and systems such as New Core will be to empower leadership to continue setting managerial prerogatives without being burdened by or being held responsible for exploitation. In principle, therefore, leadership can thus float around from one issue to another without leaving a trace.

In this case, I would argue, universities are operationalizing what has been called the 'tyranny of structurelessness' – whereby 'informal' structures visible or invisible to their members come to mask imbalances of power, and in so doing place democratic accountability at one remove from decision-making (Freeman 1996: 1–3). Indeed, with New Core, workers will be expected to bring everything forward to their managers, allowing the latter to administer co-operation behind workers' backs. Accordingly, workers would 'enter relations with the capitalist, but not with each other' (Marx 2004: 450–451). Ultimately, this co-operative and distributed form of 'touch-and-go' intellectual leadership gives 'capital the credit for organizing production and reproduction' (Caffentzis 2010: 29): managers move to abolish the habit of working in isolation, and seek legitimacy for establishing coercive forms of teamwork.

However gloomy this picture may be, it does not constitute a sufficient basis upon which to reject the possibility of mass intellectuality. But while it is important not to conflate estimations of the growing or shrinking cognitive competences of academic labour with those of intellectual leadership in general (Harney and Moten 1998: 177), it is also crucial to realize that universities are one of the many institutions with the power to enclose the general intellect (De Angelis and Harvie 2009; Lindenschmidt 2004; Pirie 2009). This is exemplified by the fact that the circulation of the general intellect in universities gives rise to a form of co-operation that is subsumed under capitalist accumulation and which constitutes 'almost as important a source of counter-revolutionary energy as commodity fetishism' (Caffentzis 2010: 29).

This points to the necessity of struggle in and against the university, without which it would be impossible to confront this counter-revolutionary energy, and therefore develop mass intellectuality beyond the university. For this to occur, I want to conclude, a form of self-taught intellectual leadership capable of abolishing universities is needed. Furthermore, this kind of auto-didacticism need not be the effort of a single individual, but also of a self-taught mass capable of abolishing universities by abolishing itself. Therefore, I demand that this kind of intellectuality explores new points of leverage, and destructive forms of industrial action that can strike at the heart of the university once and for all.

Against the methodological university

The dialectical relationship between commons and enclosure is perpetually enacted through enforced exclusion. Within the methodological university, this process of enclosure appears as would a music box, preserving its content to the point of formalism. The emptiness of content is the product of a closed circuit of self-perpetuating, self-affirming banalities. The mechanical model of the methodological university as such contains this vicious cycle as an active process of enclosing knowledge, where knowledge neither knows itself nor its object. Through the imperatives of the market, caught up in a system that does not account for itself reflexively, the often stressed convergence of theory and practice is muted. As such, the reproductive model of the methodological university is still founded upon a seemingly unshakeable positivism, where 'the forbidden fruit of lived experience flees or disappears under the assaults of reductionism; and silence reigns around the fortress of knowledge' (Lefebvre 2008: 134).

From the gilded walls of the university, commons emerge as cracks. They shake the foundations of knowledge that denies itself. We propose that we, the students and workers, are the impulse of the commons – a form of social co-operation that takes a critical stance against the production of knowledge, against the hegemony of method. It is a political potential that tears through the *a priori* of objective validity with an experiential pause. Rather than making commons functional to the existing system, we propose the commons as the university's negative imprint, that which already exists in resistance to enclosure.

Our guiding principles for the educational commons are thus: mutual recognition; good conversation; and practical reflexivity. These are the basis for the new 'sensibility' that we wish to build (Gunn 2015: 14–33). These concepts form a constellation, each of them implying the other, comprising a whole which we call the de-mediated autonomous university. By mutual recognition we mean that we view each other as totalizing subjects, as others situated within the world with valid experiences, seeking to conceptualize and communicate them (Gunn 1989a: 71–77). Mutual recognition suggests that we come to know ourselves through the interplay of our view with the views of others – as a unity through difference (Gunn 1989a: 71–77). This mutual recognition is the essence of the 'good' conversation, itself a dialectic of recognition and critique. Our experience, instead of being denied, is seen as internally related to our conceptualizations, meaning theory and practice are moments elaborating each other, rather than externally related spheres (Gunn 1989b). This allows our experience to be the basis from which to develop meaningful (abstract) categorizations as well as providing experiential grounds for interrogation and critique.

Commons stand against the methodological university, the domain of specialist knowledge production, which promotes a formalistic, monological approach to knowledge production mirroring factory production lines, and embodying the fragmentation and separation inhering in society through the ever-intensifying division of labour. To become socially valid intellectual labourers, we are trained for the production of knowledge. We are told, as Scholasticus once said, 'never venture into the water until you have learned how to swim' (cited in Rose 1995: 44). This entails contradiction, for we arrive *in medias res* and are confronted in the classroom with the supposed governing rules of our own intellectual experiences. In fact, more is governed by these rules: they delimit the very object of knowledge itself, given validity by reference to these rules alone. Therefore, society is reified – reflected as a 'second nature', a predetermined object of study – and methodology fetishized, as possessed with the power to delimit the valid object of science while deriving, from this self-same movement, its own internal validity. Hence the vicious circularity: methodology drawing legitimacy from and justifying itself through its reification of society. In the undergraduate textbooks we see the schematic of this knowledge production process as the movement 'from theory to hypothesis to operationalization to research design to data collection, and finally to analysis and findings' (Burnham 1992: 5), reiterated *ad nauseam*, regardless of actual experiences in research which, instead, call for reflexivity to dissolve the façade. We stand opposed to all this for, in the words of Gillian Rose: 'The limitation of "justified" knowledge of the finite prevents us from recognizing, criticizing, and hence from changing the social and political relations which determine us' (1995: 45).

Therefore, our concern with practical reflexivity is not simply a concern for the rigour of knowledge, but a concern for the rigour of opposition. Only when we place our position as critics of society within the society in question can we begin to examine whether our theoretical categories reflect or copy the hermeneutical composition of capitalist society and thus reinforce (remediate) what we are seeking to overcome (Gunn 1987: 43–46). Practical reflexivity is the means by which we critique the forms of appearance of capitalist society, and it thus provides the non-methodological basis of militant conceptualization (1987). Furthermore, practical reflexivity promises an end to dogmatism, as it maintains and emboldens a theoretical openness to empirical complexity (Bonefeld 1987: 36; Burnham 1992: 3–8). The principle of doubt inherent in practically reflexive theorization allows us, as militants, to take account of 'the open and contingent process of class struggle, its changing forms and conditions' (Bonefeld 1987: 34) through an eternal return of concepts to experience. Mutual recognition enables this process to encompass the variety of experiences present in struggle, metabolizing these through good conversation, whose organizing principle is the self-determining movement of practice and theory.

No institutional imperative guides the good conversation. The only principle is internal to itself – the deepening of critique through a process of its own reflection into itself, into its content, into the historical experiences of capital's permanent recomposition around labour's refusals (Bonefeld 1987: 36–37). The only means by which we may keep critical pace with these transformations, without falling into methodological formalism, is to renew the historical nature of our concepts by enfolding them back into our practical existence.

What is Marxism for anyway?

The tradition of independent working-class education has a long history. As communists we are encouraged not only to reflect on this history in order to place ourselves contemporaneously, but also to think of ourselves as active agents with capacities and needs that are conditioned by the uniqueness of our respective struggles. As a result, the form that independent working-class education takes in any historical moment should change to keep abreast of the latest developments, as should the content of this education. This necessitates a sober re-evaluation of both the need to educate, agitate and organize on an explicitly communist basis, as well as the technological capacity to materialize this political will. Both of these factors are present in our historical moment. As such, the project of reimagining independent working-class education finds fertile ground in our current conditions. However, despite this need to reimagine and bring up-to-date, the real content of independent working-class education is the same as it has always been. It is the struggle of labour against capital, of the worker against the boss. Likewise, the form is always the same in its barest essence. It is the presentation of knowledge in a manner that takes into account our living and working conditions as workers, as well as the particular educational needs that emerge from these conditions. For example, the contemporary hegemony of the flexible working arrangement in the form of zero hour and part-time and temporary contracts currently acts as a blockage to the adoption of the standard evening class model that has historically been the preserve of workers. This move towards flexible contracts has been described by Naomi Klein as follows:

> For other employers, however, part-time positions are used as a loophole to keep wages down and to avoid benefits and overtime; 'flexibility' becomes a code for 'no promises', making the juggling of other commitments – both financial and parental – more challenging, not less. (2000: 248)

Massive Open Online Courses (MOOCs) provide a potential twenty-first century solution to the difficulty of learning when working flexibly. They are described in a white paper published by the Association of Governing Boards of Universities and Colleges as follows:

> MOOCs use Web-based tools and environments ... Learning is accomplished via a 'flipped classroom' model, whereby the instructor employs the Internet and other technologies to allow students to gain knowledge that used to be delivered via a lecture format and then use time in the classroom to work on problems together. (Voss 2013)

The potential for MOOCs to provide a radical and emancipatory education, given the current conditions of tuition fees and unpredictable working hours, is obvious. Regarding the orthodox bricks and mortar university, the university factory in its current neoliberal manifestation as an 'accelerated' academy exists to reproduce the student as compliant worker-in-training on a daily basis. Housebroken by debt into a future of precarious work, the students' true status as exploited labour-power being hidden from them by their wageless status. As a result, students' intellectuality is internally related to the working class as opposed to being an external force. There is no 'going to the people' because there is no 'people' to go to, and the false distinction between intellectual and manual labour is invalidated. As such, MOOCs provide the potential for the communist student to make intellectual resources appropriated from the university more widely available.

However, it is important to remember that the world of education is hierarchical, and technological developments such as MOOCs do nothing to challenge this in and of themselves. It is not the technology itself but the manner in which it is used, and the way in which teachers and learners relate to each other, that provides the basis for an emancipatory education. The key problem with the museum piece Marxism taught within universities is that the teacher–student relationship is perceived as a static relation between unequal subjects. The curriculum remains dry, dull, and boring, unresponsive to the daily experience of the living subject under capitalism. The curriculum is therefore nothing more than a dead weight, weighing heavily on the brains of the living. Writing on MOOCs, Hall states that they 'need to be critiqued from inside the system of production/consumption in which they emerge ... and the systemic need to seek out new spaces for that profitability' (2015a).

In contrast, a collaborative approach to producing a curriculum creates a process in which teacher and student are co-producers of knowledge. Reciprocity in learning can be easily facilitated by the internet. Online forums could enable activists to share information with each other and link up struggles. In order to bring teachers and students together there could be a section built into the course with advice on how to run a local reading group based on the course material so that any student can potentially become a teacher. The MOOC itself should only be the first point of contact. This is vital because the alternatives are unthinkable. The notion that the MOOC is enough in and as of itself is reactionary. It actively reproduces the learner as the perfect atomized neoliberal subject, sat behind their laptop, learning by themselves, cut off from the social relationships that make the process of learning enjoyable and transformative. The other alternative notion, that an emancipatory Marxism can be found in the neoliberal university, is to be given no quarter either due to a curriculum that crushes Marxist theory into mere essay fodder and the hegemony of a teacher–student relationship which brutalizes both parties by reducing their lived experiences into spectres that must be left at the door in the name of 'scientific objectivity'.

Therefore, the technology is not to be fetishized but expropriated and used to facilitate the building of a commons of sense predicated on a mutual recognition of experience that reduces the role of the technology itself to a facilitator role. This process of expropriation begins with an undercommoning of the university, with stealing from the university those intellectual resources required to develop independent working-class educational projects (Harney and Moten 2013). In other words, the first step in this process of expropriation is an organized academic bank job. Since the technology is there as is the political imagination, the task of reinvigorating the tradition of independent working-class education is far from impossible.

Conclusion

We have argued that it is no longer possible to imagine a university and a society in a different image unless all those who valorize it mutually recognize each other as such. This insight has shed light on the fact that there is a whole world of conditions that remain to be discovered and which desperately need to be analysed in order for emancipatory strategy to renew itself. As we indicated, this kind of militant research could start by elucidating a critique of how the condition of self-doubt is essential to the functionality of the university.

For us, such a critique must start by plotting the destruction of the methodological university – an institutionally bounded form of thinking that reproduces the seemingly insurmountable cognitive fissure between universities and the ever-changing forms and conditions of capitalist society. The demand for the abolition of the methodological university thus demands a form of practical reflexivity which abolishes the separation between theory and practice by intellectually reconstructing their unshakeable historical unity. In this way, it may become possible to overcome some of the ambivalence of the technological mediations of capitalist social relations, and turning them into the weapons of a reinvigorated independent working-class education.

To do so, we have argued that the disjuncture which exists between the overcoming of theoretical and practical barriers should not discourage people from seeing the necessary role that the intellect must play in the undoing of capitalist social relations. However, this insight also belongs to a form of unburdened intellectual leadership that currently dominates universities and posits the spontaneous emergence of a fetishized form of mass intellectuality which is divorced from the question concerning the ownership of the means of production. Without a more thorough critique of this kind of leadership it remains difficult – if not impossible – to talk of mass intellectuality. Thus, we conclude that this phenomenon cannot achieve a critical mass unless it is concerned with the abolition of the university as we know it.

11

Reconciling *mass* Intellectuality and *higher* Education: Lessons from the PPE Experience

Joel Lazarus

> *We need to found a new politics not on nostalgia but on the power to organize the time and space of knowledge production that has been by an accident of history invested in us all.*
>
> Fred Moten and Stefano Harney (1999: 28).

Introduction

A fundamental challenge for radical academics working to democratize higher education (HE) worldwide is that of trying to overcome, theoretically *and* practically, the immanent contradiction between *mass* intellectuality and *higher* education. While the belief in and pursuit of mass intellectuality is rooted in ideas and values of *in*clusivity, indeed universality, the term '*higher* education' expresses an unavoidably *ex*clusive concept and practice. Here, I argue that this 'higher-mass contradiction' is a central functional element of and, hence, irresolvable within, the capitalist ideology and system. As such, any attempts to establish truly democratic pedagogical organizations and institutions must be *post*-capitalist in both their ends *and* means. To this end, I present here both a theoretical and very practical proposition for overcoming this higher-mass contradiction.

I begin with theory, journeying from Marx, via Gramsci, on to Lazzarato, in order to trace the historical co-evolution of two core concepts: the 'general intellect' and 'mass intellectuality'. I argue that, because the general intellect is, as Virno puts it, the 'public intellect', radical academics must avoid inadvertently perpetuating the capitalist 'higher-mass' contradiction by locating the general intellect exclusively within the university and the academic labour process. Instead, I argue that since, echoing Gramsci, all labour has an intellectual element and that, therefore, knowledge is produced by *all*, the democratization of higher education equally necessitates the cultivation of mass intellectuality.

This brings me to practical considerations. Clearly, the democratization of higher education would require the deep rooting of the university and the academic labourer within their local community and wider society. This would suggest, in response to recent discussions concerning the optimal path for pursuing the democratization of higher education, that our primary focus should be on the creation of alternative, co-operatively constituted organizations. To bolster this argument, I share the experiences of a community education project I co-founded in 2012 in my own town, Oxford, called 'PPE' (People's Political Economy). I show how the project has had some real successes, but has also been impeded by those very foundational constituents of capitalist reality – space, money and particularly time – that we seek to critique, reimagine and reconfigure. Consequently, I suggest that perhaps the only real way to sustain and institutionalize such community pedagogical projects might be to establish them as either the 'outreach' arm or, ideally, an integral element of a co-operative university, serving that institution's own democratic, emancipatory agenda. In this way, projects like PPE could access the resources they need to institutionalize their activities, while, at the same time, they could be built up into sturdy, resilient two-way bridges that link the co-operative university and its community. It is this bridging function, I argue, that could facilitate the overcoming of the contradiction between higher education and mass intellectuality. At last, the university, liberated from capital, becomes no longer an 'instrument of dehumanization', but an institution contributing to our collective 'humanization' (Freire 1970: 51). It functions both as a centre for scientific expertise and exploration that serves society, locally, regionally and globally, while simultaneously functioning to facilitate opportunities for all to come together in dialogue to 'name' and 'remake the world' (87). It is in this way, I argue, that the co-operative university, and its subsumed community education programmes, might most powerfully serve the democratic cause, contributing not just to the democratization of higher education – the *emancipation* of our 'general intellect' – but to the flourishing of mass intellectuality – the *democratization* of that general intellect itself.

I recognize that I do not problematize the possible nature and outcomes of a co-operative university in this chapter. Other chapters in this volume and elsewhere do this (Cook 2013; Neary and Winn 2016; Winn 2013a,2015a). Here, I focus on the possible and what would need to be done and avoided to make this possible.

Higher education and mass intellectuality

The 'higher-mass contradiction' set out above is an unavoidable and necessary contradiction constitutive of the capitalist system of education and knowledge production. The most obvious reason for this is that capitalism simply could not continue in liberated conditions of mass intellectuality. Capital's other ideological requirement met significantly by the university is a distinct category of intellectual labourers to reproduce the ideology, theories and research that legitimate, justify and naturalize the social order. The construction of the university fortress also reflects the authoritarian requirements of capital to control the production and dissemination of knowledge. The structural hierarchy of social relations must be reflected in and constructed by a similar structural hierarchy of the institutions of knowledge production (Newfield 2010).

Beyond these cultural-political necessities, the enclosure of expertise and scientific knowledge within the university serves the economic division of labour requirements of capital, particularly in the age of the global 'knowledge economy' (DBIS 2016): a few, more capable (read privileged) types undertake the essential innovative, entrepreneurial and strategic work; some more do less thoughtful, but essential intellectual work; the rest do supposedly unthinking manual work (Newfield 2010). Thus, the contradiction between higher education and mass intellectuality is irresolvable within capitalism because it *is* capitalism; that is, it expresses and embodies the way in which capital divides us: 'the intellectuals' from society; thinkers from doers; and theory from practice. It also expresses and embodies the way in which knowledge's social use value is subordinated to its exchange value. Knowledge under capitalism is a commodity (Mirowski 2004,2011).

The separation of the university and the academy from people has always been pronounced. Yet, perhaps, in our era of globalized capitalism, never has the higher-mass contradiction been both so extreme and extensive. The university's gaze is oriented outwards and upwards. It solicits its producers and consumers on the world market. It looks downwards to its local community for little more than the manual labour required for its daily reproduction – cooks, cleaners, security and handymen – yet, even such labour is often provided by cheap foreign migrants. The university's location is significant only for this requirement and to the extent that its locality can attract academics, students and corporate partners. Finally, the increasingly precarious, low-paid and overworked nature of academic labour within the capitalist university is increasingly well documented in recent years (Hall andBowles 2016; UCU 2016).

This is the house of learning that capital built. Consequently, any genuine attempt to democratize higher education must be post-capitalist in its objectives and its practices. It must also be socially embedded in order to overcome, rather than perpetuate, the higher-mass contradiction. I will now explain why this is so theoretically through the exploration of the etymology of two key concepts: the general intellect and mass intellectuality.

The general intellect and mass intellectuality

Marx's contradiction

We begin with Marx's (1993:1519) note in the *Grundrisse* commonly known as 'Fragment on Machines'. Here, Marx focuses our attention on the way in which, '[i] n machinery, the appropriation of living labour by capital achieves a direct reality'. We are asked to take in the material world around us, to witness the 'development of fixed capital' and, in so doing, to appreciate 'to what degree general social knowledge has become *a direct force of production*' and 'to what degree ... the conditions of the process of social life itself have come under the control of the general intellect and been transformed in accordance with it'. In identifying capitalist development as a cumulative and ever-intensifying process, Marx envisages a point in history at which 'all the sciences have been pressed into the service of capital' and 'invention ... becomes a business'.

Marx's analysis helps us to recognize the contemporary neoliberal university as the institutionalized exploitation of our general intellect, of our 'power of social production'; an exploitation approaching totalitarian characteristics and proportions. Yet, we must also recognize that these powers of social production are indeed *ours;* that they are of awesome magnitude; and that their potentiality actually increases with every intensification of their exploitation. This is the contradiction that Marx (1993:1518) so presciently identifies:

> On the one side, then, [capital] calls to life all the powers of science and of nature, as of social combination and of social intercourse, in order to make the creation of wealth independent (relatively) of the labour time employed on it. On the other side, it wants to use labour time as the measuring rod for the giant social forces thereby created, and to confine them within the limits required to maintain the already created value as value.

The repression of our ever-increasing powers of scientific knowledge necessitates ever more sophisticated and socially and psychologically invasive techniques of discipline, manipulation and control. Why? Because, in stark contrast to the misanthropic individualist depictions that assault us, it is in the joy of 'social combination' and 'social intercourse' that this knowledge is produced. Thus,

> if we conceive teaching and learning as the expenditure of student and teacher labour-power in the production of the knowledge commodity, we begin to recognize that the exchange relation between teacher and student, where each consumes the labour-power of the other, is a productive relation too and not simply one where knowledge is being distributed to consumers in a market for higher education. (Winn 2015b: 10)

Within the university, therefore, knowledge is *co*-produced by academics and students. Furthermore, because of knowledge's essential imaginative, intellectual properties, these co-productive interactions cannot be controlled and overseen to the minute extent that more manually oriented, repetitive processes can be. As a rule of thumb, we might posit that the less directly alienated the process of collective value production is, the greater becomes the need for bureaucratic intervention. Thus, the university today is, and must be, a site of 'extreme regulation' (Harney 2009:319): it attracts and cultivates 'all the powers of science and nature' in social combination, yet, in order to ensure the continued exploitation of the 'giant social forces thereby created', it applies an ever firmer 'measuring rod' to regulate its workers and their time. The UK Conservative Government's recent plan to introduce the new 'Teaching Excellence Framework' is a perfect example of the measuring rod in question.

At this historical moment, when socially necessary labour time remains a central source of value (as an expression of life – the universal source), our immense productive powers reveal this as a 'miserable foundation' upon which to base wealth.

It is in the very process of social combination that produces knowledge – the process at the heart of university life that we call 'academic labour' – that we can locate 'the material conditions to blow this foundation sky-high' (Marx 1993:1518). Liberate our academic labour and we can liberate the university from capital. But, as the term '*general* intellect' suggests, that would be just half the job.

Gramsci's declaration

Gramsci's vital contribution to this tantalizing insight lies in his broader and fuller politicization of our understanding of knowledge and its production and, by extension, his more explicit democratization of our conception of intellectuality. In 'Fragment', we see Marx conjecturing over an alternative, more directly sociological (rather than political–economic) dialectical way in which the historical process of capitalist development itself generates the conditions for its own transcendence – this time through knowledge and the development of the general intellect. In Gramsci, we find a powerful analysis of how knowledge functions not just in harnessing capital's (that is, our) productive powers, but in producing the vital *cultural and ideological conditions* necessary for the very continuation of capitalist social relations. It is from this vantage point that Gramsci identifies the crucial function of 'the intellectuals' – that group of idealist thinkers who posit themselves philosophically and sociologically as 'independent', 'endowed with a character of their own' – in generating the theories legitimating and, most crucially, naturalizing the social order (Gramsci [1971] 2005: 139). Gramsci rejects this claimed independence, identifying the intellectuals instead as 'organic', that is constitutive of and operating for the hegemonic bourgeois class. This opens the way for him to famously reclaim intellectuality for us all:

> All men[1] are intellectuals, one could therefore say: but not all men have in society the function of intellectuals. When one distinguishes between intellectuals and non-intellectuals, one is referring in reality only to the immediate social function of the professional category of the intellectuals, that is, one has in mind the direction in which their specific professional activity is weighted, whether towards intellectual elaboration or towards muscular-nervous effort. This means that, although one can speak of intellectuals, one cannot speak of non-intellectuals, because non-intellectuals do not exist. (Gramsci 1971: 140)

By rejecting the intellectuals as a distinct class, and intellect as the attribute of a select few, Gramsci pronounces the most radical and sacrilegious of speech acts; one that 'could stand as definitive of Marx's emancipatory project, opposing the life world of communal reciprocity to the alienated-institutionalized world staffed by intellectuals, professionals, "priests" of all kinds claiming esoteric knowledge and monopolizing power usurped from the social body' (Critchley 1997: 22).

Here, Gramsci in no way jettisons, but instead reinforces, Marx's materialist foundations. From rejecting the idealist and idealized intellectual, he swiftly moves to reunite the intellectual with the physical, head with heart, theory with practice. It is the *combination* of intellectual activity and 'muscular-nervous effort' that constitutes the 'general practical activity, which is perpetually innovating the physical and social world'. Gramsci insists on the need for the 'critical elaboration of the intellectual activity that exists in everyone' if this general practical activity is to serve as 'the foundation of a new and integral conception of the world' (Critchley1997: 141).

Thus, it is Gramsci who opens the door to radically democratic and materially grounded interpretations of and practical attempts to realise what has subsequently been called 'mass intellectuality'. The foundation of this radical democracy is Gramsci's philosophy of praxis – this reunification of intellect and body, of theory and practice – that affirms us all as potential agents of history. Far beyond the walls of the university, beyond the intellectuals, it is the collective intellectuality of *all* that produces knowledge for capital's appropriation. Consequently, beyond the emancipation of merely academic labour, since intellectuality is a component of *all* labour, of all humanity, the democratization of the general intellect necessitates the cultivation of *mass* intellectuality.

Lazzarato: The contradiction intensifies

Italian autonomist scholar, Maurizio Lazzarato, draws on Marx's initial dialectical insight to articulate powerful analyses of the central reproductive function of our mass intellectuality in contemporary post-Fordist capitalist society (Lazzarato's 1996). Central contribution lies in the concept of 'immaterial labour', which he defines as 'the labour that produces the informational and cultural concept of the commodity' (1996: unpaged). For Lazzarato, the profound restructuring of socio-economic organization since the 1970s has engendered a whole 'new nature of productive activity'; one in which old dichotomies between 'mental and manual labour' have been rendered ambiguous. Instead, what we are confronted with today is a process of valorization in which '[t]he split between conception and execution, between labor and creativity, between author and audience, is simultaneously transcended'.

The further we move into the realms of the 'post-industrial' sectors of our contemporary economy – into the services and financial sectors and, particularly, into 'audiovisual production, advertising, fashion, the production of software, photography, [and] cultural activities' – the more we enter the domain of immaterial labour. Here, informational, cultural commodities are 'continually innovated' through dynamic, fluid networks of authors and audiences engaged in 'immediately collective' 'processes of communication'. This realm 'gives form to and materializes needs, the imaginary, consumer tastes, and so forth, and these products in turn become powerful producers of needs, images, and tastes'. In this world, the division between base and superstructure, between economics, culture and society, is significantly dissolved; cultural and ideological production *has become* the economic process of valorization *and* the social process of 'producing the capital relation itself'. This process of economic, cultural and social (re)production occurs within what Lazzarato calls the 'basin of immaterial labor'. The further we transition from the factory to the basin, 'it becomes increasingly difficult to distinguish leisure time from work time. In a sense, life becomes inseparable from work'.

There is no doubt that for those, like academics, engaged in immaterial labour, Lazzarato's words ring painfully true, particularly when he describes the fragile existence of the contemporary immaterial worker:

> Precariousness, hyper-exploitation, mobility, and hierarchy are the most obvious characteristics of metropolitan immaterial labor. Behind the label of the independent 'self-employed' worker, what we actually find is an intellectual proletarian, but who is recognized as such only by the employers who exploit him or her. (Lazzarato 1996: unpaged)

Lazzarato's insights also evoke a sense of *ex post facto* intuition over a historical process of capital accumulation that evolves from first exhausting absolute surplus value onto the external extraction of relative surplus value and on in turn to a situation in which relative surplus-value extraction has become a (largely subconscious) collective endeavour in which the workers internalize responsibility for exploiting themselves. Lazzarato paints a profoundly disturbing landscape:

> The fact that immaterial labor produces subjectivity and economic value at the same time demonstrates how capitalist production has invaded our lives and has broken down all the oppositions among economy, power, and knowledge. (Lazzarato 1996: unpaged)

The more immaterial our world becomes, the more ideology *becomes* communication *becomes* capital accumulation *becomes* our very collective subjectivity and experienced reality *becomes* our very soul!

There is no doubt that taking immateriality too far risks detaching us from the material foundations of human life. The online 'basin' of immaterial work remains wholly sustained by a physical infrastructure constructed by material labourers under appalling working and living conditions. Qualifications aside, however, Lazzarato's depiction of an increasingly immaterial world sheds much light on the evolution of the dialectical contradiction first uncovered by Marx. Even despite its relative success in internalizing its reproduction within the very soul of the immaterial labourer, capital does not purge itself of this contradiction. As Lazzarato himself recognizes,

> In fact, employers are extremely worried by the double problem this creates: on one hand, they are forced to recognize the autonomy and freedom of labor as the only possible form of cooperation in production, but on the other hand, at the same time, they are obliged (a life-and-death necessity for the capitalist) not to 'redistribute' the power that the new quality of labor and its organization imply… The subjugation of this form of cooperation and the 'use value' of these skills to capitalist logic does not take away the autonomy of the constitution and

> meaning of immaterial labor. On the contrary, it opens up antagonisms and contradictions that, to use once again a Marxist formula, demand at least a 'new form of exposition'. (Lazzarato 1996: unpaged)

The more capital's reproduction brings us together in co-operation and co-production (and this is intensified in networked immateriality), the more our general intellect drives capital accumulation, and the more our potential collective emancipatory power is harnessed. With this, we return once more back to the heart of Marx's emancipatory project, to Gramsci's declaration: we *all* can, we all *must* eat the fruit of the Tree of Knowledge, for the Tree is ours, cultivated by our common efforts. The Tree is our collective general intellect and our mass intellectuality.

The practical task: Beyond the university

Thus, the immediate task for all radical pedagogues, for humanity itself, becomes clear – to emancipate our general intellect from capital not just within the university, but far beyond; in short, the overcoming of the higher-mass contradiction. Conceiving of the task in this way makes, I believe, a forceful intervention into recent debates about whether our efforts to democratize higher education should be concentrated within or beyond the university (Hall 2014; Social Science Centre 2014; Winn 2015a). Since the objective is to break and transcend capital, we are clearly also talking about organizations constituted by the institutions of collective ownership and co-operative participatory governance and founded, of course, on a radical reconceptualization of labour – not just academic labour, but all labour required in the organization's reproduction. In short, we are talking about the establishment of a co-operative university. Winn (2015a: 44), who has led these recent considerations, presents us with three paths to its establishment:

1. Conversion: Constitute existing universities on co-operative values and principles.
2. Dissolution: Constitute co-operatives at the level of the department, research group, and curriculum
3. Creation: Build new co-operative experiments in higher education.

The choice is not absolute. The struggle occurs within and beyond the university. That said, that there are several powerful arguments to be made for option three – creation. First, the near-totalizing nature of capitalist social relations makes it more realistic to achieve and cultivate greater autonomy outside of one of its central institutions. It is not that capitalist social relations do not exist outside of the university, but that I see alternative organizations as more autonomous and flexible, more conducive to serving as both embodied critiques of the capitalist school or university, and a more powerful 'laboratory for the creation of forms of social cooperation and subjectivities that arguably would form the basis of a post-capitalist world' (Shukaitis 2010: 62–63). Furthermore, I believe that the creation of a co-operative university would constitute a fuller recognition and utilization of what Winn (2015b: 10) calls 'the significant productive capacity of our existing historical conditions'. In other words, it is incumbent on us now to transcend any undialectical strategy of mere internal resistance and release the potential of the capitalist university – our own potentiality – in a new organizational form.

However, the final and decisive point relates to the vital overcoming of the higher-mass contradiction. Right from its extroverted, autonomous and socially grounded origins, the creation route would facilitate, necessitate even, the cultivation of broader and deeper co-operative and creative relationships with local communities and beyond. In this way, the establishment of a co-operative university could be a hugely significant step not just towards the disruption and ultimate supersession of capitalist academic labour, but also towards the equally vital cultivation of mass intellectuality.[2]

Freireian foundations

But, if the 'character of the revolution' is 'eminently pedagogical' (Freire 1970: 66), what concrete form does this radical democratic pedagogy take? Here, Paolo Freire's contribution is vital. Freireian methodologies enshrine and, crucially, operationalize Gramsci's declaration of mass intellectuality. Here are Freire's foundational pedagogical principles as I understand them.

1) *Revolutionary pedagogy begins not in abstraction, but from people's own lived experiences.*
2) *Revolutionary pedagogy is 'dialogical from the outset'.* Dialogue constitutes 'the encounter between men, mediated by the world, in order to name the world' (1970: 87).
3) *Revolutionary pedagogy is non-hierarchical* (84). This does not mean that the teacher is not a figure of authority, but that this authority is reflective not of institutional power but of personal qualities and is mandated by the learning group.
4) Since it expresses her total faith in people's own capacity for critical discovery and transformation, *the role of the counter-hegemonic teacher is facilitative, not directive* (60–1).
5) *Revolutionary pedagogy is prefigurative.* Thus, 'preoccupation with the content of dialogue is really preoccupation with the program content of education' (95), and '[w]hat distinguishes revolutionary leaders from the dominant elite is not only their objectives, but their procedures' (166).

Though its Freireian roots were explicit from the start, in no way was the community education project that I co-founded in 2012 on the kind of philosophical conceptualization of mass intellectuality set out here. Our project instead constituted a practically oriented response to very material developments – the economic crisis, austerity and the occupy movement. Nonetheless, the ultimate vision was similar – the cultivation of mass intellectuality as catalyst for revolutionary democratic transformation. In the following section, I describe our activities and analyze their outcomes.

The PPE experience

In the Summer of 2012, four friends with academic and activist backgrounds came together to set up a community education project in Oxford. Two of us, Neil Howard and James Sevitt, had helped to establish the 'Tent City University' at the Occupy London site that previous Autumn. This initial 'Political and Economic Literacy' project was later renamed 'People's Political Economy'. Being also the acronym for 'Philosophy, Politics, and Economics', Oxford University's infamous elite-producing conveyor belt, the choice of the 'PPE' acronym also constituted 'an act of reclamation, a direct, subversive challenge to the elitist model of education … associated with Oxford' (PPE 2013: 3). Our goal was to set up learning groups in community organizations at the sharp end of austerity. In this way, we sought to bring people together to learn about and respond to the structural factors constraining their lives and opportunities.

Our first year

Here, I will only briefly outline the activities of our first year's 'pilot phase', details of which are provided in our comprehensive inaugural report (PPE 2013). We managed to establish learning groups with four community organization partners: a homeless charity; a mental health organization; a City Council-funded programme for young adults; and a secondary school. We also ran a group for graduate students at the University's Department of International Development. At the same time, we recruited and gave some rudimentary training to ten students and academic colleagues to help them 'facilitate' these learning groups in pairs. We elaborated an initial syllabus, but soon discarded it.

The learning groups ran with mixed levels of success. Due to a complete lack of institutional support, the school group attracted just two regular participants. Nonetheless, those two found the experience rewarding and important. Our groups at the homeless and mental health charities went reasonably well, but the main factor impeding their development was the inconsistency in participation caused primarily by the very unstable and precarious nature of participants' own lives. The stand-out group was the young adult group which ran weekly for almost a whole year. The two facilitators of this group did sterling work. Their pedagogical and ideological approach differed significantly from ours. Nevertheless, the participants expressed their excitement at learning about political and economic issues. The highlight of that year was undoubtedly a debate on education organized by the City Council between group participants and local Labour and Liberal Democrat Councillors.

When we reflected on our first year, we felt confident enough to conclude that: 'PPE works and can grow … Many people want to learn about the political economy of this crisis – the political economy of their lives – and many people were attracted by our democratic, critical approach to learning' (PPE 2013: 18). That said, we also fully recognized that our successes were very limited in both scale and depth. This pilot phase had given us only mere glimpses of the possible, and had, at the same time, revealed to us just how hard it would be to go further.

My life my choice

By 2014, three of the four co-founders had left Oxford and, in 2014, I headed abroad for a year. It became too difficult to sustain, let alone build on, our initial efforts. However, one learning group, set up by myself in late 2013, has continued to run weekly for almost two years now. My Life My Choice (MLMC) is an outstanding self-advocacy charity run for and by people with learning disabilities. The learning group is small – around ten regular participants – but its intimacy has made possible transformative learning experiences.

In the fourteen months that I have facilitated the group, we have spent two months covering the 2015 general election; looked at benefits, work and the universal basic income; and spent several months on the issue of power. We plan to produce a film that not just reveals MLMC members' tortuous daily navigations through the benefits system, but gives them a platform to articulate and demand an alternative, just world. We have used brainstorming, watched films, devised and performed role plays, and used theory to develop our learning.

MLMC's Project Development and Training Coordinator, Alex Brooks, has been instrumental in supporting the PPE process. Alex described how MLMC members unconsciously 'wear the labels' that society gives them.[3] She has seen group participants gradually becoming able to question these labels and to reconsider who they really are and what they really think. This process has been aided by our facilitators providing participants with the information they require and helping them to analyze it.

To give a concrete example, on the issue of benefits, by sharing their personal stories and by analyzing media output, participants have been able to begin to recognize and challenge the structural violence they endure as disabled people and benefits claimants. Prior to this, as Alex put it, 'there was a total belief in many members that they were the only ones in their situation'. Their work here has informed one of MLMC's major ongoing campaigns, its 'We Will All Benefit' campaign, that aims to challenge the dominant narrative attacking the welfare system and those it supports.

The significance of this sense of empowerment for a group of people who Alex describes as being 'historically very oppressed and dictated to', and who generally must submit to the 'big rules that govern their lives' is profound. Alex talks about how PPE has brought a positive energy into MLMC, about how PPE and politics are talked about in the office, in group meetings, and on 'Stingradio', MLMC's own online radio show.

The PPE process has been contributing directly to the political actions of MLMC members. The tragic and entirely avoidable death of eighteen-year-old Connor Sparrowhawk[4] at Slade House, an NHS assessment and treatment unit in Oxford, in July 2013 has triggered demands for justice, accountability and hugely improved standards in such facilities. MLMC members have been at the forefront of this campaign, both locally and nationally.

Though this review of PPE's activities ends on a high, this must not detract from the huge obstacles that make it so hard to institutionalize projects like this. I now explore these issues.

Difficulties in institutionalizing PPE: Space, money and … time

The nature of the difficulties that we faced in trying to institutionalize our project come down to those three constituent components of capitalist reality – space, money and time – and the lack thereof. The first thing to declare is that in terms of these three resources, PPE itself had absolutely nothing. It was an entirely voluntary project. Since we felt that our autonomy was entirely non-negotiable, we were wary of applying for funding and particularly trapping ourselves within the perpetual NGO funding cycle.

PPE organizers and facilitators gave very generously of their time. Organizers spent time meeting, recruiting facilitators, establishing new learning groups, building relationships with partner community organization staff, and preparing and running facilitator training sessions. There were also reports to write, websites to build and online and real-life networks to cultivate. Facilitators needed to dedicate their time to training and, of course, to convening a weekly learning group during term time. In short, the time required to sustain and develop PPE was considerable, particularly for already-overstretched students and academics.

Time was a significant issue for our community organization partners too. We found that it was absolutely crucial to the success of any learning group that we received strong, consistent support from influential, senior people within partner community organizations. It was sometimes hard to develop relationships with organization managers because they themselves were so busy. On one occasion, it became impossible to establish a learning group because the key manager there was too busy trying to find funds to replace those cut by national or local government. In short, it was austerity that was impeding us from running learning groups about austerity.

For group participants, time was also a huge issue. It was entirely unsurprising that it was groups with more spare time – in our case, the young and unemployed – that have proved most successful. However, such participants invariably face precarious employment, benefits or housing situations and, unsurprisingly, poor mental health. These factors make it very hard indeed to build a learning group capable of real transformative potential, since this requires a consistency over time in participation. This is exacerbated by the fact that Oxford University's three terms are very short and intense affairs, so student facilitators are often out of town for long periods.

For me, all barriers are insurmountable. Yet, to surmount them takes time and sustained dialogue. Space can be found. As academics and students, we have access to areas in departments or colleges to hold meetings. With regard to holding learning groups, we intentionally partner with organizations with their own spaces available. For meetings, there are also public spaces – libraries, community centres, parks, even homes or pubs at a push. They might not always be ideal, but some kind of space is still available. However, in late capitalism, there is no such thing as public time and almost no such thing as public money anymore.

In conclusion, the PPE experience established pedagogical processes with transformative potential, but it also demonstrated how that success is absolutely contingent on people investing very considerable amounts of time – in organization, in relationship building, in developing pedagogical methods and workshops, in recruiting facilitators and participants and in actually participating in learning groups. Those group participants who do have time invariably lack the stability and self-confidence to commit to a regular learning process. In light of this, and at a critical historical moment such as this, this conclusion leads us to think seriously about how we can go beyond voluntarism in order to really instigate a nation-wide process of cultivating mass intellectuality.

Bridging higher education and mass intellectuality

This chapter contributes directly to current activities and future plans concerning the creation of post-capitalist forms of higher and mass learning. I believe that the creation of a co-operative university would constitute the most potent strategy for challenging capital's hegemonic grip on academic labour and the enclosed and commoditized general intellect. The co-operative university would also be far better placed to overcome the higher-mass contradiction; that is, to democratize the general intellect through the cultivation of mass intellectuality. What I wish to briefly set out here, then, is a vision for how community projects like PPE might operate alongside or, ideally, within a co-operative university towards this end.

The relationship between community projects and a co-operative university could be mutually productive. From the project's perspective, a properly funded co-operative university could provide the (very modest) resources needed to enable project organizers to build the kind of long-term relationships necessary for transformative outcomes. At the same time, such community projects might reach those sections of society that other capitalist universities cannot reach. Here, community projects might form the bridge between the co-operative university and its host community, bringing academic- and student-scholars into fruitful collaboration with local individuals and groups, allowing both university members to serve their local community and the local community to be directly involved in running their local university. Clearly, the main channel of cross-collaboration would be for community projects to consciously evolve into a collaboratively designed and implemented programme of participatory action research. In this way, the co-operative university could contribute its expertise to the co-production of strategies designed to address concrete social problems. In this very concrete way, the contradiction between higher education and mass intellectuality – irresolvable within the capitalist university – could begin to be overcome in post-capitalist practice.

In terms of reaching a critical tipping point for social transformation, I believe that several years of partnership with a wide and varied range of community organizations in a given city or town could generate hugely exciting outcomes and offer those around the UK and beyond a model demanding replication.

Conclusion: 'Time' to act

Citing Lefebvre (2008: 350), Neary and Amsler (2012: 108–119) approach the central problem I have addressed in this chapter from a different angle. Since it is space time that constitutes the 'supreme good', the goal of radical pedagogy is to 'detonate' 'value in motion' – the capitalist social relation that reduces knowledge to (exchange) value and students/scholars to its co-producers. I wholeheartedly agree. Yet, as I envisage the process, any actual 'detonation' would, like any political revolution, only constitute the dramatic climax of a slower-burning, sustained and growing process of collective praxis. I have argued in this chapter that community education projects like PPE housed within and supported by a new co-operative university might constitute the optimal organizational and institutional catalyst for such a process.

Though it is true that to contribute positively to even a single person's life is reward enough, the crisis of democracy we face is so profound that the stakes we must play for are far higher. We urgently need global revolutionary, democratic transformation. To declare this as our objective is synonymous to proclaiming as our objective the cultivation of mass intellectuality. With time inextricably linked to money under capitalism, and with funding limited and scarce, it is hard to imagine community projects sufficient in size and scope that they could collectively contribute towards mass intellectualization on a scale necessary to reach a societal tipping point. At the same time, under the kind of increasingly precarious conditions that university academics currently labour, it is hard to see the movement for the liberation of academic labour and the general intellect taking place solely within the university.

The contradiction between higher education and mass intellectuality is constitutive of and irreconcilable within the capitalist ideology and social system. Theoretically, I have argued that the democratization of higher education necessitates the democratization of the general intellect – the cultivation of mass intellectuality. Practically, I have argued that the creation of a properly funded, collectively owned and co-operatively governed university would be the most effective vehicle for pursuing this objective. Leading the efforts to generate mass intellectuality would be community-embedded pedagogical programmes supported by the university. In this way, the co-operative university would create a bridge between itself and society – the physical embodiment of the overcoming of the higher-mass contradiction.

The challenges standing in the way of establishing a co-operative university are daunting. PPE was hard enough to set up and run. However, if ever there was a time to throw caution to the wind, it is now. I for one would be willing to play my part in the creation of such an organization.

Notes

1 Gramsci, of course, says 'men', but I will assume this to mean all human beings.
2 I recognize the insufficient problematization of the reality of establishing and running a co-operative university. These challenges are taken up by other authors in this volume.
3 Interview with Alex Brooks, December 2014.
4 See 'Why did Connor Sparrowhawk die in a specialist NHS unit?', *The Guardian*, 19th March2014. http://www.theguardian.com/society/2014/mar/19/connor-sparrowhawk-death-nhs-care-unit-slade-house-learning-disabilities.

12

Somewhere Between Reform and Revolution: Alternative Higher Education and 'The Unfinished'

Gary Saunders

Introduction

In 2010, the UK Coalition Government announced a series of reforms to higher education (HE) in England. Among these reforms were: (i) raising the cap on tuition fees to a maximum of £9,000; (ii) removing block grants for teaching to the arts, humanities, business, law and social sciences; and (iii) changing the regulation around granting the title of university to 'level the playing field' and encourage more 'alternative providers' to enter the sector (DBIS 2011; McGettigan 2013). These reforms were based on the findings of the *Browne Review: Independent Review of Higher Education Funding and Student Finance*(IRHEFSF 2010), and were articulated *both* in a statement made to Parliament by the then Minister of State for Universities and Science David Willets (Hansard 2010) *and* in the government's White Paper, *Higher Education: Students at the Heart of the System* (DBIS 2011). Made during a period of global economic uncertainty, and as part of a raft of austerity measures outlined in the *Government Spending Review* (2010), the Coalition's reforms were proffered as the best way of ensuring that English universities would be able to continue to offer a 'world-class education' (DBIS 2011), while putting into place a sustainable system of financing HE that would supposedly lighten the burden on public finances, be more responsive to the needs of students, and enable the sector to expand to meet the increasing demands for student places (Brown and Carasso 2013; IRHEFSF 2010; McGettigan 2013).

While the full impact of these reforms is yet to be played out, they have unquestionably shifted HE in England towards a more financialized and marketized model of provision (Brown and Carasso 2013). Integral to this has been an attempt to shift the burden of funding the sector from the state to the student through cutting block teaching grants and increasing student tuition fees (financialization), and the imposition of market principles through the (re)emphasizing of the rhetoric of 'student as customer' (marketization) (Boden and Epstein 2006; Molesworth et al. 2009; Naidoo et al. 2011). Underlying these reforms has been the logic that embedding market principles into the sector will drive up the quality of provision and improve value-for-money by increasing competition between institutions for student numbers, with the latter gravitating towards the most popular, well-run courses, forcing less popular courses to improve the quality of their provision, reduce prices or simply go out of business (Callender and Scott 2013; Thompson and Bekhradnia 2011; Wyness 2013).

This shift towards a financialized and marketized model of provision has been influenced by the logic of neoliberalism, which is characterized by a rolling back, or hollowing out, of the welfare state, deregulation, privatization and placing an emphasis on the market provision of formerly public goods and services (Larner 2000). The influence of neoliberal ideology on HE can be increasingly detected in successive reforms to the sector since the 1970s. These include experimentation with more centralized and managerial forms of governance (see for instance the influence of industry at the university of Warwick, in Thompson 1970) and the UK Conservative government's introduction of fees for international students alongside its cutting of the HE budget by £100 million days after coming into power in 1979 (Canaan 2012).[1] These reforms put increasing pressure on universities to do the following: (i) contribute towards economic growth through the creation *both* of an increasingly skilled workforce *and* of new technology and knowledge through academic research (DBIS 2011); and (ii) respond to a governmental drive for greater efficiency, effectiveness and accountability as part of an attempt to reduce public sector spending (Henkel 2000). In short, these reforms promote privatization and the interests private enterprises to accumulate profits without necessarily providing a public benefit (such as social, cultural and economic needs of communities) (Boden et al. 2012) and, more generally, form part of an attempt to (re)produce the conditions needed for continued capital accumulation (Somerville and Saunders 2013).

In terms of leadership, this has had a significant impact on universities' governance structures and organizational culture as HE institutions (HEIs) have not only modified their management systems through the imposition of new public management (NPM) (Deem et al. 2001,2007; Radice 2013; Scott 2013; Shattock 2008; Tapper and Salter 2003), but also their strategies to cope with the new funding environments (Callender and Scott 2013). This has led to a redistribution of power within universities (Lomas 2005), which has seen a shift away from the more traditional collegiate model, referred to here as a form of collaborative and mutually supportive decision-making by scholars (Bacon 2014), to a more centralized, hierarchical and corporate model that shifts the control of universities from scholars to managers (Boden et al. 2012; Callender and Scott 2013; Halffman and Radder 2015; Shattock 2008). This has resulted in a 'democratic deficit' within many HEIs, which essentially underutilizes academic knowledge and expertise, leaving around half of all academic staff in UK universities feeling that they are unable to make their voice heard within their institution (Bacon 2014; McGettigan 2014). These reforms have been described as 'a fundamental assault on the critical and radical traditions of academic activity, and an act of vandalism against "the idea of the University" as a progressive sociological and political project' (Neary 2011), which have fundamentally 'disfigured' the sector (Warner 2015) and left the idea of the university in 'ruins' (Readings 1997).

The reforms to the sector have also challenged the nature and purpose of HE so that for students, it is increasingly being posited as an individual investment in human capital rather than as a, albeit somewhat vague, 'public good' (Holmwood 2011). Moreover, students commencing their studies since 2012 can now expect to accrue increased amounts of debt *circa £51,600*[2] for a three-year degree programme (Lewis 2016), which may be further increased for some once maintenance grants are replaced by a new loans system in 2016/17. Consequently, this has started to *distort* the way students, especially those from poorer backgrounds, choose what and where to study as they sensibly attempt to reduce debt and ensure favourable career prospects (Atherton et al. 2015; Tomlinson 2014). Nevertheless, despite an initial dip in applications to study in HE in 2012, numbers reached an all-time high during the 2015 application cycle with 411,420 applications, including the highest recorded number from students from disadvantaged areas (UCAS 2015). However, there has been a slight dip overall in applications for 2016 cycle down to 408,990 (2016). Where increased tuition fees have had the most impact appears to be on adult and part-time learners with a 40 per cent and 14 per cent reduction in numbers, respectively (HEFCE 2013). This has had a significant impact for some HEIs, one example being the Open University, which has traditionally recruited mature and part-time learners and recently reported a £7 million deficit and a further decline in student numbers (HESA 2016).

For academics, the reforms appear to have reinforced a process of deprofessionalization and led to increased workloads, deteriorating pay and conditions, alongside cuts to pensions (Barnett 2012; UCU 2013). Moreover, staffs are reporting increased levels of stress and mental health problems (Kinman and Wray 2013; UCU 2013) as the nature of academic labour is intensified (Gill 2009). Moreover, the new funding model is also something of a 'financial gamble' for the government, which still funds HE through the student loan book, as higher than originally predicted levels of unpaid student debt are now forecast, meaning that the new funding model may become more expensive than the one it replaced (McGettigan 2013).

These reforms have not gone unopposed and, in 2010, sparked a wave of protests across the UK, which included student demonstrations, union-led strikes and occupations of university property. Beyond these sporadic outbursts of protest and resistance, a number of groups around the UK have responded by establishing alternative education experiments beyond the university that offer free HE (Gallagher 2011; Jones 2011; Lunghi and Wheeler 2011). Focusing on the latter, what follows is an overview of the some of the main findings of research conducted with seven education experiments based in the UK. With an emphasis on leadership, I examine what can be learned from them in terms of creating an alternative model of HEI in response to the recent reforms to HE.

Methodology

The findings discussed in this chapter are drawn from research I conducted as a part of my doctoral thesis with seven education experiments based in the UK. The research consisted of two parts: (i) an extended case study using participatory action research (PAR) with an education experiment of which I am a member, the Social Science Centre (Lincoln); and, (ii) comparative research conducted with six education experiments based in the UK using a case study approach. These included the following: Birmingham Radical Education, Free University Brighton, IF Project (London), People's Political Economy (Oxford), Ragged University (Edinburgh) and The Really Open University (Leeds). All seven education experiments were selected using a 'convenience sample' (Bryman 2004) and were drawn from personal networks developed through my role as an HE lecturer as well as being a member of an education experiment. The data were gathered using a mixture of participatory observation, twenty-eight semi-structured interviews with members, organizers, teachers and students of education experiments, and documentary analysis, including websites, minutes of meetings, blogs, course material and publications. The chapter is based on the aggregate findings of my research and a more in-depth analysis can be found in Saunders (forthcoming).

Summary of main research findings

The main aim of my research was to examine what can be learned from these education experiments in terms of creating an alternative model of HEI in response to the Coalition's reforms. While this aim was not shared by all of the education experiments I visited, I did find that some aspects of their working practices had the potential to inform how HEIs might be organized alternatively. With regard to addressing my research aim, perhaps the two most important aspects of working practice were the ways in which the groups had experimented with different models/ philosophies of democratic pedagogy and democratic self-organization. These allow us to think about what teaching and learning, research and institutional governance might look like in an alternative model of HEI. Overwhelmingly, these models/ philosophies were democratic in nature and attempted to question the distinctions between student and teacher, and manager and worker, in a way that challenges some of the more centralized and managerial decision-making processes found in mainstream HE. Although these philosophies/models have been adopted to greater or lesser extents by different education experiments, respondents from all groups cited them as being influential in some way.

Philosophies/models of democratic pedagogy

With regard to how the education experiments organized teaching and learning, four main philosophies/models of democratic pedagogy were cited as being influential by respondents.

1. **Do-It-Yourself (DIY) Education** is a philosophy/model of providing free education which is based on the utilization and sharing of freely available

resources (e.g. people, space, technology and books) and is characterized by its anti-capitalist, anti-consumerist and anarchistic ethos with a strong emphasis on action, or doing something to challenge the status quo (Hemphill and Leskowitz 2013; Kamenetz 2010; McKay 1998). Given the lack of funds available to the education experiments that feature in my research, it was not surprising that this philosophy/model was influential as groups attempted to make the most of the resources around them. One example of this is the IF Project in London, which uses public spaces around the city, such as museums, art galleries and theatres to support its education provision.

2. **Learning-Webs** as a philosophy/model refers to a teaching and learning approach where people within the local community are invited to meet, talk and share their skills/knowledge on a particular subject (Illich 1973). This model influenced most of the education experiments I visited. One example of where this philosophy/model was used was the Free University Brighton via its online 'Wish List',[3] which acts as a portal for people to offer their skills and knowledge or to request the types of courses they would be interested in engaging with. Another example is the Ragged University's 'Ragged Talks',[4] which attempts to connect people in the local community to share skills/knowledge with those that would like to learn them.
3. **Critical Pedagogy** is a philosophy/model of teaching and learning which challenges traditional education practices characterized by a formal teacher and student relationship, and which is often referred to as the 'banking concept' of education. Instead, it posits an approach to education that encourages *both* the critical reflection of commonly held assumptions, traditional ways of being, formal institutions, and action, *and* the subsequent, practical transformation of them (Freire 1970). This philosophy/model has been influential for most of the education experiments that featured in this research. One example of where this philosophy/model has been used is People's Political Economy in Oxford. As part of its training for new facilitators, they are offered an introductory critical pedagogy workshop before they commence facilitating classes with groups in the local community.
4. **Student as Producer** is a philosophy/model of teaching and learning that has been developed within mainstream higher education and attempts to reconnect the disparate activities of teaching and research through the concept of 'scholarship' (Neary and Winn 2009). A key part of this process is questioning the traditional relationship of teacher and student and, instead, arguing that both can learn from each other. It describes both of them as scholars in the pursuit of new knowledge. One example of where this philosophy/model has been implemented is the Social Science Centre, especially its 'Beyond Public and Private: A Model for Co-operative Higher Education' research project,[5] which attempts to engage all members of the Social Science Centre (and others beyond the education experiment) to think through what a co-operative university might look like in practice, which is anchored within five key areas: pedagogy, governance, legal considerations, business models and global solidarity.

Philosophies/models of democratic self-organization

Not all of the education experiments were sufficiently large enough (in terms of members/organizers) to warrant a formal model of democratic self-organization. Decisions were often made by a small number of people through consensus, although respondents stated that some philosophies/models were still influential in this process. The philosophies/models of democratic self-organization that were cited as being influential by respondents were as follows:

1. **Horizontalism** is an approach to self-organization which is based on the concepts of autonomy, direct democracy, mutual aid and empowerment, which attempts to challenge social inequality, oppression and power through the adoption of non-hierarchical, leaderless and consensus-based decision-making processes (Sitrin 2014). The research found that this philosophy/model had been influential for most of the education experiments. One example where it had been embedded into working practice was the Social Science Centre, which has constituted a formal model of consensus decision making.
2. **Open Marxism** is a tendency within Marxism which emerged as a response to the crisis experienced by 'orthodox' Marxism in the late 1970s. Open Marxism re-emphasizes the importance of the 'dialectical dimension' of Marx and has as its starting point the struggle between capital and labour. Re-emphasizing the primacy of class struggle implies a constantly changing social reality and social forms (Bonefeld et al. 1992). Open Marxism is more than a critique of capital from the standpoint of labour, and it is a negative critique of labour within capitalism (Postone 1993). This philosophy/model was cited as being influential by the Really Open University[6] and the Social Science Centre.[7]
3. **Workerism** is a tendency within Marxism that places an emphasis on the autonomous, self-organization of the working class as a site for radical social change (Wright 2002). This model of radical self-organization is distinct from 'orthodox' Marxism, which tends to posit trade unions, vanguard political parties and the State as indispensable mechanisms for the overthrow of capitalism. This philosophy/model was cited as being important for the Social Science Centre, whose name was inspired by the Social Centre movement that emerged out of the European Autonomia (workerism) movements of the 1970s.
4. **The Co-operative Movement** has a rich history as a model of democratic self-organization. The values and principles that underpin the co-operative movement, which were formalized by the Rochdale Pioneers in 1844, include self-help, self-responsibility, democracy, equality, equity and solidarity. Co-operatives exist in a variety of different forms, which include producer co-operatives, consumer co-operatives, housing ownership and management co-operatives, community benefit societies, development trusts, co-operative consortia and credit unions and can exist as unitary entities or can be networked or federated with other co-operatives (Somerville 2007). One example of where this philosophy/model had been influential is the Social Science Centre, which was constituted as a co-operative in 2011.

Discussion of main findings

While the research found some useful insights into how alternative HEIs might be organized, these were not without their problems. As they tended to be run on a voluntary basis, members dedicated their time for free, which meant the education experiments were often small scale and experienced a high turnover of members as people suffered from fatigue or had other commitments. Moreover, they also tended to exist outside the HE sector, by which I mean they had not been legally granted university status, nor did they have degree awarding powers, although some education experiments attempted to circumvent this by offering their own informal qualifications at the 'level of higher education'.[8] Nevertheless, existing outside the sector has been beneficial in some respects as it has provided these education experiments with the freedom to move and develop alternative models of democratic pedagogy and democratic self-organization without having to worry about quality audits or metrics such as the National Student Survey. Moreover, they tended to have better connections with the local community, often situated or occupying public spaces within their locality, which meant that they were more visible and accessible to the general public.

In this sense, these education experiments have been important in helping to prefigure an alternative model of HEI and how it might be organized more democratically and inclusively of the general public in a way that speaks to the main tenets of mass intellectuality by attempting '…to build solidarity and sharing related to the social and co-operative use of knowledge, skills and practice that we create as labour' (University of Utopia n.d.). Nevertheless, existing outside the sector means that these education experiments are unable to offer an education provision that can compete with mainstream HE. As a result, they can be easily marginalized, or ignored, for being either too radical or not relevant, which is evidenced *both* by the increase in university applications despite the increase in tuition fees (UCAS 2016) *and* by the fact that many of the education experiments that emerged *circa*2010 have tended to disappear.

Thus, these education experiments have had very little impact on reforming the sector to date. In an attempt to address this point, I draw on the work the work of Thomas Mathiesen (1974) who offers a Marxist framework for institutional change, which is conceptualized in his notion of 'the unfinished' or 'competing-contradiction'. Using Mathiesen I argue that an alternative model of HEI should, at every opportunity, attempt to compete against and expose the contradictions of the current model of HE in a way that cannot be either dismissed for being too revolutionary or easily absorbed into the current system (reformist), but instead be positioned somewhere between reform and revolution.

Mathiesen and 'the unfinished'

In his book, *The Politics of Abolition* (1974), Mathiesen outlines what he refers to as a 'sketch' for penal reform in Scandinavia during the 1970s. Mathiesen's work is part of a rich tradition of abolitionism (Bianchi and van Swaaningen 1986; Christie 1982;

Cohen 1988; Davis 2003; Morris 1998) that extends beyond the confines of modern prisons to include the endeavours of many who have fought for the abolition of the death penalty (see National Coalition to Abolish the Death Penalty) and slavery (see the American Anti-Slavery Society), not only in the United States but as part of a continued struggle around the world (Nicolau 2013). While it may seem odd that the work of a prison abolitionist should appear in a chapter concerned primarily with HE, Mathiesen's framework is set at a high level of abstraction so it can be applied to the abolition of other capitalist institutions, including the capitalist university (Mathiesen 2015; Neary and Saunders 2016).

Mathiesen's framework for abolition is conceptualized in his notion of 'the unfinished – also referred to as "the sketch" or "the alternative" and emerges from within and against already-existing societal systems: a society whose legitimacy is based on the satisfaction of human need' (Mathiesen 1974: 22). Mathiesen provides further detail on the nature of the unfinished which must both 'compete' with and 'contradict' the institution one is attempting to abolish so that it is able to expose 'the insufficiency of being satisfied with the system' (Mathiesen 1974: 14). For Mathiesen, this is a negative rather than an affirmational critique (Neary and Saunders 2015). The alternative emerges out of a fundamental disagreement with the representatives of the established system, in an attempt to make them conscious of the fact that they are 'necessarily faced with a dilemma: through the conscious experience of, in fact, having to choose between a continuation of the prevailing order (possibly with minor changes) and the transition to some which is unknown' (Mathiesen 1974: 25).

Mathiesen then outlines a framework for making those parts of the current system conscious that they face a dilemma. This framework is made up of two parts: (i) 'the message' and (ii) 'its inception and maintenance'. However, the practical implementation of this framework is not without its problems. Mathiesen highlights a number of potential pitfalls that groups engaged in creating an alternative might encounter, such as being marginalized or ignored for being too radical (revolutionary) or, by being absorbed into the established system, for not being radical enough (reformist). What this means is that an alternative must reside somewhere between reform and revolution so that it can keep the relationship between the long-term goal of abolition and short-term improvements open: 'A choice between "revolution" and "reform" constitutes a hopeless dilemma. You therefore look for a road which may lead around the choice, and which may maintain the state of the unfinished on this dimension' (Mathiesen 1974: 33).

The first part of Mathiesen's framework, 'the message', is how the alternative is conceptualized and shared with others: 'it is vital not to remain silent concerning that which we cannot talk about; it is vital to express the unfinished' (Mathiesen 1974: 16). Mathiesen (1974: 14) argues that the message must be able both to 'compete' and 'contradict' with the institution one is attempting to change 'in terms of goals or in terms of means together with goals'. To do this, an alternative must be based on its own premises and be different to those that underpin the current institution. Moreover, the message must be 'a sketch', not a complete or fully formed drawing, but unfinished. If the message is not based on its own premises then it is already part of the current system and, thus, is not contradictory. Mathisen (1974: 15) argues that the alternative can then be easily dismissed as already existing and constitutes a 'fictitious competition'. In addition, the alternative is unable to compete with the established system if it is finished as it can be easily dismissed or marginalized for being too radical or not relevant and can be disregarded as being permanently outside of the system. 'The main problem, then, is that of obtaining the combination of the contradicting and competing; the main problem is that of avoiding that your contradiction becomes non-competing and that your competition becomes agreement' (Mathisen 1974: 14).

Mathiesen outlines some of the pitfalls that one might face when trying to convey the message of an alternative from within the institution one is attempting to abolish. One of these pitfalls is the use of language or 'persuasion'. Mathiesen argues that there is often pressure to explain what the alternative might look like, how it will work in practice, and what impact it will have. While these are sensible questions, Mathiesen argues that once an attempt is made to explain the alternative in this finalized language it becomes 'finished' or 'fully formed' and, even before it has a chance to be implemented, it can easily be marginalized as 'irrelevant', 'unachievable', 'extreme' or 'too revolutionary' and, thus, no longer competes with the current system.

Another potential pitfall is the pressure to provide an 'example' of what the alternative looks like in practice. If unable, or unwilling, to provide an example of how the alternative works in practice it can easily be dismissed as 'unachievable'. If one decides to provide such an example, it can be done in two ways: (i) from within the institution one is attempting to change[9] or (ii) from outside the institution. Those examples that operate within the institution usually attempt to achieve short-term reforms while at the same time working towards a more long-term revolutionary goal of abolition. Nevertheless, Mathiesen argues that these examples are usually absorbed within the institution either by the following: (i) 'incorporation' – where the alternative is only allowed in a reduced form and therefore the long-term revolutionary goal is easily broken down; (ii) 'initiation' – the 'rebel' is initiated into the current system by being given privileged position, which dilutes their interest in change and usually results in the alternative being abandoned; or (iii) 'being held responsible' – working within the institution people may try to initiate the alternative, but because they are responsible for performing their duties within it, the consequences of failing to carry them out guides their actions and moves them away from their long-term revolutionary goal of abolition.

Another potential pitfall is attempting to carry the alternative into effect outside the institution one is trying to change. Those alternatives which are situated outside the current system can either be developed in (i) 'splendid isolation' or (ii) by 'performing raids on enemy territory'. The problem with creating a new institution in splendid isolation is that the alternative is outside the established order and therefore finds it difficult to compete and can be easily marginalized as not relevant, or labelled extreme or revolutionary. In response, the alternative created in splendid isolation has to rely on persuasion as a way of convincing people that they should accept their alternative.

While Mathiesen is generally critical of initiating change from outside the institution, he argues that an alternative might be able to effect change from outside if it tries to abolish the current system by 'exposing or unmasking the establishment, and so on' (Mathiesen 1974: 21). Rather than trying to persuade or using an example, Mathiesen proposes something more radical and suggests that those involved in the alternative should 'perform raids in the enemy territory of the establishment, contributing to crises which have a generally alarming effect on members of the establishment' (Mathiesen 1974: 21). Mathiesen's point here is that the alternative should, at every opportunity, expose the contradictions in ways that do not allow the message to be either avoided as being either revolutionary and beyond the mainstream, or reformist and not challenging enough (Neary and Saunders 2015).

It is only when the message is both foreign and contradictory that 'we break with the established order and at the same time face unbuilt ground' (Mathiesen 1974: 25). Mathiesen argues that it is at this point that we begin to think about the second part of the alternative, its 'inception and maintenance'. The importance of this stage is how to keep the alternative unfinished once it has been created: 'how the sketch may be maintained as a sketch, or at least prolonged in life as a sketch' (1974). Mathiesen states that after the inception of the alternative it is important that it is maintained as unfinished – this as a process of 'perpetual abolition, rebuilding, re-abolition on continually new levels' (Mathiesen 1974: 28). To do differently, he argues, would only 'crystallize new structures that would imprison us in the same way as the ones we sought to abolish in the first place' (Mathiesen 1974: 22). Mathiesen argues, therefore, that those involved in the alternative need to perpetually reflect, evaluate and theorize the alternative. It is the latter process that keeps the alternative unfinished, which can be achieved through a form of 'action research', that is itself part of an unfinished process where 'theory is improved by information, whereupon the gathering of information is improved, whereupon the theory in turn is improved and so on' (Mathiesen 1974: 29).

Co-operative education and a new model of HEI

One potential source for developing an alternative model for HEIs is the growing academic literature around co-operative forms of HE (Cook 2013; Matthews 2013; Somerville and Saunders 2013; Sperlinger 2014; Winn 2015a).While the idea of a co-operative university is not new, there are very few actually existing examples of this model around the world (see Mondragon in the Basque Region of Northern Spain and UNICOOP in Mexico as existing examples). Within this literature, there are a number of different co-operative models including worker co-operatives (Winn 2015a), social co-operatives[10] (CICOPA 2011), trust universities (Boden et al. 2012) and the commons university (Halffman and Radder 2015). Here, I explore the idea of a social co-operative university, which I consider to be more appropriate for an alternative model of HEI. This is because while the other models tend to focus on the production of goods and services, worker ownership and control; the social solidarity model explicitly defines a social need or general interest mission as its primary purpose (in this case, it could HE and research, which provides a public benefit) and carries out this mission through the production of goods and services (CICOPA 2011). Moreover, rather than focusing solely on worker ownership and control, social co-operatives tend to have a multistakeholder membership, which better reflects the divergent university community, such as academics, professional staff, students and local community (CICOPA 2011).

The emerging idea of a social co-operative university also fits well with Mathiesen's framework for institutional change as it offers a message that both competes and contradicts with the current model of HE. It does this by exposing the limitations and contradictions of centralized and hierarchical leadership (see earlier comments about serving private interests, 'democratic deficiency' and the impact this has on staff) while proposing an alternative model of HEI that attempts to address the shortcomings of the managerial university. Moreover, given the historical tradition and theoretical development of the co-operative movement, which can be traced back to the Rochdale Pioneers in the 1840s, and that currently employs over 100 million people and has over a billion members worldwide (Birchall 1994; Nolan et al. 2013), it means that the idea of a social co-operative university would be difficult to marginalize as being beyond mainstream (revolutionary). Yet, its organizational form contrasts distinctly from the current model of HE (foreign, or based on its own premises as per Mathiesen) in that it encompasses worker/user-ownership, worker/user-benefit, and worker/user-control.[11] As a result, it cannot be easily dismissed for not being challenging enough or easily absorbed into the current system (reformist) meaning that it occupies the middle ground somewhere between reform and revolution. As co-operatives are run democratically, either on a one person one vote system, multistakeholder and/or representative democracy, their inception and maintenance means that they could potentially remain an infinitely unfinished project as members decide the direction of the organization in perpetuity.

In practice, a social co-operative university would be owned by its workers and controlled by both its workers and users using a multistakeholder membership structure. This could be organized in a similar way to Mondragon University using a 'General Assembly' to make general decisions (e.g. finances, investment, infrastructure projects) and decide the strategic direction of the university, which would consist of the following: (i) academics and university staff, (ii) students and (iii) participants (local community local councils and other organizations) (Wright et al. 2011). As part of this model academics and university staff would both own and control the university while students and participants would have a different membership that would preclude them from ownership, but involve them in the decision-making process. This seems to be the most logical approach given that the former have a long-term interest in the university whereas students and organizations may have more short-term interests, although local councils might be an exception to this rule.

Although each member would have a vote in the decision-making process, votes would be weighted so as to equally represent the three different categories of membership (outlined above) otherwise students, who are likely to be the greater number, would have more of a say in running the university. The outcomes of the General Assembly would be actioned by a Governing Board and Executive Board which are made up of representatives from each category of membership. Those on both boards would be elected at the General Assembly by members and accountable to them. Members of both boards may be recalled at any time and have restricted remuneration differences. At Mondragon, this has resulted in significant information sharing, discussion, debate and conflict. This encourages an attitude of dissensus towards the idea of the modern university (Readings 1997) and would help develop more democratic and participatory leadership and governance in response to carrying out the mission of HE and research.

Nevertheless, creating a social co-operative model of HEI is not without its problems. To receive university status and have degree awarding powers would mean that a social co-operative university would still be subject to the same bureaucracy as other HEIs (e.g. Quality Assurance Agency, Research Excellence Framework and potentially the proposed Teaching Excellence Framework) and compete for student numbers based on NSS, key information sets (KIS) and Destination of Leavers from Higher Education Survey (DLHE). Although external quality mechanisms might be something, a social co-operative university might want to move away from in the future (especially when they are connected to the State) at least how to respond to these demands in the short-term could at least be decided more democratically. Including students in the decision-making process and running of an HEI as members of the co-operative could improve student satisfaction.

It is not clear how a social co-operative university would be funded (publicly, privately or philanthropically) and whether students would still have to pay tuition fees (in part or in full). One option is that a social co-operative university could be funded in a similar way to Mondragon University, which receives funding from three different sources: (i) investment from new members, (ii) a levy paid by all Mondragon co-operatives towards education and (iii) student fees. In the UK, a social co-operative university could be funded, in part, by Co-operatives UK which acts a network for co-operative businesses and could potentially agree with members to charge a levy to fund an HEI. Students could also pay a reduced fee that could be subsidized through the levies raised by Co-operatives UK, a reallocation of a percentage of surplus profits with any shortfall being made up by payments from students using the current student loans system. Any tuition fees paid by the students could be considered as an investment into the social co-operative university, but how this would work in practice is an area that requires further research.

Conclusion

How then to create a robust response to the financialization and marketization of HE? My argument has been that the lessons learned from these education experiments need to be embodied within an organizational form that can both compete with and contradict mainstream HEIs by offering a viable alternative. This could take the form of a social co-operative university which could potentially avoid the pitfalls for institutional change outlined by Mathiesen by being in, against and beyond the current HE sector. In so doing it can expose, at every opportunity, the contradictions of the current system in a way that cannot be avoided for being too revolutionary or not challenging enough. While not without its problems, a social co-operative university has the potential to occupy this middle ground somewhere between reform and revolution and, given its democratic principles, could remain a potentially unfinished project *pace* Mathiesen. While in terms of its implementation and maintenance the idea of a social co-operative is still embryonic, there is a growing body of research under way into how it might work in practice (Cook 2013; Neary and Winn 2016; Saunders forthcoming). The importance of the idea of the social co-operative university is that it challenges current university leadership and governance models and offers an alternative possibility. This not only fosters more co-operative and democratic forms of leadership, but also promotes the production and dissemination of forms of socially useful knowledge, or mass intellectuality, as part of its general interest mission to create and disseminate knowledge that provides a public benefit.

Notes

1 See also the *Jarratt Report* (CVCP 1985), the *Croham Report* (1987), the *Dearing Report* (1997), the *Lambert Report* (2003), the *Higher Education Act 2004*, the *Browne Review* (IRHEFSF 2010), the *Higher Education White Paper 2011* (DBIS 2011) and the proposed Higher Education White Paper Higher Education: Teaching Excellence, Social Mobility and Student Choice as further examples of the neoliberalization of higher education.

2 This figure is based on a three-year degree course priced at £9,000 pa and living costs of £8,200 pa. Nevertheless, the debt accrued will not necessarily be the amount paid back. For more detail about this, see Lewis (2016).

3 For more information about Free University of Brighton's 'Wish List' see: http://freeuniversitybrighton.org/wish-list/.

4 For more information about Ragged University's 'Ragged Talks', see: http://www.raggeduniversity.co.uk/category/about-ragged/ragged-talks/.

5 For more information about this research project, see: http://socialsciencecentre.org.uk/blog/2015/03/30/beyond-public-and-private-a-model-for-co-operative-higher-education/.

6 See The Really Open University's 'Reimagine the University' event for influence of this philosophy/model on the group's thinking: https://reallyopenuniversity.wordpress.com/2010/11/12/join-us-and-reimagine-the-university/.

7 See the Social Science Centre's 'Beyond Public and Private' research project for influence of this philosophy/model on the group's thinking: http://socialsciencecentre.org.uk/blog/2015/03/30/beyond-public-and-private-a-model-for-co-operative-higher-education/.

8 See Social Science Centre's 'Original SSC Statement': http://socialsciencecentre.org.uk/original-ssc-statement/.

9 I write about institutional change from within higher education elsewhere – see: Neary and Saunders (2016).

10 Social co-operatives are also referred to as 'social solidarity co-operatives', 'social initiative co-operatives', 'solidarity co-operatives' and 'collective interest co-operative societies' (CICOPA 2011).

11 See Cooperative Principles for examples: (i) Voluntary and Open Membership; (ii) Democratic Member Control; (iii) Member Economic Participation; (iv) Autonomy and Independence; (v) Education, training and Information; Co-operation Among Co-operatives and (vi) Concern for Community (International Co-operative Alliance 1995).

13

Permaculture Education as Ecology of Mind: The Head, Hands and Heart of Transformation

Thomas Henfrey

This chapter considers permaculture education as a form of 'mass intellectuality', in the sense of being radically critical of dominant educational paradigms, particularly in higher education (HE), and the institutions, practices, implicit politics and cultural assumptions that support them. In doing so, it counterposes permaculture education to a caricature of university-based education as monolithic, centralized, hierarchical, top-down, elitist, and hence striving to entrench and undermine opposition to neoliberal values, with the imposition of subjective uniformity a key strategy. This is, of course, a great simplification: present-day university education is far from uniform, and all of the foregoing features are actively contested within the academy, as well as without (Bailey and Freedman 2011; Maxey 2009). However, it is sufficiently true to act as a guiding analytical approximation for our present purposes, which themselves will reveal some of its nuances.

Permaculture, in contrast, I present here as a linked philosophy and practice of celebrating, nurturing and making practical use of diversity, that is human as well as ecological and socio-ecological. Permaculture education is hence simultaneously learner-centred and socially and environmentally conscious: it supports individuals to identify and mobilize their own unique qualities, in ways that enable them to make their fullest possible contribution to serving societal and planetary needs. Furthermore, learning is not an isolated or bounded activity, restricted to specific settings or contexts, but is a fundamental and perpetual quality of being, evident in all permaculture practice, whether individual or social, as relevant for lifelong practitioners as for complete beginners.

This chapter first describes permaculture as a social movement, life philosophy and set of practices. It then goes on to consider: prevalent pedagogic philosophies, methods and practices within permaculture and the closely related ecovillage and Transition movements; the wider role of these approaches to learning in constituting and socializing people into and within the movements; and their dialogue with formal education, including efforts towards formalizing learning processes. A short closing section relates this material back to the main themes of the volume. It concludes that approaches to teaching and learning in permaculture are an example of mass intellectuality: A popular education initiative with potentially transformative power for formal education and wider society, in concert with other movements for radical social change. It identifies as central to this forms of intellectual leadership that are very different from those within the academy: highly distributed and networked, with individual intellectuals working less for individual achievement than for their contributions to the collective good.

Permaculture: A global action learning community

Permaculture defies straightforward and uncontroversial definition. My preferred current definition is a design system for sustainable human habitats, rooted in ethics of environmentalism, humanism and equity, and seeking consciously and as appropriate to learn from and emulate the features that promote productivity and resilience in biotic systems. Ferguson and Lovell (2014) identify this design framework as one of four main aspects of permaculture, all relevant to our treatment here. The other three are: an ongoing process of exploration of best practice in application of this framework; a worldview that both derives from and underpins the operational framework; and a global social movement of (normally) self-identified practitioners.

Underpinning all these aspects of permaculture are its three core ethics, which can be simply stated as Earth Care, People Care and Fair Shares. Permaculture lies at the intersection of these three ethics, in efforts to instantiate them through design frameworks inspired by nature, through the people who apply these frameworks in service of these ethics, and in the philosophical and existential space that permaculture practitioners co-create through their lives and work. Specific techniques not contextualized in such a design framework and a worldview that subscribes to these ethics, may superficially resemble permaculture, but are not permaculture in a truly meaningful sense (Aranya 2012).

While best known through its applications in agroecology and other forms of ecological agriculture, and indeed often conflated with these, permaculture design has applications in many areas of human endeavour. In addition to practical areas such as soil restoration, water management, green building and settlement design, these include a range of social fields, including governance and community organization, business, conflict resolution and indeed education (Henfrey and Penha-Lopes 2015). Social permaculture is an expanding field, and recognizes that any activity to which permaculture is relevant has personal and interpersonal dimensions, which permaculture design can help reveal and improve (MacNamara 2012). In this view, the garden as agroecological formation becomes a powerful metaphor (Henfrey 2010). Just as a permaculture gardener seeks to understand the properties and needs of the land and resident biota, and create a context that not only reconciles but synergizes these with human interests, so a proficient exercise in social permaculture creates a context where each individual can flourish and grow on their own terms while at the same time maximizing their contribution to needs emergent at the level of the group.

In the context of education, this translates into an approach where the educator is less a teacher in the conventional sense of a conveyor of knowledge than a supporter of processes of individual and collective learning, akin to a gardener employing agroecological methods. A well-designed permaculture garden creates microhabitats amenable to all desirable species and interacting complexes of species, whether deliberately planted or arising of their own accord, and interlinks these in ways that ensure they complement each other and in some way contribute to addressing the needs or wishes of the people who tend and use it. Agrodiversity – among cultivated plant species and varieties, and plants, animals and microbes naturally present and vital to the growth of productive species and vitality of the agro-ecosystem overall – is the key resource in permaculture when applied to food production. Similarly, interpersonal diversity – of knowledge, perspective, experiences, aspirations – is the key resource in permaculture-based learning. A skilled permaculture teacher facilitates processes where every learner experiences creative, mutually enhancing interactions among their own knowledge and interests, those of the other learners, those of the teacher and recorded in books and other learning resources, and new knowledge and ideas derived from direct observation of natural and social phenomena.

This approach mirrors wider social processes within permaculture as a movement, in which learning is at the heart of practice at all scales from the smallest to the largest. The core questions permaculture is posing globally – of what a society based on the three ethics would look like, and how we begin to move towards such a goal – are open-ended, divergent and offer no fixed answers. They can be approached not from positions of authority based on certainty, but only through ongoing processes of learning through experience. Permaculture design builds in ongoing cycles of action learning, equally relevant to examining how it can organize as a global movement, why a particular plant or animal has chosen to live in your garden and what it contributes to its ecology, and to what a teacher and learner or group of learners have to offer each other at any particular moment.

Such learning is built in to social processes with various degrees of formality. People are socialized into the movement largely through courses: structured series of learning events convened and facilitated by teachers recognized to have the appropriate skills, knowledge and experience to do so, and who, regardless of their own level of knowledge and experience, approach such events as important learning opportunities for themselves. Permaculture events and meetings combine talks, workshops, practical exercises, spontaneous discussions and conversations, all in a spirit of mutual learning and ongoing enquiry. A visit to a permaculture site or project – or in fact any conversation among people involved in permaculture – inevitably becomes some sort of learning exchange. A common practice among permaculture practitioners, advocated in much of the key literature, is to spend time alone in wild space purely for the purpose of learning from nature. Organizations such as the UK Permaculture Association and permaculture businesses build spaces for reflection, sharing and mutual learning into their operations. These learning processes are, on the whole, inclusive and democratic, not restricting the level, nature, or influence of any individual's input based on their position in pre-existing authority structures.

Permaculture education thus bears little resemblance to that within a traditional university. It has far more in common with the radical pedagogies of Ivan Illich and Paolo Freire. It enacts the vision of Illich whereby the production and sharing of knowledge take place largely in contexts that are institutionalized only loosely, if at all, and widely distributed in terms of both physical location and authority to teach (Illich 1973). It fits with Freire (1970) in taking as the starting point the circumstances, knowledge and aspirations of learners rather than a predetermined curriculum. As a result, relationships with the mainstream academy – substantive, conceptual and political – are nuanced, dynamic and laced with controversy, as the next section begins to describe.

Permaculture as feral ecology

Permaculture has been vividly described as a 'feral ecology': a scientific subject that has broken free of the academy in order to find and follow its own nature (Morris 2012). Its spread and uptake within related social movements have been marked by the emergence of distinctive approaches to education and forms of intellectual leadership. While very different from those prevalent in conventional academic settings, each to some degree remains in dialogue with these.

Permaculture originated in Australia in the late 1970s in a collaboration between Bill Mollison, then a lecturer at the university of Tasmania, and David Holmgren, a student in environmental design at the Tasmanian College of Advanced Education, leading to the publication of two introductory volumes (Mollison 1979; Mollison and Holmgren 1978). Mollison and Holmgren both subsequently abandoned formal academic work, Mollison to concentrate on propagating permaculture through teaching and writing, and Holmgren to exploring its practical applications and conceptual refinement through work as a theorist and designer.

Sparked by Mollison's work and those of people he trained and inspired, permaculture grew rapidly as a movement in Australia and beyond through the medium of popular education. Anecdotal accounts within the movement suggest this began rather informally, qualifications and authority to teach largely awarded at Mollison's discretion. Veteran permaculture teacher Robyn Francis, one of the earliest of Mollison's students, reports that formal processes were first put in place at the first International Permaculture Convergence (IPC-1) in New South Wales in 1984 (Francis 2015). IPC-1 agreed a basic two-tier structure that remains the basis of permaculture education in much of the world today, with the seventy-two-hour Permaculture Design Certificate (PDC) course as a basic training and the diploma as a more advanced qualification based on independent design work. It also established a Permaculture Institute to issue certificates and diplomas and keep registers of graduates, and a 'College of Graduates' to review and recommend changes to PDC curricula. National permaculture movements in other countries have adopted similar models. For example, the UK Permaculture Association issues certificates to those completing training with recognized independent teachers and runs the national diploma programme, while in Germany the Permakultur Institut and Permakultur Akademie operate as closely linked organizations.

As it has grown, permaculture has become intimately linked with other radical sustainability and social justice movements, notably ecovillages (Dawson 2006) and Transition (Hopkins 2011). Ecovillages grew out of the marriage between longer-standing experiments in intentional communities as critical responses to the failings of mainstream society and emerging movements in environmentalism and bioregionalism. In the process, many adopted permaculture as a tool for practical action (Lockyer and Veteto 2013). The Transition movement (formerly and still commonly known as Transition Towns) of locally led efforts to promote sustainability and well-being originated when a group of permaculture students designed a community-based response to peak oil as their end of course project (Hopkins 2005). Transition retains permaculture among its key methodologies and in some respects represents the transfer to existing communities of ideas and techniques developed in ecovillages, which provide environments conducive to social and technical experimentation (Lockyer 2010; Seyfang and Smith 2007).

Education and learning are also central to ecovillages and Transition. As in permaculture, each to some degree formalizes, and remains in dialogue with, ongoing action learning that is built into social, developmental and operational processes. The Global Ecovillage Network has developed an extensive curriculum for Ecovillage Design Education (EDE), some forms of which incorporate a full Permaculture Design Certificate. In 2005, Gaia Education came into existence as an educational offshoot of GEN and main delivery body for the EDE, whose curriculum is freely available online.[1] Transition Network, the coordinating and support organization for the Transition movement, has developed a multilayered training programme and established an international network of over a hundred recognized trainers. Training, information sharing and fostering processes of lateral and informal learning within the movement are among Transition Network's key roles as an organization, and seen as crucial to Transition's emerging status as a global learning network.[2] Transition Network has consistently recommended that Transition initiatives embed permaculture among their core competencies: having a holder of a PDC within the core group was a criterion in the (now largely defunct) process of endorsing initiatives as 'official'. Its training portfolio at times includes specialized courses on permaculture for Transition.[3]

Embedded learning processes in the permaculture, ecovillage and Transition movements all also incorporate elements consistent in function with research, formalized to greater or lesser degrees. The UK Permaculture Association employs a Research Coordinator, has initiated collaborative research projects on various core practical techniques and developed a suite of resources including a Research Handbook for permaculture practitioners wishing to deepen existing processes of onsite experimentation.[4] It has also nurtured emergence of a new Permaculture International Research Network, with several hundred members in over fifty countries worldwide.[5] Analysis from within the movement identifies these and related developments as a natural maturation of the movement: the emergence within a learning network of a capacity to study itself (Sears et al. 2013). The ecovillage movement is experiencing parallel growth in levels of interest (internal and external) in and capacity for research, both self-directed and in collaboration with the academy, and continuous with existing processes of technological and social innovation within ecovillages (Andreas and Wagner 2012; Kunze and Avelino 2015). The Transition Research Network grew out of the Transition movement in response to the evident affinities between Transition and formal and informal research processes (Henfrey and Brangwyn 2013). When organizations representing permaculture, ecovillage and Transition at national and international levels came together to form the ECOLISE meta-network of community-based sustainability initiatives, founded in 2014, they invited a number of research organizations to join as specialized members.[6] The founding statutes of ECOLISE identify Knowledge and Learning among the four main pillars of its work.[7]

Intellectual leadership in the permaculture, ecovillage and Transition movements takes diverse forms. These overlap, echo and challenge those of mainstream academia in various ways and degrees. Mollison in particular has been a significant intellectual figurehead for permaculture, around whom exists something of a cult of personality not dissimilar from that of the celebrated academic. Several other prominent permaculture teachers and writers (almost all of them men) also model something closely resembling conventional forms of intellectual leadership. Alongside this - and recognized within the movement as at least equally important - quieter forms of leadership facilitate the generation, documentation, evaluation, sharing and discussion of new knowledge in more distributed ways through grassroots learning processes of the type described below in the section Learning as socialization. Such leadership is vested in both individuals and organizations, including national associations and networks and professional teaching organizations such as Gaia University (2016) and the Integral Permaculture Academy (2016). Its focus is not advancement of the individual or organization showing leadership, but to create opportunities for individual and collective learning to support more effective action towards the three permaculture ethics.

A similar phenomenon within Transition is perhaps exemplified by the work of its originator Rob Hopkins, now 'Catalyst and Outreach Manager' at Transition Network, which represents another form of intellectual leadership highly dissimilar from those in the academy. His books show a trend from how-to manuals - drawing on an increasingly broad base of experience from the movement as it grew and deepened (Hopkins 2008, 2011) - to telling inspirational stories of increasingly diverse and creative projects from a movement as it spreads and deepens (Hopkins 2013, 2015). This key body of work increasingly reflects a common metaphor for the work of Transition initiatives in their home communities - and their interconnections in regional, national and international networks - as *mycorrhizae*. These are networks of fungal filaments in the soil that invisibly connect trees and other plant life, exchanging nutrients and information in ways that foster optimum growth for the ecosystem as a whole. Intellectual leadership in the Transition movement, accordingly, is not about personal acclaim but about contributions to nurturing common interests.

Approaches to research in permaculture and Transition also emphasize the decentralization of intellectual leadership. That of the British Permaculture Association

(2016) considers all permaculture practitioners to be *de facto* researchers, and hence aims to nurture and support the collective intellectual capacity of this community of practice. That of the Transition Research Network (2016), which developed alongside and in dialogue with that of the Permaculture Association, also seeks to democratize knowledge production through more participatory approaches to research. These collaborations value academic skills without assuming their primacy, treating them as one among many forms of valued expertise necessary for successful intellectual endeavour.

All three movements considered in this section thus place an emphasis on learning and embed learning processes within their group cultures and working methods. However, they do so in ways that greatly differ from, and hence challenge, conventional academic regimes. In effect, they raise questions of what methods and institutional forms are appropriate both for supporting transitions to more sustainable, socially just and equitable societies, and as models for how such societies will perform knowledge creation and communication functions currently exercised largely by universities. The next section examines how permaculture education is addressing these questions in practice.

Learning as socialization

Permaculture education operates at multiple levels, and pedagogic approaches reflect this. This can be considered an example of stacking – organizing a single activity so that it fulfils multiple functions – an important permaculture design technique. A classic example of stacking is the forest garden, a permanent agroforestry system comprising up to seven distinct layers of vegetation from roots up to tall trees (Jacke and Toensmeier 2005). This vertical stacking in space allows the same ground area to accommodate greater numbers and variety of plants than a structurally simpler formation. Different layers support each other's growth: for example, ground-layer plants cover, protect and nourish the soil in which trees, shrubs and bushes grow; trees provide shade to herbs that prefer cool conditions, and a support up which vines and creepers can grow. Elsewhere I have employed the forest garden as a metaphorical illustration of the contrast between conventional approaches to research, narrowly focused on yields of high-impact publications and grant funding, and those emerging in Transition and permaculture, which also pay attention to softer, social and more localized outcomes (Henfrey 2014).

The same is true of education in permaculture and related fields, which combines divulgation of information with multiple other yields. Generic and widely applicable information – on permaculture ethics, principles and design methods, and techniques for their application – is packaged and in mutually supportive interrelationship with multiple layers of context. These contextual layers include the life experiences and circumstances of learners, the specific site/s at which training takes place and the wider permaculture movement at local, regional, national and/or international levels. Effective permaculture teaching involves establishing these layers during convening of, preparation for, delivery of and follow-up to a course, and cultivating and maintaining interconnections among them throughout all these phases (Morrow 2015).

Specifics of delivery are tailored to the skills as well as needs of learners. Teachers, convenors and facilitators of courses survey these skills and learning needs during recruitment and monitor them on an ongoing basis during delivery. Learners are encouraged to draw upon and contribute their own knowledge and experience, and use the novel framework provided by permaculture to understand them in different ways. Delivery formats and methods are mixed in order to accommodate diverse orientations and learning styles of participants, and often change flexibly as a course develops and new needs, interests and possibilities come to light. Some courses operate without a set curriculum, instead agreeing learning goals and activities through ongoing group discussion. In these ways, a course becomes a microcosm of the wider action learning processes that constitute and develop the permaculture movement.

Most permaculture courses are hosted either at recognized permaculture sites[8] or other community resources, allowing beneficial relationships to emerge between participants and their immediate physical setting. The physical setting provides a demonstration of principles and techniques in practice (and/or their absence and the complications of moving from theory to practical applications), and a site for practical training, including execution of learners' design projects. It benefits from the insights learners provide, income and voluntary labour associated with the course, and establishing relationships, which are often ongoing, between the site and its resident community and the transient learning community assembled for the course. Many people who complete permaculture courses go on to work at, establish or convert existing sites to permaculture projects, extending this network of people and places.

In addition to socializing people into embedded learning processes and relationships to place, permaculture teaching is an exercise in community building. Most PDCs involve around twelve teaching days, which may be delivered as an intensive residential immersion or spread out over a longer period of as much as a year. Whatever the format, as it develops any such course acquires an increasing sense of community as participants (learners, teachers, hosts…) learn together, play together, eat together and, on residential courses, live together and develop close bonds of familiarity and friendship. Newcomers to permaculture within this learning community find ready connections to the wider permaculture community through teachers, site residents and workers, and other old timers involved in the course, many of whom attend and help organize the projects, events and networks through which this community constitutes itself at local, regional, national and/or international scales.

Through use of inclusive pedagogies combining multiple techniques suiting diverse learning styles, backgrounds and skill sets, and rooted in the specifics of place and moment, permaculture education seeks to contribute to building as diverse a movement as possible. The data that exists on educational outcomes shows this to be partially successful. Unpublished research undertaken by Joe Atkinson, Learning Coordinator at the UK Permaculture Association, shows people with dyslexia to be unusually highly represented in permaculture. Some dyslexic permaculture practitioners point out the potential advantages of a different perspective that may, for example, be better attuned to identifying and working with patterns in complex systems.[9] Anecdotal reports from permaculture teachers suggest that many learners alienated by their experiences of formal education flourish and prosper in the different environments they offer.

It is equally true that many adult learners of permaculture come to it with prior experience of university-level studies. A survey of permaculture practitioners showed general high levels of educational attainment, with proportions of respondents holding post-secondary academic qualifications at all levels higher than national averages (Ferguson and Lovell 2015). This study has an acknowledged methodological bias (being based on voluntary responses to an online survey available only in English, thus excluding people without internet access and English-language competence),[10] which may have inflated these figures compared with those in the movement as a whole. Australian permaculture teacher Robyn Francis (pers. comm.) estimates 35–40 per cent of people taking PDCs are university graduates, still a significant number. Francis reports that many of these people find that permaculture integrates ideas and their application in a way their university studies did not. In a workshop on new higher degrees in permaculture at the International Permaculture Conference in September 2015 Andrew Langford, founder of permaculture-based online learning organization Gaia University, suggested that the success of permaculture as an overlay to undergraduate training endorses its value as a discipline of academic as well as practical merit.

The multilevelled pedagogic approaches characteristic of permaculture are designed to embrace, nurture and cultivate diversity in all respects. This includes catering for learners with varying levels and experiences of formal education, and other types of knowledge, skills and life experiences. It also includes various initiatives towards engagement with formal systems, the subject of the next section.

Formalization and permaculture education

Efforts to formalize permaculture education for adults in various countries have encountered considerable challenges. The controversies they inevitably generate are highly instructive about values and attitudes within the permaculture movement. Here, I interpret them as centring on the issue of diversity, and the perceived threat to diversity posed by formal procedures for validation and accreditation.

The first documented discussion about higher degrees in permaculture took place at the third International Permaculture Convergence in New Zealand in 1989 (Francis 2015). In the same year, the Australian Permaculture Institute began to deliver advanced courses on topics beyond the scope of PDCs (which tend to have fairly broad curricula) and not well covered in more conventional forms of training. Reflecting general approaches to vocational training in Australia at the time, these sought to strike a balance between knowledge and its practical applications. Accreditation became more important from 1995, when the Australian government limited eligibility for state funding to formally accredited courses. This stifled many important teaching initiatives, for example in indigenous Australian communities and to other cash-poor groups of learners. The introduction of Accredited Permaculture Training (APT) in 2003 allowed students on many bachelor's courses to receive credit for permaculture designs. It also allowed delivery of an elective module on permaculture within Australia's main horticultural college.

The UK has seen both coordinated and isolated efforts to create formally recognized qualifications in permaculture. The Permaculture Association has created mechanisms to accredit PDCs and some introductory courses at secondary level through the Open College Network, with the longer-term intention of an accredited diploma and, eventually, courses at levels equivalent to undergraduate and graduate degrees. Independently, permaculture has entered undergraduate degree curricula at a small number of UK universities, in each case due to the initiative of specific staff members and in none gathering sufficient institutional support to persist.[11] Accredited masters degrees including permaculture-based content are taught in the Centre for Agroecology, Water and Resilience (CAWR) at Coventry University[12] and at Crossfields Institute[13] and Schumacher College.[14] CAWR is part of a network of advanced permaculture teaching organizations and sympathetic universities in several European countries, led by the Permaculture Association and the Science Faculty Foundation at Lisbon University, who are collaborating on developing a new formally accredited Masters in Permaculture Design.

Discussion of such initiatives in permaculture circles, such as that took place at the twelfth International Permaculture Convergence in London in September 2015, inevitably raise various concerns. These can be seen as a wish to protect diversity at movement level. The perceived threat to teachers' livelihoods raised in connection with APT in Australia reflects a concern that the existence of formal and/or accredited programmes could undermine the perceived legitimacy of teachers operating outside these. This would additionally hold a danger of privileging the content, skills, knowledge and teaching methods of formal programmes and those teaching within them, meaning that perceived authority over knowledge and its transmission becomes restricted to certain institutions, pedagogic methods, programme structures and ways of knowing. In scenarios such as this, the greater power of the academy – in financial, institutional, political and cultural terms – would allow it to recapture its feral offspring. This would lead to the effective colonization of the permaculture movement, either restricting it to forms amenable to control by centralized authority structures (c.f. Scott 1998) or appropriating its energy and creativity in forms that support global political agendas incompatible with the ethics of earth care, people care and fair shares (c.f. Hardt and Negri 2000).

The opposite scenario is of permaculture engaging with the academy as a disruptive element that reconnects it with its core sense of purpose: by posing, and then seeking to answer, the question of what HE would look like if its basis was the three permaculture ethics. This firstly makes visible the largely covert premises of HE as it predominantly operates at the present moment – to accept, normalize, perpetuate, expand and entrench a global system based on systematic increases in inequality supported by ongoing destruction of environmental and social capital. It then seeks directly to subvert these premises by developing and operating alternatives with explicit ethical roots, and offering these processes (and, under suitable conditions, the outcomes) as models that can inspire and inform radicalizing initiatives elsewhere in the academy. In terms of Walter Wink's (2000) liberation theology, as adapted by Alistair McIntosh (2004), it seeks to reveal the powers, engage the powers and reclaim the powers: exposing where corrupt institutions have lost sight of their original social purpose, and initiating change processes that restore them to this.

A small example of how this could look in practice arose in a two-day externally facilitated learning event that took place in the Faculty of Arts at the University of Wales Trinity St. David (UWTSD) in February 2016. UWTSD has excellent recognized sustainability credentials relative to the rest of the HE sector, in the 2015 People and Planet Green League it was the highest ranked of Welsh Universities and eighth in the UK overall.[15] However, both students and some staff experience gaps between curricula and students' interest in taking practical action on sustainability. My colleagues and I were therefore asked to deliver a series of workshops that could help address this.

Our approach, based on my experience in permaculture teaching, eschewed prescribed content and instead sought to hold a space that allowed free self-expression and the natural unfolding of ideas and plans based on the students' own knowledge, concerns and interests. Our team augmented this with selective reference to specialist and technical knowledge in the literature as we felt appropriate and helpful – always in response to the emerging content. Our documentation and analysis of these discussions showed them to cover almost every key area in the recognized sustainability literature; learning, interestingly, was the single important omission. By the end of the first day, the group had agreed a small number of key topics of interest for further exploration. By the end of the second day, it had developed action plans based on a number of these, which ongoing self-organized processes are taking forward. The result was a *de facto* instance of Freire's model of self-directed, issue-led pedagogy, very different from anything the students had experienced elsewhere in their university education. In my view, it gave a hint of the potential power of harnessing the institutional resources of universities via flexible and engaged approaches to teaching and learning.

The tension between diversity-centred permaculture pedagogy and dominant pedagogic regimes in HE that tend towards uniformity, when the two seek to interact, is potentially both dangerous and productive. The danger is of forcing conformity upon flexible, adaptable and constantly evolving methodologies characteristic of permaculture. The potential is for these methodologies to subvert established approaches in HE and act as a transforming force. The latter can be an important part of wider processes of societal transformation that recontextualize globalizing forces in embedded relationships with place, as the following section briefly considers.

Permaculture as ecology of mind

Permaculture, in my view, is a paradigmatic example of a conceptual and practical 'ecology of mind' (Bateson 1972, 1979; Bateson and Bateson 1987): a set of integrated measures to protect and cultivate diversity in both mind and nature, that is, in subjective and objective aspects of phenomena, operating at multiple mutually contextualizing levels. Its approach to learning aims at supporting action to work creatively with ecological diversity, and mobilizes social and cultural diversity as its interdependent and therefore necessary correlates (c.f. Guattari 2000). Central to this are pedagogic methods that work with and seek to encourage diversity in many different respects: of outlook and approach among learners and teachers, among specific features of teaching sites, among applications in different fields of activity, among practitioners within the community. Each teaching event – formal, informal or aformal – is emergent upon specifics of the exact time, place and social context at which it arises, arising as a unique interchange, enriching to all taking part and impossible to replicate. The permaculture movement as a whole is a rich, complex, dynamic tapestry of such events, interweaved in layers of meaning and consequence in ways as utterly as possible distinct from the tendencies towards uniformity evident in much conventional HE.

In postulating and seeking to apply globally relevant ethics and design principles, to be contextualized as appropriate in the momentary specifics of place and time, permaculture echoes the contrast between the 'immutable mobiles' of modern science and the 'mutable immobiles' of traditional agricultural knowledge (De Walt 1994). This relationship tends to be productive when bearers of traditional knowledge encounter science from a situation of empowerment, in which they are able to interpret and apply it on their own terms (e.g. Toledo 2001). Some indigenous groups have adopted permaculture on just such a basis: as a tool to re-evaluate and adapt as necessary traditional knowledge systems threatened by environmental, social, political and/or economic change (Henfrey and Penha-Lopes 2015: 27–29; 77–79). Globally, preservation of this knowledge, and the diversity of perspectives on nature and ecologically embedded lifestyles and economies it supports, is vital to the continued existence of biotic and ecological diversity: an interdependence captured in the term 'biocultural diversity' (Maffi 2001).

Among practitioners in industrialized settings, permaculture addresses the issue of biocultural diversity from the other side, so to speak: of restoring to local and regional economies a sense of geographical rootedness and consequent coherence with the social, cultural and environmental idiosyncracies of place (Cato 2013). It is one among many social movements worldwide (and a valuable tool within many others) seeking to countervail the ongoing depletion of ecological and cultural diversity by a rampantly destructive global economy (Henfrey and Kenrick 2015). These assaults on global diversity are sustained, in significant measure, by the normalizing tendencies of the educational systems within which its leaders, operators and citizens are socialized into largely unquestioning compliance, based largely on ignorance of alternatives. As a form of mass intellectuality that embeds in all its social processes forms of learning that explicitly promote multiple forms of diversity, permaculture is an important example of emerging alternatives.

Acknowledgements

Thanks to all my permaculture teachers, especially Wilf Richards, and other colleagues in the permaculture world, especially Robyn Francis, Rosemary Morrow and Andrew Langford, all of whom provided invaluable advice.

Notes

1 www.gaia.org/gaia/education/curriculum/.
2 http://transitionnetwork.org/do-transition/training/trainings/.
3 http://transitionnetwork.org/do-transition/training/trainings/.
4 www.permaculture.org.uk/research.
5 http://pirn.permaculture.org.uk/.
6 http://www.ecolise.eu/?page_id=1024.
7 www.ecolise.eu/?page_id=24.
8 For example, those in the LAND Network of permaculture demonstration and learning sites supported by the UK Permaculture Association.
9 http://permateachers.eu/rakesh-rootsman/.
10 It is also worth noting, as an aside, that the same survey showed ethnic diversity among respondents to be far lower than national averages, with strong biases towards self-identification as white/caucasian. While methodological bias will again have influenced this figure, certainly internationally (e.g. excluding most participants in largely grass-roots, farmer-led permaculture movements in various African, Asian and Latin American countries) and perhaps nationally, it certainly indicates significant underrepresentation along ethnic lines in the countries from which most responses were forthcoming (the United States, Canada and Australia). This is a recognized issue within permaculture and related movements such as Transition (see https://transitionnetwork.org/resources/7-ingredients-just-fair-inclusive-transition-inner-transition-guide/).
11 A long-standing example in the United States is taught by Will Hooker at North Carolina State University: http://cals.ncsu.edu/hort_sci/people/faculty/pages/hooker.php.
12 www.coventry.ac.uk/course-structure/engineering-environment-and-computing/postgraduate/agroecology-and-food-security-msc/.
13 www.crossfieldsinstitute.com/higher-education-research/courses-programmes/researching-holistic-approaches-to-agroecology/.
14 www.schumachercollege.org.uk/courses/postgraduate-courses/ecological-food-systems.
15 https://peopleandplanet.org/university-league/2015/tables.

14

Mass Intellectuality from the Margins

Sara C. Motta

Indigenous women and women of colour are subject to ontological and epistemological invisibilization in which their perspective on community life and liberation is generally denied. If it is heard, it is as Lugones (2006: 78) describes, represented 'as insane or deviant, as inferior, or as threatening'. They, like indigenous peoples, black communities and excluded communities, are the 'non-subjects' of capitalist coloniality, denied visibility, humanity and the capacity to know. Yet such subjects articulate a voice from the margins which speaks the unspeakable. They are at the heart of a reinvention of an 'other' emancipatory politics of knowledge, which decentres the imperial subject of knowing and being of coloniality, and instead enacts a decolonizing praxis that reinvents revolutions (Motta 2014).

For the non-subjects of coloniality to become visible as thinking subjects means exceeding the epistemological logics that structure and reproduce coloniality. This involves critiquing the invisibility and non-being of the colonized other, 'a subject lacking the capacity of gift' reproduced in such a politics of knowing. Arguably, this means decolonizing autonomist Marxism's concept of mass intellectuality whose site of enunciation – internal to modernity – presents a particular view from *the included* as the global universal framing of emancipation (see Dyer-Witheford 1999 for an overview of the concept). Such totalization reproduces the ontological logics of coloniality in its reproduction of the non-being, invisibility and inability to give, of the excluded and absent–present other.

It is not enough therefore, as Nick Dyer-Witheford (1999: 506) argues, to maintain the concept of the general intellect but add on questions of gender and race, or admit that 'the wretched of the earth ... are not powerless to appropriate [the mechanisms of high-technology production]'. Rather a decolonizing project that enables the voice, visibility and very possibility of being *of the colonized* requires as Nelson Maldonado-Torres argues (2007: 261)

> [a] break with monologic modernity ... to foment transmodernity ... [as] an invitation to think modernity/coloniality critically from different epistemic positions and according to the manifold experiences of subjects who suffer different dimensions of the coloniality of Being.

This decolonizing project embraces multiple subjects of knowing, multiple literacies and multiple grounds of epistemological becoming (Motta and Cole 2014). It re-embodies and reimagines what it means to speak, to think, to theorize (Anzaldúa 2007: 81). This project, whilst maintaining the concept of mass intellectuality, enacts a radical decentring that transgresses the limits of coloniality which are reproduced in Autonomous Marxism's conceptualization. Thus, it does not seek to finish 'the unfinished democratic project of modernity' but rather to realize 'the unfinished project of decolonisation' in which the wretched of the earth become the primary agents of transformation (Maldonado-Torres 2007: 262).

My contribution will thus focus on the praxis of two experiences of women in the movement in the global South, with the global South understood not as a geographical place but rather a relationship with patriarchal capitalist coloniality, in which racialized and feminized communities are produced as non-subjects (Mohanty 2003; Motta 2013). The first is the Escuela Política de Mujeres Pazficas (Political School of Pazifica Women) in Cali, Colombia, formed in 2000 with the aims of developing nonviolent, feminist proposals and practices, to denounce and make visible the violences which mark Colombian society and politics, and to affirm and co-create a post-patriarchal politics of emancipation. The second, a younger network formed in early 2014, is the Family Inclusion Strategy Hunger (FISH) collective based in the Hunter Valley, Australia. FISH emerged out of growing concern of the lack of voice and representation of marginalized families in out-of-home care processes, and the increasing practice of child removal from Aboriginal, refugee and poor white families. The group converged on a commitment to addressing these issues with a parent-centred approach to facilitate the voice, visibility and agency of families, so as to foster reflexive and inclusive practice and transform/reform the discourse within which the politics of child removal is framed.

Both involve the emergence of the racialized and feminized non-subjects of patriarchal capitalist coloniality, whose onto-epistemological[1] experience is constituted through: invisibility as subjects; the white gaze of suspicion which asks 'are you truly human'; and the denial of the capacity of gift[2] (as onto-epistemological denial), in which systematic denial that there is anything to learn from such non-subjects is reproduced. Here, as Maldonado-Torres explains:

> coloniality survives colonisation. It is maintained alive in books, in the criteria for academic performance, in cultural patterns, in common sense, in the self-image of peoples, in aspirations of self, and so many other aspect of our modern experience. In a way, as modern subjects we breathe coloniality all the time and everyday. (Maldonado-Torres 2007: 243)

Both respond to this onto-epistemological denial and forced absence through politicizing the collective and individual soul wounds enacted by this social system to transform these into: a politics of knowledge of the reconstruction of 'other stories and memories to tell'; decolonizing subjectivities and pedagogies; and a praxis of mass intellectuality from the margins (see also Motta and Cole 2014, and Duran et al. 2008 for further discussion of the concept of 'soul wounds').

Visibilising emergences

The Escuela emerged out of the experience and recognition of the denial, invisibilization and delegitimization of women's voices in Colombia politics, and in particular peace dialogues that had occurred in early 2000 in which the voices of women combatants were absent. As Norma Bermúdez (10 April 2012) explained to me, when recounting how the idea for the Escuela emerged:

> In the early 2000s peace-talks were occurring between the government and armed guerrillas in which women's voices and experiences were excluded. There was no space to talk of the politics of motherhood, relationships and loss, love and desire within the experiences of female combatants. There was no place for a humanising of combatants. So we decided to write a letter to the women guerrillas to hear their stories of motherhood, of loving and loss within conditions of war and conflict. We sought to open a dialogue that could break the logics of patriarchal capitalism in Colombia in which politics is an extension of war and war and extension of politics.

Appearing in public, through their collective letter, as political subjects with distinct voices, histories and experiences acted as a moment of rupture which disrupted politics as normal in Colombian society and opened space for the creation of the Escuela. Women who were used to men deciding everything – writing and directing the scripts of politics and power – began to realize that they could be active agents in Colombia's future. This involved a process of unlearning subjectivities in which women were objects of other's discourses and represented as passive victims of the violent logics of Colombian politics. It involved creating new forms of sociability when women came together to support each other's acts of speaking. This experience began a process which re-rooted subjects within their own agency and dignity. As Norma continues (Bermudez 2013: 243–244):

> From the beginning we knew that the debate and dialogue we had opened would have major consequences for us and for moving beyond the old formulas of politics. We were facing something deeper: to question the meaning of politics, its objectives and its means; to question the meaning of power, and the idea that power is enacted not only in parliaments and battlefield, but also in social relations, on the streets, in the square, at home and in the bedroom.

FISH similarly emerged in relation to the denial, invisibilization and pathologization of racialized mothers and families in the out of home sector[3] and the resultant reproduction of historic practices of child removal. Critical practitioners participating in the network were also resisting their silencing by a policy discourse in which they were positioned as implementers of particular programs lacking the intellectual capacities to become co-participants in the praxis of community social work (Family Inclusion Network (FIN) 2007; Rogowski 2015; Thorpe 2007). FISH knew that they had to change the terms of the conversation structuring state interventions and relationships with racialized, subaltern women and communities, by fostering the voices, experiences and knowledges of these subjects who were otherwise denied agency and rationality (Cocks 2014).

Contrary to Autonomist Marxism's framing of mass intellectuality, the emergence of these subjects of the commons and communing does not derive from shifts towards immaterial, networked production, which shapes and enables the emergence of subjective (collective) autonomy (Dyer-Witheford 1999: 486–488; Lazzarato 1996). Rather these new emancipatory subjects emerge out of historic and contemporary experiences in which they are produced as the non-subjects of modernity. They/we have thus always been subjected to processes of subjectification and legitimated interventions onto their/our bodies, communities and lives (Lugones 2010). Such emergence is not ontologically determined and then politically actualized (Hardt and Negri 2005), but rather it is an existential, immanent practice of becoming subjects who are against and beyond processes of onto-epistemological denial and dehumanization (see also Motta 2015).

These emergences disrupt the Global Design present in the conceptualization of Autonomist Marxism, visibilizing its raced, gendered and classed particularity, alongside the unidimensionality of its framing of the ways in which capitalism alienates both oppressed and oppressor, colonized and colonizer. As such, their imagining of the subject and practice of mass intellectuality and the transformations this politics of knowledge might foster become reinscribed into the logics of coloniality. Arguably, it is only through a decentring and decolonizing of such unidimensional universality that a horizon of hope-filled and heart-felt possibility for a pluri-diversality of multiple grounds of epistemological becoming can emerge.

The power to name

Both movements are committed to practices of epistemological prefiguration (Motta 2011) that decentre representational knowledge practices of coloniality, in which the word is separated from the world, the knower from the known and the thinker from the doer. This means that they ground their praxis in a commitment to collectively co-produced practices of knowledge creation. Here, knowledge is practised as a verb as opposed to a noun. Transformation is thus immanent to the process of knowledge creation itself and is weaved through the embodied knowledges of the racialized, subaltern woman and her allies. This practice of mass intellectuality suggests that the promise of epistemological pluri-diversality lies in the body of the non-subjects of modernity.

The Escuela build on the lived knowledges and experiences of participants, and nurture new pedagogical practices that enable a collective and critical reading of the world and women's experiences of oppression, violence and displacement (Motta and Cole 2014). Organized into a four-month diploma, the first month begins with a dialogue of knowledges in which sacred space is created for a sharing of participants' experiences and knowledges. Women sit in circle and call in their ancestors and spirit guides to be with them and as Jacqui Alexander (2005: 269) describes more generically but applicably here:

> become fluent in each other's histories, resist[ing] and unlearn[ing] an impulse to claim first oppressions, most devastating oppression, one-of-a-kind oppression, defying-comparison oppression.... Unlearn an impulse that allows mythologies about each other to replace knowing about one another... cultivate a way of knowing in which we direct our social cultural, psychic and spiritually marked attention to each other.

An example of this is around the seemingly everyday and 'apolitical' agency of a woman making nutritional recipes for her children and self in challenging material conditions. The woman shares this experience and acknowledges her knowledge and resilience in creating this through telling her story orally to the group, but also opening another kind of dialogue of sharing knowledges in which the group collectively make the recipe, taste it and share similar experiences. The speaking of her truth and being witnessed in a nurturing and loving way enables an opening to a critical reflexive process in which this mundane act becomes a door into the possibilities of autonomy and food sovereignty. As Norma describes:

> We then link this experience of making the recipe to the conditions of her life and questions such as food sovereignty. We read texts, watch videos about food sovereignty movements in Colombia and other places. We also talk about the neoliberal crisis and how this increases the weight of labour on women's shoulders. We explore alternative forms of economy such as the feminist economy.

Everyday practices of active subjectivity and wisdom are visibilized. These are then connected to other processes of collective resistance and transformation to foster critical reflexivity and the power to name the world, which as Freire argues is the power to change the(ir) world (1970: 69). This gives *character* to history, demonstrating how social relationships and meta-processes of political, economic and social dispossession are deeply rooted and made real in the everyday lives of raced and gendered subaltern subjects (Levins Morales 1998: 3). The embodied and embedded knowledges of racialized and feminized subjects become epistemologically pivotal in the construction of the existential knowledges out of which transformation emerges, is nurtured and sustained.

FISH too is committed to collaborative and dialogical knowledge processes with parents and families facing the disciplinary (neoliberal) state and its historic and contemporary dehumanization of racialized and feminized mothers and communities. Accordingly, its first public forum was organized to explore family inclusion in and out of home and child protection processes, and was orientated around the stories of four parents who had interacted/were interacting with these systems. They were the experts and invited to share their stories, expertise and knowledges of the system and to provide advice to practioner participants about what had worked well and what needed changed. They participated in the entire forum as experts contributing to the ongoing discussion with practitioners. The remainder of the day was organized around participatory methods of knowledge construction, which included world cafe and open space technology methods (for further information about the methodology and the outcomes, see Cocks 2014).

The ethical and epistemological praxis of FISH enacts a decolonization of the monologues of intervention as they have, and continue to characterize dominant state intervention on the body and in the family and community of racialized subaltern mothers, children and their families (Roberts 2012; Robinson and Paten 2008; Salmon 2011). FISH's practice enacts a radical disruption of the implicit hierarchies of knowledge and rationality on which they are premised, and decentres the terms of the epistemological and politically violent conversation of capitalist coloniality in Australia. This affirmative dialogical praxis, like the Escuela, does not seek to (re-) enclose the conversation into a homogeneous and unidimensional solution. Rather there is an embrace of epistemological complexities and multiplicity. Importantly the embodied lived experiences of racialized and feminized subject become sites of expertise and knowledge as opposed to spaces of lack, criminality and deviance.

This involves disruption of dominant embodied performances of expertise and professionalism in which the knower is the deplaced academic who empowers the practitioners to intervene into the infantilized and pathologized lives of subaltern racialized women. Deplaced and disembodied hierarchical distance becomes transfigured and prefigured with placed and embodied dialogical intimacy and connection (see Lugones 2010; Motta 2014, 2017a for theorization of critical intimacy). Key to this is a commitment to deep listening. This listening is epistemological as it disrups the coloniality of knowing–being and instead nurtures the emergence of 'other' forms of speaking, theorizing and listening (Gonzalez de Allen 2006).

This politics of knowledge turns the assumptions of Autonomist Marxism in relation to mass intellectuality on their head. It is not changes in social relations of production which create the conditions of possibility for the creation of onto-epistemological practices of emancipation. Neither is it the disembodied intellectual that creates the universal view out of which we might come to know such onto-epistemological possibilities. Rather it is the lived experiences of the embodied subject, and the tensions between processes of subjectification and active processes of subjectivity 'that gives life to her agency' (Lugones 2010: 746). The knower here becomes *not* the prophetic knowing-subject of modernity but rather the embedded storyteller of prefigurative encounters (see Motta 2014 and 2017a for further discussion of the storyteller). To embody and embed critique in this way, as Lugones (2010: 746) suggests,

> is to enact a critique of the racialised, colonial and capitalist heterosexualist gender oppression as a lived transformation of the social. As such it places the theorist in the midst of the people in a historical, peopled, subjective/intersubjective understanding of the oppressing-resisting relation at the intersection of the complex systems of oppression.

Finding (our) serpent's tongues

An 'I' exists even when this existence is denied... it is a form of listening... that functions like the talking drums across communities... awareness of one's situation is awakened and enhanced by hearing the 'call of other' like beings whose voices

> *reverberate knowledge about existence... new forms of understanding are acquired; the epistemic directives which aid in understanding what is known and how it is known begin to emerge from the shadows. (Gonzalez de Allen 2006: 2–3)*

The dominant script of the political and the knowable denies racialized and feminized subjects' intelligibility rendering them non-subjects. Thus, both movements are involved (to differing degrees) in a process of creating their own languages, which Stoler (cited in Agathangelou and Ling 2004: 41) suggests requires recalling 'other kinds of memories... and stories to tell'. This has involved reimagining what it means to think, theorize and represent and involves embracing multiple literacies which reconnect the word to the world.

In the work of the Escuela, pedagogical practices are multidimensional embracing and enacting a healing of the multidimensionality of the wounding and alienation of patriarchal capitalist coloniality onto their bodies, spirits, emotions and minds. They work through the erotic, which as Audre Lorde (2000: 1) describes, 'lies in a deeply female and spiritual plane, firmly rooted in the power of our unexpressed or unrecognized feeling'. It is a deep knowing which forms the basis for an articulation of voice and political subjectivity which once experienced cannot be forgotten and redenied. Such a deep knowing is chiselled into being through critical reflection on the alienations and violence of the soul wound (Duran et al. 2008) as individually and collectively experienced. Importantly this is put into dialogue with other critical experiences and theorizations. Centrally such decolonizing praxis is existential as it involves the very coming into being of subjects who have both experienced onto-epistemological denial and internalized such denial and lack of self-worth (Maldonado-Torres 2007; Motta 2017a; Motta 2017b). Their pedagogical practices include ritual, the senses, dancing and bodywork, storytelling, visual art and representations, singing, sacred touch combined with more traditional textual practices (for further details of body-work and sacred touch, see Motta and Cole 2014; Motta 2014). These build the conditions for participants' reoccupation of their selves and of the world, foregrounding their ability to make visible and heal from multiple oppressions and create the conditions for 'other' ways of be-ing and knowing.

Collective processes of storytelling that are multidimensional in this way create links of solidarity and (re-)connection, and enable monologues of isolation to become dialogues of understanding, voice and pleasure. As Pilar Restrepo, one of the participants in the Colectivo, explains: 'Telling stories is a way of reconstructing reality, and sometimes, it also enables the healing of deep wounds' (author interview 2010). Importantly, ways of knowing are also ways of inhabiting and creating the world and each other. To re-enchant the world with these multiple embodied knowledges therefore enacts not merely a discursive reappearance in the world but enables the flourishing of multiple grounds of onto-epistemological be-ing otherwise.[4]

FISH is at the beginning of its journey of creating other languages and stories to tell. However, in its recognition of the wounds enacted upon racialized and feminized subjects there is a strand of work that focuses on collective healing using multiple modalities. Much of this work is contextualized through the lens of feminist narrative therapies in dialogue with traditions of popular education (White 2007). This has resulted in the creation of collective spaces for mothers and families experiencing the 'system' to journey with their experiences. The ethics and commitments of this praxis are to facilitate the development of critical reflexivity to disrupt individualized and normalizing/pathologizing accounts and discourse of violence, marginalization and addiction, by situating them within broader conditions and causes, as well as disrupting hegemonic framings of subaltern families which devalue and pathologize.

Storytelling as an epistemological practice comes to the centre, and involves not merely cognitive knowing and representation but also the use of metaphor and symbolic representation and expression (as onto-epistemological prefiguration). Part of this process involves witnessing of the participant's story. As a witness, one is asked to reflect on the resonances in the story and how the experience of healing and reflecting on her story is transformative. The methodology seeks to disrupt the internalization of individualized and pathologizing discourses of deficiency and turn towards recognition of agency, understanding wisdom and resilience.

The praxis is based in a method of deep dialogue, which transgresses the self and other binary upon which the entire matrix of state interventions upon the racialized and feminized body politic is premised. It invites reflections on the way in which the story of the 'other' actually has implications and resonances for 'our' stories. The affectivities of decolonizing storytelling work through critical intimacy and an ethics of care in which vulnerability is strength. Witnessing in this process troubles any simplistic binary framing of such practices, for in these encounters participants become both witness of an 'other' but also to 'our' selves (see also Zembylas 2006, for a similar discussion of witnessing in the context of classroom space). Such practices enable the shared co-creation of other stories to tell, the creation of our own relational heart languages, and dislodge borders of difference and separation, to create unexpected empowering recognitions, encounters and connections.

Anzaldúa (2007) tells of her coming to healing and voice, she speaks of her right to have her serpent's tongue, to speak her own language and no longer be confined within the terms of the conversation of patriarchal capitalist coloniality. Both the Escuela and FISH, in differing ways, are involved in such a process of finding their own languages; of developing their serpents' tongues. By necessity this involves rupturing with the politics of knowledge of coloniality and exceeding its logics of being and knowing. For these onto-epistemological logics enact a violent monologue of denial and dehumanization. As de Sousa Santos (2014: 19) writes, 'it seems as if colonialism has disabled the Global North from learning in non-colonial terms'. Perhaps it becomes clearer now, why the framing and creation of the concept of mass intellectuality as emerging out of the site of enunciation of the works of Autonomist Marxism is in need of decolonizing, to avoid its complicity into these onto-epistemological logics. The knowing subject is not merely a cognitive subject of autonomy, and the possibility of knowing about the possibilities of revolution in our times is not merely a representational act about such possibilities. It is itself an onto-epistemological expressive coming into being that takes multiple forms and embodies multiple literacies (see also Maldonado-Torres 2007; Motta 2015).

Becoming subjects in our own right

The work of critical intimacy embodied and embedded in the praxis of the Escuela and FISH enables participants to 'resignify' themselves and their communities in which those shamed, silenced and delegitimized become dignified co-creators of their histories, communities and selves. Such resignification occurs in the safe and intimate spaces and through the prefigurative, epistemological pedagogies outlined in the previous sections, in which participants build the conditions together for their emergence as political subjects enacting public pedagogies that disrupt and re-imagine the dominant script of the political.

In the work of the Escuela, their appearance as political subjects resignifies the public and political away from a patriarchal capitalist logic of power-over and control of the other, and towards an understanding and practice of power-within and power-with. Here, the public becomes a space of commonality and recognition, and a practice of re-creating space and reclaiming of women's power. An example of such resignification is the 'Broken Dolls' ritual which visibilizes, challenges and transforms gendered violences. Filling a public space with broken dolls to represent the wounds enacted against women by gendered violence, the women and allies of the Escuela enact a ritualistic embodied creation, in which these wounds are given healing balm as participants lovingly and collectively put the dolls back together (personal communication October 2015).

Such public pedagogies enact multiple prefigurations. The women participants, many victims of gendered violence, reoccupy their bodies and selves. Here, dominant discourses, which either pathologize (as guilty) or infantilize (as passive) victims of gendered violence, are disrupted as victims become active agents of their healing, together weaving their own stories of dignity, voice and possibility. Such onto-epistemological coming into be-ing of the political subjectivity of the non-subject disrupts the terms of the conversation, as they have structured the public and political. They create a feminist ethic of care in embodied action and relationship, in which collective and collectivizing care becomes a central axis around which new 'publics' emerge and are tenderly nurtured into being. This enacts a move away from an idea of emancipatory subjectivity and practice from the figure of the warrior towards the figure of the mother-gardener birthing, tending and nurturing the new post-patriarchal world into being.

FISH is at the beginnings of its journey of public pedagogies. However, as its praxis places the expertise and voices of racialized and feminized subjects and their allies at its heart, it enacts a radical disruption of the violent terms of the conversation as they structure Australian politics and polity. The non-subjects of the body politic emerge as the knowers and co-creators of an emergent possibility of a new politics, in which their embodied knowledges are valorized, dignified and spoken. The very act of appearing as political subjects shifts and is a moment that dislodges the ontological and epistemological wounds of coloniality and nurtures the relationships and the conditions upon which our/their serpent's tongues might begin to speak and flourish.

Mass intellectuality from/of the margins

Both the Escuela and FISH exceed the onto-epistemological logics of coloniality for they foreground the emergence of other logics of being-knowing which in their emergence challenge the rationalities, subjectivities and ways of life of patriarchal capitalist coloniality. Emerging out of the experiences of the multiple wounds of patriarchal capitalist coloniality, the racialized and feminized subjects on and of the margins are decolonizing emancipation. Their praxis co-creates prefigurative epistemologies which foster multiple literacies and nurture the grounds of multiple epistemological becomings. They reimagine the nature of the political, the meanings and practices of intellectuality and the logics and relationships of emancipation. Their return to an ethics of gift invites a practice of decolonization of self and other in which as Franz Fanon (1968: 165) describes we 'quite simple attempt to touch the other, to feel the other, to explain the other to [ourselves]'.

Their praxis thus sheds light on the unidimensionality and dehumanizing particularity of the conceptualization of mass intellectuality of Autonomous Marxism. It has a message for us all for it sheds light of the depths and multidimensionality of the alienating wounding created by capitalist coloniality, and suggests that the work of epistemological decolonization is for everyone, for we are all wounded in differentiated ways by coloniality. Such decolonization entails as Mignolo describes 'a shift in the geography of knowledge and history. It is not just about having a different interpretation of the same set of events but about voicing another paradigm that emerges across' the epistemic colonial difference' (Mignolo 2011: 48). The voicing of 'other' onto-epistemological visions emerging from the epistemic colonial difference, create the possibilities of encounters in the borderlands through which to decolonize internal territories of pain, fragmentation and alienation so that we might make ourselves and our communities anew.

I end therefore with an invitation to unlearn dominant knowledge practices and subjectivities, and enact epistemological decolonization through entering the epistemological margins and borderlands, which form sites 'of creativity and power, that inclusive space where we recover ourselves, where we move in solidarity to erase the category colonized/colonizer... Enter that space. Let us meet there. Enter that space' (hooks 1990: 152).

Notes

1 Here the dominant epistemology of Coloniality is embedded in the coloniality of being (Maldonado-Torres 2007). This is understood as being constituted by and through the creation of particular subjects and practices of knowing, which seek to universalize a particular and parochial praxis of knowing-being. This is premised on the making absent and denial of other ways of creating the world and alternative perspectives, and other ways of inhabiting subjects of knowing (Mignolo 2011; Motta 2017a).

2 Here, gift relates to the idea that the non-subject is not legible within the terms of the conversation of being–knowing of coloniality, and thus is denied key elements of

being of that terrain, which is the capacity to gift. Such a capacity enables her to be a knowing–being subject who can contribute to the social, political and so on.

3 This refers to that sector which works with children who have been removed by the state from their families, the foster families and institutions that care for the removed children, and the parents and family of these children.

4 Lugones among others use the hyphenated term 'be-ing', as opposed to being, in order to suggest that life is not fixed but comes into be-ing. In this argument, our task is to come into be-ing, for we cannot be contained by the violent onto-epistemological logics and rationalities of patriarchal capitalist-coloniality.

Conclusion

Politics, Aesthetics and Democracy

15

Practising What We Preach? Writing and Publishing In, Against and Beyond the Neoliberal University

Gordon Asher

Introduction

This chapter focuses on the processes and engagements of the project that has produced the book *Mass Intellectuality and Democratic Leadership in Higher Education*. It provides an exploration of the lived realities of the process we engaged in based on discussions with the contributors to the book. These dialogical reflections explore our engagement in an alternative, critical project of writing an academic book for a mainstream academic publisher. Doing so in ways that reflect the wider values and objectives espoused by the contributors, namely radical democracy, participation, dialogue, co-operation, empowerment, mass intellectuality, and democratic leadership.

In what follows, I draw on dialogues between contributors, and with the editors, that I facilitated and mediated, in order to draw out themes. This addresses both the responses to specific research questions posed to all authors by email and dialogues undertaken in-person and online. Responses to my questions were received from authors of eleven of the fourteen chapters, including both editors. The focus is on critical reflection, with a view to generating possible lessons *both* for ourselves and our future projects *and* for others across academia attempting to work, in, against and beyond the neoliberal university.

It is worth emphasizing the heterogeneous nature of the contributors. They form a broad range of voices, from a wide range of positions in terms of their relationships and engagements with the academy. They include Undergraduate, Masters and Postgraduate students, Postdoctoral workers, Graduate Teaching Assistants, others employed on precarious and part-time terms, full-time lecturers, senior lecturers and professors from a wide range of subjects and disciplines, support staff, staff in management roles and others engaged with but not studying at or employed by the academy. There are many overlaps between these categories, and changes to roles and engagements in and with the academy over the three-year period of the book project.

The project emerged from a request from the Series Editors for an alternative perspective on intellectual leadership. The book's editors drafted a contextualized response to the call, and canvassed for interest and abstracts via email lists and blog posts. In all, twenty-two responses were received, and interested parties were then invited to a workshop to discuss which proposed chapters should be included, and the structure for the book. In all, eleven prospective contributors attended and all bar-two were included in the agreed structure. Following this workshop, the editors refined the draft of the proposal, which was then shared for revision with all contributors. On receiving feedback from the series editors, the editors again refined the proposal, and shared this with all contributors to amend.

Contexts

The project has been taking place in contexts of ongoing integrated crises (Haiven 2014), both caused by and causing (Klein 2008) an intensifying neoliberalization of society (Springer et al. 2016) – and integral to that, of the Higher Education (HE) sector (Canaan 2013) – alongside counter-hegemonic struggles, in response, for democratization and eco-social justice (Amsler 2015).

The university is being restructured and refocused as the driver of and for competition, markets and the short-term economic needs of the state and corporations. Central is the (re)production of students as customers and consumers (with degree programmes as investment projects (Lawrence and Sharma 2002) focused on 'employability' (Chertkovskaya et al. 2013)), staff as service providers and research entrepreneurs (Kelly 2013), and both as forms of academic labour (Winn 2015b). As 'edufactories' (Edufactory Collective 2009), universities are businesses with CEOs, corporate strategies and branding, business plans and partnerships, cost-benefit analyses and key performance indicators (Bok 2009); and all labouring within this set of relations are reified and valorized as human capital (Bourdieu 2010). It is important to appreciate that universities are not merely victims of local and global pressures from corporations and states in 'the restructuring of universities as competing capitals' (Hall 2015b). They are not merely being neoliberalized. Rather, they are themselves central to a growing network of institutions, bodies and organizations responsible for neoliberalizing themselves and wider society (Ball 2012). They are not merely complicit in, but initiate and promote 'the academic capitalist knowledge, learning regime' (Cantwell and Kaupinnen 2014).

Under neoliberalism competition and commodification colonize both epistemic and relational frameworks and values (Naidoo 2016), directing attention and time to that deemed measurable and important (by neoliberalism's state–corporate nexus) and thus serving to deflect attention, time and resources from all other aspects that might be considered of (social) value in university life and engagement. One aspect of such academic capitalism (Slaughter and Rhoades 2009), of specific relevance to our project, is the developing contemporary political economy of Higher Education writing and publishing. The most pronounced and influential factors in its neoliberal restructuring being the tyranny of the Research Excellence Framework (REF) (Williams and Roberts 2016) and the related, increasingly dominant, influence of corporate academic publishing and technology firms (Fuchs 2013; Lariviere et al. 2016). Together, they are the two central pillars shaping and controlling demands and imperatives. Through doing so they foreclose possibilities for criticality and creativity in research, writing and publishing – while encouraging their 'structural over-production' (Williams and Roberts 2016) – and hence also with regard to much public engagement, across the Higher Education sector. Research is increasingly instrumentalized and measured, centrally mandated and programmatic, focused on proliferating certain forms of output for the REF and for income generation that may only incidentally be of value in addressing contemporary crises.

However, the university is also a contested site and a terrain of struggles for democratization and eco-social justice (Giroux 2014). In Freire's terms, the university embodies simultaneously the potential both for 'liberation' and 'domestication', for both transformation and reproduction. We locate our project within, and as hopefully contributing to, such struggles. These contexts situate our project as lying within an inevitable (given our choices) position of tension and contradiction, taking place with regard to both institutional imperatives (such as the REF) shaping our academic labour, and as attempting to contribute to a critical dialogue of knowledges, practices and relations that speak to moving beyond 'the neoliberal order of things'. To this end, our focus is on developing democratic and co-operative ways of working, of writing and publishing, research and public engagement, and hence evolving mass intellectuality.

The project and process: Mass intellectuality?

A central question in our reflections was how, and to what extent, our experiences of the process can be viewed as embodying our perceptions of mass intellectuality?

Most contributors emphasized a genuine attempt to do so, which in many ways was successful given the restrictions and limitations that we were in general working with and that came with our decision to publish with a mainstream academic publisher:

- '[A]s much as is possible under the circumstances that we work/live';
- 'Not fully, but it's a quantum leap from the usual process... the constraints of time and space have limited its radicality as a project in and of itself';
- '[I]n all likelihood, the process was as good as could be expected given everyone's constraints';
- 'The limitations... seem to be the inevitable results of working within and/or at the margins of current regimes, rather than outside them. Most people involved are dependent for their livelihoods on university employment, with all the institutional pressures that entails; the collection would probably have been weaker, less relevant and less credible had we not. We made the decision to publish with Bloomsbury, and stuck with it despite the problems this created

(which were themselves a useful learning process); this will hopefully ensure the book reaches a wider range of audiences and achieves more significant influence than publishing independently. Engagement is full of such dilemmas; addressing them creatively and with conscience is a vital part of creating change';
- 'The nature of what and how we chose, was very much a reflection of what was practical and feasible rather than merely desirable'.

Engagement in the process waxed and waned across the project, with contributors' abilities to engage influenced by time, geography and work and life commitments. With fifteen chapters and twenty-one authors involved there have been 'a lot of people with complicated lives to co-ordinate'. Many factors influenced whether authors were able to participate collectively and to what extent. Some have hardly been able to participate at all beyond contributing their chapter, whilst others have consistently and very fully been involved in the process from the initial meeting, by contributing to discussion online and via email, and through engaging in peer review. Some, including myself, have been able to engage fully at times, and not at all at others.

Many commented on the effect of our contexts of work and wider life, as having foreclosed and limited time, energy and space for both collective participation in the process and individual/collective writing/peer reviewing. For instance, the entirety of my engagement, from response to the call for chapters and initial meeting, through the research for and writing of this chapter, to the process of peer review, had to be pursued outside my role in the university. Such work is viewed as 'not a priority' and thus to be engaged with entirely in our own time and at our own expense. Further, I was one of a number of contributors who were not just swamped with work and struggling to find time and space to give to the book, but had to be signed off work, due to the effects and affects of working in our respective universities. 'We have had at least four people off due to serious work-related illness, a flooded house, three people pull out'. Contributors commented on the editors' invaluable support and encouragement for those who were struggling with writing and participating for a host of reasons, including those of us who were ill for significant periods. 'I have been left with a real sense of their humanity, solidarity, and with their commitment to working in ways that are co-operative, and democratic'.

The importance of the initial face-to-face meeting was emphasized by a number of contributors, for starting the process in a manner that foregrounded 'democratic working and an inclusive, participatory, co-operative approach' and putting in place a mutually agreed process which 'evolved, dialogically and democratically as it went'. It was also seen as constructive in developing relations, helped by a range of interconnections between many of the authors, and served to generate an initial kernel of the kind of trust and respect that is essential to working together in a democratic and co-operative manner (Brookfield and Preskill 2008).

All decisions were made, at the initial meeting and subsequently through email and shared Google docs, in a manner that was clear, transparent, accountable and co-operative, with everyone given the opportunity to voice their opinion, engage in dialogue and have a say in final decisions and choices. As such leadership during the process was, as much as possible, democratically shared amongst contributors;

from initial decisions as to inclusion of chapters, through the reworking of the book proposal, to engagement with publisher's concerns and opportunities to comment on others' chapter contributions. Contributors also emphasized that this ongoing communicative process helped to develop further dialogical connections and thus trust and respect – relations – amongst authors.

The final prepublication period was a process of dialogical open peer review, including virtual consultations, reflecting our prefigurative intentions; with each draft chapter being sent to another contributor for review, as well as being made available through Google docs for others who wished to comment. As such, the peer review was valuable, both as a dialogical process of feedback – invaluable for 'getting some really generous and thoughtful criticism' – and as creating and evolving further co-operative connections and relations amongst the contributors.

Most contributors commented on what was viewed as the vital and central role of the editors in making the process work, in a manner that clearly attempted to reflect our values and intentions, to the extent possible given our circumstances. When it seemed necessary, the editors, as co-ordinators of the project, have 'taken the lead', without objections and always with the opportunity for others to comment and propose alternatives, with no final 'decisions around the book made without consulting the authors via the mailing list first'. While the editors 'may have taken the lead on negotiating with Bloomsbury, or in finding new authors ... we have always returned to the group to discuss and validate any decisions'. As such an inevitable, practical balance was struck 'between autonomy and control'. The editors 'have clearly worked hard to make this an open, transparent, participatory process':

- 'While Joss and Richard steered the project and coordinated it, decisions were made in a collective fashion that brought a democratic approach to the book. Everything from shaping the table of contents through to the internal review process was conducted collectively and co-operatively';
- 'I feel Joss and Richard have shown the appropriate style of leadership, having held the process with integrity and shown consistent conviction to co-operative and democratic principles, acted as transparently as possible and always sought to make decisions inclusively';
- The editors 'encouraged all of us to participate as fully as we could in this process' and 'facilitated rather than led on the project' though a consequence of this was that 'they ended up doing so much of the work themselves'.

Commenting on the lived realities of putting our intentions into practice, one contributor noted:

> this has been limited by constraints arising from engagement with dominant academic regimes: Bloomsbury's procedures and the limited availability of most participants (myself included) for attending meetings and actively taking part in email discussion, collaborative reviewing and other collaborative procedures. I feel the process has been steered with the appropriate balance of pragmatism and idealism necessary to navigate such contradictions.

More than one contributor voiced worries as to potential consequences of our choice to publish with a mainstream academic publisher:

> As I *loathe* the neoliberal concept of leadership that suggests that some should lead others as they participate in a competitive, marketised, individualised university, I feared that this was what the publishers were demanding, I was concerned that this might mean that we would be contributing to a book that served such a model.

However, all agreed that the actual process as well as orientation and content, allayed such worries, such that 'the book did seem to be [...] produced co-operatively and democratically'.

One aspect of the writing of the chapters that deserves attention is the decision to co-author chapters. The contribution from Birmingham Autonomous University was written with seven authors and ten contributors who initially tried to find one voice, but moved to a position of preserving all voices as speaking in dialogue, something only made possible by geographical and temporal opportunities to meet regularly:

> We have preserved all the voices in the chapter. We met periodically. We started with a meeting where each of us mentioned the main idea they wanted to focus on. Then we wrote drafts which we subsequently read out and discussed at other meetings and via Facebook. We collectively edited the chapter and agreed on the order of the section ... the process embodied my perception of mass intellectuality as we democratically co-operated and made decisions regarding the content and shape of the chapter.

This foregrounds some of the main issues and challenges in terms of finding the necessary time, space and opportunity to engage in wider aspects of collaborative co-production that speak to our espoused values and objectives.

Further potential benefits of co-writing/production/working were also commented on:

> we found the process of co-authoring our chapter very beneficial. This is because it provided us with the opportunity for us to do a bit of co-mentorship across our different areas of research and teaching and learning (these are often kept separate or even set against each other is some HE environments).

Some of the elements and consequent benefits, in terms of co-operative and collaborative co-writing, were felt to be mirrored by approaching peer review though an open, dialogical process in which authors were paired on the grounds of shared interests/expertise:

- 'I liked that the reviewers were other authors of chapters in this book,[1] as it makes the project more collaborative';
- 'the process of editing one another's work, has been really affirming';

- ‘Knowing and having a relationship with the peer reviewers was really positive, as it led to a much more discursive approach, with editors and authors knowing that they shared the broad values and objectives of the book and wider project’.

Again, a centrally important aspect of the process concerns the dialogical building of social relations, based on critical dialogue, reflexivity, trust and authenticity.

Responses suggest that if we had possessed greater freedom in terms of time and opportunity to meet regularly, face to face and online, different paths and opportunities would have been possible, including a greater degree of co-writing and wider peer reviewing. Doing so would also have entailed being able to share the workload of the editors more equitably, and in a manner that would have spoken to greater levels of democratic participation and co-operation across all aspects of the book’s production. Further, this would have also spoken, again, to greater connectedness, trust, authenticity and the evolution of more democratic social relations across the group.

For reasons of time, travel and finance it was not possible to meet as a group after our initial meeting. However, it was widely viewed as desirable to have done so:

- ‘It would have been amazing to have created an event for us all to come together to truly co-produce our ideas and support each other’;
- ‘the collaborative approach to editing is fantastic, but it’s just a big leap forward towards what could be an even greater model of intellectual co-production’.

A number of authors suggested that it might have been desirable to have engaged much further in experimenting with co-writing, including the possibility of writing the entire book in such a manner, whilst acknowledging that such a process would necessarily have involved greater commitments of presence and engagement, time and energy. The general feeling conveyed by the contributors though, was that they were happy with the contextualized decisions we made, and that compromises reflected the inevitable limitations of the tension of being ‘in’, within the framing of our work as ‘in, against and beyond’ the neoliberal university.

Post-publication plans and possibilities

From the outset, it has been clear many of us believe that what occurs post-publication is vital in reflecting our espoused values and objectives. If we are aiming to practice a dialogical and democratic production of knowledge and relations, and to do things counter-hegemonically in asking how this research and writing might be genuinely, socially useful, then planning prefigurative, post-publication actions is vitally important:

- How do we utilize our writings *and* the connections and relations we have evolved, to engage in the forms of praxis that we have been writing about? ‘The question is how to take the work on mass intellectuality into wider society’?

- How do we get the writings and our experiences of the process accessibly 'out there', through: distribution of the book/chapters; rewriting and re-pitching for different audiences; and the organization of and engagement with events in and beyond academia?
- Can we co-operatively organize a series of dialogical and participatory events and engagements across the UK with different groups of the authors, as well as individually and collectively contribute to pre-existing conferences and other events?

My hope, clearly shared by others, is that we 'continue the dialogue of doing and making together into the future', informed by our reflections. One contributor said:

> Hopefully this survey comprises something of a backloop in an action learning cycle – gathering feedback that can enable collective reflection on the successes and limitations of the process and indicate changes that could be made in order to work better in the future. In my view, these built-in learning processes are the most vital part of all action towards societal transitions and transformations: the basis on which we are operating, that of institutions that have lost sight of their true social purpose and a wider sociocultural context that is in many key respects toxic, is too flawed to expect our processes to be anything other than highly imperfect. What is important is that we do our best in the circumstances and with the resources available to us, learn from the consequences and seek to act upon them.

The suggestion has been made that we have the option to turn the production of the book into a wider and longer-lasting project. That if we could physically meet, to 'come together and articulate a truly shared vision then we might be able to form a community that could grow'. With one proposed consequence of doing so being that '[w]e might be able to agree that when individuals go and present their work they do so as individuals, but also expressing and sharing the goals of this community and inviting others to join and come together for new projects':

> I wonder if more concerted effort could be made to build a wider community, with open processes for writing, commenting and editing and integrated activities for networking and co-operation among initiatives for mass intellectuality (whether employing that term or not).

This might involve a greater focus on:

- 'working towards a more solid concept of what education should be rather than merely what's wrong with what it is';
- 'stimulating some real discussion on a range of issues around Higher Education and I would love the book to be a tool for promoting such discussion and potentially action. Involving UCU [the trade union] would be interesting';

- 'I think there are a number of themes, one of which is the market oriented nature of knowledge production, the other is the value of mass intellectuality in and of itself, the other is how one dialogues knowledges ... the other is about the democratization of higher education institutions, and the other about the meaning of leadership in these contexts';
- '[b]roader approaches to co-operative decision making and leadership need to be taken outside of the publication sphere. Thinking about Joss' work in particular on co-operative forms of higher education revitalises my thought that the new Alternative Provider legislation being brought in could be co-opted by positive interests that do not share the government's agenda to marketise HE'. (See Winn 2016a)

One group of authors have already organized an event, that included other book contributors, as part of the British Sociological Association's Activism in Sociology Forum, and this provides a possible model for future collaboration. A number of authors have discussed the possibility that collective book launches would provide opportunities to 'reflect on how we are bringing this process, and the book contents, further in our own work. Perhaps this participative event could help us all deepen our appreciation of the book's and the project's significance – and "move us on"'. Moving on includes developing deeper links with emerging higher education alternatives, such as the Social Science Centre (http://socialsciencecentre.org.uk/) and the Centre for Transformational Learning and culture (http://utlc2016.wix.com/home).

Our experiences and reflections have also informed individuals' future plans within and through the academy: 'the book gives me the head-space/motivation to consider how to re-enter academia and to write in/contribute to that space'. Another contributor views the experiences of this project, and that of peer reviewing in particular, as positively influencing their future plans: 'It has influenced the way I am thinking about facilitating a special issue about motherhood and academe in that I think peer-reviewing is a great way to engage with each other meaningfully and that meeting together (where possible) also opens creative possibility.' However, a number of contributors commented on the barriers and problems experienced in finding the time, energy and opportunity to reflect and plan for post publication:

> We have each had personal stuff to deal with during the production and publication process, and this leaves the potential for discussing alternatives/what next somewhat limited. Energy and time are central, and the conflicts or tensions between home, work and personal life, or between work and not work, leave the space for activism stretched or closed down.

Hopefully, sharing the responses to my research questions with all contributors can spark a collective critical reflection on the process to-date and inform new possibilities.

A possible model?

The final set of issues we explored related to the extent this project could be considered a feasible model for working in (against and beyond) Higher Education. Is it likely to inform our future engagements and projects? Does it have potential relevance and resonance for others struggling in, against and beyond the neoliberal university?

There was considerable range of opinion about how and to what extent our project could be seen as a feasible future model, for ourselves and for others across academia. Many of the contributors have spoken and commented on their appreciation of the dialogical and empowering nature of the process of co-production, in which all felt encouraged to have a voice and a say in decisions. There was great tentativeness as to the extent to which it could be conceived, itself, as transformational or revolutionary:

- 'I don't think it changes anything structurally… [i]t's perfectly accommodated by higher education as it exists today'
- '[i]t is what it was/is and it comes from a particular conjuncture and time and place'.

However, it was seen as a constructive response to the alienation of much academic work:

- 'a preferable way of working';
- as providing 'a therapeutic space because it sits against the structures of the University' when '[s]o much of HE practice requires that we compete with one another, but when we co-operate we see a far larger return';
- 'the book gives me the head-space/motivation to consider how to re-enter academia and to write in/contribute to that space'.

A central challenge, commented on by many, was such a project's demand for time, contact and slower ways of working and building relationships, obstructed by the demands of contemporary academia (Mountz et al. 2015). This was 'only feasible where authors/editors are willing to work more deliberatively. It is slower and therefore sits uncomfortably against commodified and accelerated academia'. Even those most enthusiastic about the model, tempered their enthusiasm: 'the question is raised as to how we do so given the profound alienation, work-intensification and precaritization in the current university'. This represents a recognition of the difficulties of co-production given the intensified time and work pressures of the neoliberal institutions we have been critiquing. However, making the choices we did enabled many of the authors to meet institutional requirements to publish, with related benefits in terms of distribution and perceived 'impact' (in part to meet the tyrannical publishing imperatives of the Research Excellence Framework (REF) (Butler and Spoelstra 2015)). For some contributors, this also meant the possibility of at least some time, (head)space, support and resources for working on the project, without which their engagement would have been most difficult, if not impossible.

A further challenge related to working with a mainstream academic publisher. It is worth emphasizing that our choice, deliberated at length along with alternatives to it at our initial meeting, was made with an awareness of the role of mainstream academic publishers in the contemporary political economy of Higher Education and some of the issues this might raise (Eve 2014). We believed we would have sufficient freedom to produce the kind of work we desired, in the manner of our choosing, because the project emerged through an approach from the Series Editors to the book editors, based on an awareness of their critical work, writings and engagements with radical projects such as the Social Science Centre, Lincoln. Issues arose during the process, with the publishers expressing concerns as to our chosen title for the book and regarding our political balance or bias. Considerable discussion, involving most contributors, ensued and limited compromises were made that served to reassure the publishers. Overall we were satisfied that we could proceed with a project that bore close resemblance to that which we had intended.

Communications and relations between the editors and contacts at the publishers were generally supportive throughout, as to both our content and approach, as well as with regard to the delays in the book's production. Some of these related to the deliberative nature of co-production, including the discussions engaged in to democratically respond to the publishers' concerns. To a great extent we think we have produced the book that we envisaged through the supportive contexts in which we were working and making decisions. One suggestion from contributors is that future projects might choose to 'allow the model to be developed further and more fully'. Doing so would have to address institutional imperatives and the foreclosure of available time and resources to engage with research and writing.

Perhaps the use of the term 'model' was not ideal in my question, as we did not set out to create a model in the sense of a blueprint that could just be picked up and copied by others. Rather, we viewed our project and reflections on it as a contribution to ongoing dialogues that might have resonance and relevance for others if adapted contextually:

> I didn't experience it as a model, or as a suggestion that it was a model, but rather as an experiment in trying to navigate a conservative and capitalist publishing industry in a way that maintained in process and product our ethics of democratizing practice.

This was viewed as signalling to others:

- 'that other ways of producing/publishing knowledge are available';
- 'I believe it will make a creative and critical contribution that will be of use for other collectives, communities and individuals in struggle for another education, another epistemology and another world'.

Contributors have already been asked about the project by colleagues, who are considering adopting aspects of it for their own forthcoming projects. It foregrounds certain possibilities, hopefully brought out in part through this chapter. One author noted that 'I really like the way this chapter is being developed – creatively and with contributions and reflection from the authors.' We hope and believe, from the responses of colleagues to date, that this project's process will have resonance and relevance for others working similarly.

Social relations and the production of subjectivities

A strong emphasis, moving the book beyond its content and critiques, was on the process as building and evolving social relations. This is a central aspect of any project oriented towards transformation for democratization and is deeply pedagogical in nature (Giroux 2013):

> The two integrated aspects of the project and process that I appreciated the most were; the emphasis on socially-useful research and writing and the doing so in a prefigurative manner; through democratic and collaborative decision making and relationships – a welcome, and much needed, focus on social relations in, against and beyond the neoliberal university.

This concerns the creation and evolution of relations of trust and authenticity. Especially difficult when the time, (head)space and resources (financial and otherwise) necessary to engage and develop the necessary co-operative and democratic relations of trust and authenticity is increasingly foreclosed by academic imperatives (Wanggren and Milatovic 2015), with the well documented attendant impact on mental and physical health (Hall and Bowles 2016). One of neoliberalism's tactics, and consequences more widely, is this shutting down of time, space and resources for autonomous activity and struggles of resistance and alternatives – 'Neoliberalism is a global pedagogical project aimed at the dispossession of free time so that all of life becomes productive, and education is a central institutional means for its realisation' (Hall 2016b). Not only were many of us choosing to become familiar with other contributor's writings that were relevant to our own work and interests, but also their wider projects and engagements. This led to several authors being involved in or attending collaborations and events beyond the project, with the clear intention amongst many of us for further such engagements in the future. This has expanded our social relations beyond the other book contributors, into wider networks of solidarity and struggle in, against and beyond the university.

The production of subjectivities and relations is inherent in the socialization of all education. Neoliberal Higher Education does not merely produce knowledge, but people and networks – through the (re)production of capitalist values and desires, identities, subjectivities and relations (Roggero 2011). '[W]hat is currently being enacted... is the alienation of academic labour through the enclosure and commodification of its products *and* relationships' (Neary 2012). As such, there is a need for radical, alternative Higher Educations to (re)produce subjectivities and relations democratically, co-operatively and collaboratively, in ways that move beyond categories of identity (Holloway 2016), countering neoliberalism's (hegemonic) pedagogies of oppression and domination with (transformative) pedagogies of freedom and emancipation (Haworth and Elmore forthcoming). These critical or radical subjectivities and relations are a central aspect of mass intellectuality, and form our evolving democratic social relations – the 'we' of autonomous creativity and doing – as the forces and relations of production (Holloway 2016). We are attempting not to reform, but transform, academic work and those who work in the academy, to move *beyond* academic labour (Hall 2014); in Holloway's terms, to produce academic 'doing' as critical, creative, autonomous, socially useful activity.

Our aim has not been merely dissemination or knowledge exchange, but in part, that our writings as a process of thinking and working things through, form contributions to critical dialogues of knowledges (Sloane 2016). It has been an ongoing experiment in co-creation/production with others, which speaks to the evolution of dialogical, co-operative, democratic relations – to mass intellectuality. Here, Robin's (2016) appreciation of the reader or 'audience' as 'co-creators with – and of – the public intellectual', is important:

> When we talk about public intellectuals, not only are we talking about the audience as a recipient or reader of the text, but we are also, necessarily, talking about the audience as an independent, autonomous, and equally original and creative, co-creator of the text. (Robin 2016)

This speaks to the audience/reader as co-creators of knowledge and relations, through their active dialogical participation/engagement, and as such a shift from a conception of the researcher and writer as public intellectual towards a broader notion of mass intellectuality.

Further reflections: In, against and beyond the neoliberal university

My concluding reflections propose potentially useful ways of conceiving of our engagements that might have resonances for those struggling elsewhere in, against and beyond the neoliberal university. Within this framing I introduce the notion of being and becoming critically, academically literate, and I link this to locating, developing and expanding our individual and collective agency, as a form of mass intellectuality for radical democratization. I see strong links between our conceptions of mass intellectuality and the Scottish philosophical tradition of 'common sense' as inherently pedagogical, as an education for a 'democratic intellect where philosophical and general issues were at one' (Davie 1990; Gunn 2013).

In, against and beyond

Holloway (2010, 2016) provides a useful framing and orientation for social struggles when he advocates thinking, acting, living and relating 'in, against and beyond capitalism':

- 'In' – as we are inevitably within structures, processes and relations of capitalism and their attendant oppressions, repressions and exploitations;
- 'Against' – speaking to resistances to them;
- 'Beyond' – speaking to alternatives to them; to transformation.

Taking Holloway's framing, alongside what Cantwell and Kaupinnen (2014) have called 'academic capitalism', and an understanding of contemporary capitalism as neoliberal in nature, leads to a critical position of working 'in, against and beyond the neoliberal university' (Asher 2015). Thus, framing critical responses to our contemporary neoliberal conjuncture in Higher Education as developing understandings and orientations that are:

- 'in' – inevitably within the neoliberal university, so as to navigate, challenge and intervene in it;
- 'against' – to resist its ongoing neoliberalizations and oppressions; and
- 'beyond' – to nurture, evolve and create transformative alternatives to it.

Increasingly critical educators/students/writers/researchers and groups are drawing on this framing to inform and orientate their work and struggles (Amsler 2015; Asher 2015; Canaan 2011; Cowden et al. 2013; Hall 2014; Neary 2012; Ridley 2016; Undercommoning 2016; Winn 2014) This book project locates its production processes within such an interpretation of the critical paradigm. This helps illuminate our individual and collective positioning as situated in inevitable tension or contradiction, and orientate our work as contributing to struggles for radical democratization and eco-social justice.

The interactive and the institutional

Richard Gunn's (2014a) critique of struggle offers an alternative way of conceiving the inherent tensions and contradictions of living (with)in capitalism while struggling for a better world. This maps closely on to Holloway's notion of 'in, against and beyond'. Gunn poses a tension or contradiction between institutions and interactions through autonomous democratic social movements, co-operatives and assemblies (Gunn et al. 2015). These are revealed between the interactive choices in which individuals, groups and movements set their own autonomous, prefigurative agendas, priorities and processes (Amsler 2015) and the imperatives, limits and restrictions set by institutions.

Institutional thinking shapes and co-opts our identities and inter-personal relations – as 'state foundational individualism', such that the individual and social co-operation become conceived of in a specifically institutionalist (corporatist/statist) way (Asher and French 2012). This clouds, or mystifies, perspectives which should be interactive, autonomous, open and free, thus working against notions of the collective, the co-operative and thus genuinely participatory and democratic practices and relations (Gunn 2014b).

We can view attempts to frame and orient our engagements as 'in, against and beyond the neoliberal university' as located in this interactive–institutional tension. Our interactive (to the extent they actually are) choices and actions are in contradiction with and alienated by the institutional imperatives of the university and wider corporate structures, including their policies, strategies, practices and hierarchical relations that serve to 'entrench the neoliberal order of things' (Asher et al. 2016). The extent to which these choices exist, and can be deepened and expanded, relates to questions of agency and how and where this can be located and evolved within, against and beyond our structural contexts.

Being and becoming critically academically literate

Whatever critiques can be made of our choices, it is worth re-emphasizing that there is no possible position of purity. The question is what have we achieved, and might we achieve post-publication, from within our contextual limitations? A starting point is the present trajectory of Higher Education, and whether it becomes increasingly impossible for many to engage in radical education (Banfield et al. forthcoming). If this is the case, how do those of us positioned so find ways to (collectively) leave the university and engage in these necessary pedagogical aspects of transformation outwith the academy (Undercommoning 2016)? What might we lose by doing so, including potentially the struggle for/over the university? How do we understand and where possible broaden and extend our choices and options from within? If we choose to exit, what possibilities and potentialities might we gain (and lose) by doing so? How might there be exit or exodus, while linking with those who cannot or choose not to exit? Such questions emphasize the continual need to link struggles for and within the university to those beyond.

One central benefit of the process is that it has fed into wider, ongoing processes of our being and becoming critically academically literate (Asher 2015). The book and our plans and projects post-publication contribute to similar processes for ourselves, our readers and others engaging with us and our work. These dialogical, collective processes include evolving understandings of the past, present and likely future contexts and trajectories of Higher Education, speaking to necessary conditions for creating and evolving mass intellectuality, and for working towards the genuine democratization of Higher Education and the wider society it both shapes and is shaped by (Edufactory Collective 2009).

The minimum that might be incumbent on those of us working in or engaging with Higher Education is to problematize our specific and immediate conjunctures and contexts democratically. This aims to develop understandings of *our own* educational contexts, in ways that enable essential resistances and alternatives to the neoliberalization of the academy (to both the academy being neoliberalized and to its concomitant role in neoliberalizing itself and wider society (Ball 2012)), and thereby to be able to 'teach the university' (Williams 2012); that we should learn and teach about what the university was, is and could be, and that we need to teach critically across (and beyond) the university. Central to such a project is a focus on the formation of identities and subjectivities, and on transforming relations, such that we attempt to live, work, act, think and relate prefiguratively. This is an ongoing, iterative process of praxis, forming an always incomplete and 'not yet accomplished' project (Amsler 2013).

This relates closely to Amsler's (2013) concept of the fearless and re-politicized university:

> 'if we are to shape universities to be places in which we can actually teach and study and learn and be [...] *we need to educate ourselves about the politics of higher education, advanced research, labour, intellectual culture, space and time.* And we need to do this in a context in which thinking and speaking about the politics of any of these things is regarded as either a waste of time or a threat to economic productivity and institutional "reputation" [...] And we need to do this in an environment where perhaps many academics, by dint of profession or proclivity, have either no experience of political participation or activism, or no interest in social and economic politics at all. And we need to do all of this in an environment where many academics and some students are exhausted and insecure and are therefore in need of considerable self and collective care' ... and involves 'the capability to liberate time for solidarity actions and activities, rather than for exchange'.

This foregrounds the urgency of connecting struggles inside the university with those outwith the university, and in particular to participatory, democratic and autonomous social movements, peoples' assemblies and co-operatives (Asher et al. 2016).

Locating agency: Radical democracy and mass intellectuality

Central questions underpinning our notions of collective leadership relate to the necessary agents of change and transformation. We question where our agency might be located and most effectively used. How do we move from our contemporary 'here's' towards our utopian 'there's'? 'How do we successfully foster transformative change within the structural context of the academy? How do we continue to maintain our analysis of larger contexts (structures) that stifle or shape individual and collective possibilities for change (agency) and simultaneously implement these possibilities?' (Canaan and Shumar 2011).

Our project represents our attempt to locate, inform and evolve our individual and collective agency as fundamentally co-operative and interactive, through the formation of democratic subjectivities and relations, and in the linking of networks of struggles. Here, we work towards a radical democratization of the commons (Haiven and Khasnabish 2014) – including the educational commons (Undercommoning 2016) – across all spheres of human existence. The project and its process represent an attempt to reflect (to prefigure or foreshine (Amsler 2015)) the principles of radical democracy. This can be conceived of as the theory and practice of collective freedom (a prefigurative praxis of being and becoming (2015)), and understood as both participatory in nature (Bookchin 1990) and focused on space and opportunity for contestation, on agonistic pluralism (Mouffe 2000). It involves an appreciation of dialogue, diversity, difference and dissensus (Ranciere 2015). Through doing so we hope to contribute to the project for radical education; conceived of as evolving understandings of ourselves and others, the word and the world and the relationships between them, allied to an appreciation of our individual and collective agency, and an orientation to act in and on the world to change it for the better – to *transform* it in the interests of eco-social justice. As such, speaking to the hope that the Social Science Centre (2014) identifies as lying in the 'possibilities for associational networks' that critique higher education policy and practice, in part through their lived realities of alternatives to neoliberal Higher Education.

Radical democracy is focused on: the limits and possibilities of our material and affective contexts; and, individual and collective autonomy and agency, or 'the manner and extent to which agency is restricted or safeguarded, allowed or disallowed, encouraged or removed from day-to-day life' (Helms et al. 2016). As a result, this book project provides an example of working against and beyond neoliberalized Higher Education, that proceeded from a conscious choice of inherent tension, which we then proceeded to explore from (with)in that contradiction. This is an exploration that speaks to both individual and collective attempts to locate our agency within (and against) our neoliberal structures and contexts, and to find different ways of moving beyond them.

Note

1 The publisher also sent the complete manuscript to an anonymous reviewer and we are grateful for the constructive and supportive comments received.

References

Adorno, T. (1997), *Aesthetic Theory*, Minneapolis: University of Minnesota Press.

Agathangelou, A. M. and Ling, L. H. (2004), 'The house of IR: From family power politics to the poisies of worldism', *International Studies Review*, 6(4), 21–49.

Agents for Environmental Justice and Scandrett, E. (2003), *Voices from the Grassroots Redressing the Balance: Working Towards Environmental Justice in Scotland*, Handbook 4, Edinburgh: Friends of the Earth Scotland.

Alexander, M. J. (2005), *Pedagogies of crossing: Meditations on feminism, sexual politics, memory, and the sacred*, Duke University Press.

Allington, D., Dueck, B. and Jordanous, A. (2015), 'Networks of value in electronic music: SoundCloud, London and the importance of place', *Cultural Trends*, 24(3): 211–222.

Alvesson, M. and Spicer, A. (2012), 'Critical leadership studies: The case for critical performativity', *Human Relations*, 65(3): 367–390.

Amsler, S. (2013), 'The Fearless University', *Venturing Beyond*, 16 May 2013. Available at: http://amsler.blogs.lincoln.ac.uk/2013/05/16/the-fearless-university/ (accessed 18 July 2016).

Amsler, S. (2015), *The Education of Radical Democracy*, London: Routledge.

An Independent Review of Higher Education Funding and Student Finance (2016), Securing a Sustainable Future for Higher Education. Available at: https://www.gov.uk/government/uploads/system/uploads/attachment_data/file/422565/bis-10-1208-securing-sustainable-higher-education-browne-report.pdf (accessed 18 July 2016).

Anderson, T. (1913), *A Co-operative College. The Next Step in Our Educational Development*, Manchester: Co-op Union.

Andreas, M. and Wagner, F. eds (2012), *Realizing Utopia: Ecovillages and Academic Approaches, RCC Perspectives 2012/8*, Munich: Rachel Carson Center for Environment and Society (RCC).

Angelos, E and Dimitris, L. (2014), 'Workers' Enquiry in praxis: The Greek student movement of 2006–2007', *Ephemera: Theory and Politics in Organization*, 14(3): 413–429.

Anon (2003), 'Berlin Declaration on Open Access to Knowledge in the Sciences and Humanities'. Available at: http://oa.mpg.de/lang/en-uk/berlin-prozess/berliner-erklarung (accessed 18 July 2016).

Anzaldúa, G. (2007), *Borderlands/La Frontera: The New Mestiza*, San Francisco, CA: Aunt Lute Books.

Aranya (2012), *Permaculture Design: A Step by Step Guide*, East Meon: Permanent Publications.

Aronowitz, S. (1983), 'Mass Culture and the Eclipse of Reason: The Implications for Pedagogy', in D. Lazere (ed.), *American Media and Mass Culture*, 465–474, Berkeley: University of California Press.

Asher, G. (2015), 'Working In, Against and Beyond the Neoliberal University', Paper for Standing Conference on University Teaching and Research in the Education of Adults. Available at: https://www.academia.edu/13925922/Working_in_against_and_beyond_the_neoliberal_university (accessed 18 July 2016).

Asher, G. and French, L. (2012), 'Crises Capitalism and Independence Doctrines', in S. Hames (ed.), *Unstated: Writers on Scottish Independence*, 77–87, Edinburgh: Word Power Books.

Asher, G., Cole, P., Fuchs, C., Gunn, R. and Smith, R.C. (2016), 'Strategies moving forward: Social movements and progressive governments – A round table discussion', *Heathwood Journal of Critical Theory*, 1(2). Available at: http://www.heathwoodpress.com/strategies-moving-forward-social-movements-and-progressive-governments-a-round-table-discussion/ (accessed 18 July 2016).

Atherton, G., Jones, S. and Hall, A. (2015), 'Does Cost Matter? Students' Understanding of the Higher Education Finance System and How Cost Affects Their Decisions', NEON. Available at: http://www.educationopportunities.co.uk/wp-content/uploads/DoesCostMatter_ANEONReport.pdf (accessed 18 July 2016).

Avolio, B., Mhatre, K., Norman, S. and Lester, P. (2009), 'The moderating effect of gender on leadership intervention impact an exploratory review', *Journal of Leadership and Organizational Studies*, 15: 325–341.

Bacon, E. (2014), *Neo-Collegiality: Restoring Academic Engagement in the Managerial University*. The Leadership Foundation for Higher Education, London. Available at: http://eprints.bbk.ac.uk/11493/ (accessed 18 July 2016).

Bailey, M. and Freedman, D. eds (2011), *The Assault on Universities: A Manifesto for Resistance*, London: Pluto Press.

Ball, S.J. (2009), 'Privatising education, privatising education policy, privatising educational research: network governance and the "competition state"', *Journal of Education Policy*, 24(1): 83–99.

Ball, S.J. (2012), *Global Education Inc. New Policy Networks and the Neo-Liberal Imaginary*. London: Routledge.

Ball, S.J. (2013), 'Care of the self, resistance and subjectivity under neoliberal governmentalities', *Critical Studies in Education*, 54(1): 85–96.

Banfield, G., Maisuria, A. and Raduntz, H. (2016), *The (Im)possibility of the Intellectual Worker Inside the Neoliberal University*, Fortaleza, Brazil: Universidade Estadual do Ceará.

Barbier, Ch-h. (1951), 'A tribute to Louis de Brouckère – Co-operator', *Annals of Collective Economy*, 32(2): 113–127.

Barcan, R. (2013), *Academic Life and Labour in The New University*, Farnham: Ashgate.

Barnett, R. (2012), *Imagining the University*, London: Routledge.

Bateson, G. (1972), *Steps to an Ecology of Mind*, Chicago: University of Chicago Press.

Bateson, G. (1979), *Mind and Nature: A Necessary Unity*, London: Fontana.

Bateson, G. and Bateson, M.C. (1987), *Angels Fear. Towards an Epistemology of the Sacred*, New York: Bantam.

Bauman, Z. (2001), *Community*, Cambridge: Polity Press.

Beall, J. (2013), 'The open-access movement is not really about open access', *TripleC: Communication, Capitalism and Critique. Open Access Journal for a Global Sustainable Information Society*, 11(2): 589–597.

Beckman, G. (2005), 'The entrepreneurship curriculum for music students: Thoughts towards a consensus', *College Music Symposium*, 45: 13–24.

Begg, T. (1994), *The Excellent Women*, Edinburgh: John Donald Publishers.

Bellamy, Joyce M. and Saville, John (1972), *Dictionary of Labour Biography*, Vol. 1, Clifton, NJ: Augustus M. Kelley.

Bellamy Foster, J. and Yates, M.D. (2014), 'Piketty and the Crisis of Neoclassical Economics', *Monthly Review*, Available at: http://monthlyreview.org/2014/11/01/piketty-and-the-crisis-of-neoclassical-economics/ (accessed 10 March 2017).

Benjamin, W. (1934/1998), *The Author as Producer: Understanding Brecht*, London: Verso.

Berardi, F. (2009), *The Soul at Work: From Alienation to Autonomy*, Translated by F. Cadel and G. Mecchia, with preface by J.E. Smith, Los Angeles, CA: Semiotext(e).

Bermudez, N.L. (2013), 'Cali's Women in Collective Crossing for Three Worlds: Popular Education, Feminisms and Nonviolence for the Expansion of the Present, Memory and for Nurturing Life', in S.C. Motta and M. Cole (eds) *Education and Social Change in Latin America*, 239–259, New York: Palgrave Macmillan.

Bevington, D. and Dixon, C. (2005), 'Movement-relevant theory: Rethinking social movement scholarship and activism', *Social Movement Studies*, 4(3): 185–208.

Bhopal Survivors' Movement Study (2009), *Bhopal Survivors Speak: Emergent Voices from a People's Movement*, Edinburgh: Word Power Books.

Bianchi, H. and Van Swaaningen, R. eds (1986), *Abolitionism: Towards a Non-Repressive Approach to Crime*, Amsterdam: Free University Press.

Birchall, J. (1994), *Co-op. The People's Business*, Manchester: Manchester University Press.

Blakey, H. (2014), *CommUnity Review*. Unpublished.

Blakey, H., Chester, G. and Pearce, J. (2006), *Minorities Within Minorities: Beneath the Surface of South Asian Participation*, York: Joseph Rowntree Foundation.

Bloomsbury Group (2012), Annual Report. Available at: http://www.bloomsbury-ir.co.uk/annual_reports/2012/pdf/2012ar.pdf (accessed 18 July 2016).

Boden, R. and Epstein, D. (2006), 'Managing the research imagination? Globalisation and research in higher education', *Globalisation, Societies and Education*, 4(2): 223–236.

Boden, R., Ciancanelli, P. and Wright, S. (2012), 'Trust universities? Governance for postcapitalist futures', *Journal of Co-operative Studies*, 45(2): 16–24.

Bok, D. (2009), *Universities in the Marketplace: The Commercialization of Higher Education*, Princeton, NJ: Princeton University Press.

Bolden, R., Gosling, J. and O'Brien, A. (2014), 'Citizens of the academic community? A societal perspective on leadership in UK higher education', *Studies in Higher Education*, 39(5): 754–770.

Bolden, R., Gosling, J., Maturano, A. and Dennison, P. (2003), 'A review of leadership theory and competency frameworks', working paper, University of Exeter: Centre for Leadership Studies.

Bolden, R., Petrov, G. and Gosling, J. (2009), 'Distributed leadership in higher education rhetoric and reality', *Educational Management Administration and Leadership*, 37: 257–277.

Bonefeld, W. (1987), 'Open Marxism', *Common Sense*, 1: 34–48.

Bonefeld, W., Gunn, R., Psychopedis, K. eds (1992), *Open Marxism: Volume. 2: Theory and Practice*, London: Pluto Press.

Bookchin, M. (1990), 'The Meaning of Confederalism', *The Anarchist Library*. Available at: http://theanarchistlibrary.org/library/murray-bookchin-the-meaning-of-confederalism (accessed 18 July 2016).

Bourdieu, P. (2010), *Distinction: A Social Critique of the Judgement of Taste*, London: Routledge.

Bousquet, M. (2008), *How the University Works: Higher Education and the Low-Wage Nation*, New York: New York University Press.

Bradley, R.L. (2011), 'Oil Company Earnings: Reality Over Rhetoric', *Forbes*, 10 May 2011. Available at: http://www.forbes.com/2011/05/10/oil-company-earnings.html (accessed 21 January 2014).

Bradshaw, A. (2014), Community University Field Diary. Unpublished.

Britton, J., Deardon, L., Shephard, N. and Vignoles, A. (2016), 'How English Domiciled Graduate Earnings Vary with Gender, Institution Attended, Subject and Socioeconomic Background', London: Institute for Fiscal Studies. Available at: http://www.ifs.org.uk/uploads/publications/wps/wp201606.pdf (accessed 18 July 2016).

Brookfield, S. and Preskill, S. (2008), *Learning as a Way of Leading: Lessons from the Struggle for Social Justice*, San Francisco, CA: Jossey Bass.

Brown, P., Cabell, D., Chakravarti, A., Cohen, B., Delamothe, T., Eisen, M., Grivell, L., Guédon, J-C, Hawley, R.S., Johnson, R., Kirschner, M., Lipman, D., Lutzker, A., Marincola, E., Roberts, R., Rubin, G., Schloegl, R., Siegel, V., So, A., Suber, P., Varmus, H., Velterop, J., Walport, M. and Watson, L. (2003), 'Bethesda Statement on Open Access Publishing', Cambridge, MA: Digital Access to Scholarship at Harvard. Available at: http://dash.harvard.edu/handle/1/4725199 (accessed 18 July 2016).

Brown, R. and Carasso, H. (2013), *Everything for Sale? The Marketisation of UK Higher Education*, Oxon: Routledge.

Bryman, A. (2004), *Social Research Methods, Second Edition*, Oxford: Oxford University Press.

Bryman, A. (2007), 'Effective leadership in higher education: A literature review', *Studies in Higher Education*, 32(6): 693–710.

Bujra, J. and Pearce, J. (2011), *Saturday Night and Sunday Morning: The Bradford Riot and Beyond*, Bradford: Vertical Editions.

Burnes, B., Wend, P. and By, R. (2014), 'The changing face of English universities: reinventing collegiality for the twenty-first century', *Studies in Higher Education*, 39(6): 905–926.

Burnham, P. (1992), 'Method and myth in political research: A practical guide for research students', *Politics*, 12(1): 3–8.

Burns, S. (2007), 'Mapping Dance: Entrepreneurship and Professional Practice in Dance Higher Education', Higher Education Academy. Available at: https://www.heacademy.ac.uk/sites/default/files/mapping-dance.pdf (accessed 18 July 2016).

Butler, N, and Spoelstra, S. (2015), 'The Tyranny of Excellence Is Hurting Research', Social Science Space, 6 February 2015. Available at: http://www.socialsciencespace.com/2015/02/the-tyranny-of-excellence-is-hurting-research/ (accessed 18 July 2016)

Caffentzis, G. (2010), 'The future of "The Commons": Neoliberalism's "Plan B" or the original disaccumulation of capital?', *New Formations*, 69: 23–41.

Caldart, R.S. and the Movement of Landless Workers (2011), 'Pedagogy of the Landless, Brazil', in T. Wrigley, P. Thomson and B. Lingard, *Changing Schools: Alternative Ways to Make a World of Difference*, 71–84, London: Routledge.

Callender, C. and Scott, P. eds (2013), *Browne and Beyond: Modernizing English Higher Education*, London: Institute of Education Press.

Canaan, J. (2010), 'Analysing a "neoliberal moment" in English higher education today', *Learning and Teaching*, 3(2): 55–72.

Canaan, J. (2011), 'Critical Pedagogy in, Against and Beyond the Neoliberalised University', ESRC Seminar Global Citizenship as a Graduate Attribute, University College London, 14 October 2011. Available at: http://www2.wlv.ac.uk/celt/ESRC_Seminar/Pedagogies_for_Undertstanding_and_engaging%20_in_a_globalised_world.pdf (accessed 18 July 2016).

Canaan, J. (2012), 'Critical Education In and Against the Neoliberalised University: An English Perspective'. Available at: http://andreasbieler.net/wp-content/files/Canaan%20Critical%20pedagogy.pdf (accessed 18 July 2016).

Canaan, J. (2013), 'Joyce Canaan on the Neoliberal University, Critical Pedagogy and Popular Education', in S. Cowden and G. Singh, S. Amsler, J. Canaan and S. Motta (eds), *Acts of Knowing: Critical Pedagogy in, Against and Beyond the University*, London: Bloomsbury.

Canaan, J. (2013), 'Resisting the neoliberal university: what critical pedagogy can offer', *Journal for Critical Education Policy Studies*, 11(2): 16–56. Available at: http://www.jceps.com/archives/426 (accessed 18 July 2016).

Canaan, J. and Shumar, W. (2011), *Structure and Agency in the Neoliberal University*, London: Routledge.

Cantwell, B. and Kauppinen, I. eds (2014), *Academic Capitalism in the Age of Globalization*, Baltimore, MD: John Hopkins University Press.

Carey, J. (1992), *The Intellectual and the Masses: Pride and Prejudice Among the Intelligensia, 1880–1939*, London: Faber and Faber.

Casey, J, Hides, S. and Shaw J. (2013), 'Taking Care of Business: Reimagining the Art College in the 21st Century', European League of Arts Institutions (ELIA) publication. Available at: http://www.elia-artschools.org/documents/taking-care-of-business-reimagining-the-art-college-in-the-21st-century (accessed 18 July 2016).

Cato, M.S. (2013), *The Bioregional Economy*, London: Earthscan.

Centeno, M. (2001), 'Disciplinary Society', in M.A. Centeno and F. Lopez-Alves (eds), *The Other Mirror*, 289–308, Princeton, NJ: Princeton University Press.

Chan, L., Cuplinskas, D., Eisen, M., Friend, F., Genova, Y., Guédon, J-C., Hagemann, M., Harnad, S., Johnson, R., Kupryte, R., La Manna, M., Rév I., Segbert, M., de Souza, S., Suber, P., Velterop, J. (2002), 'Budapest Open Access Initiative'. Available at: http://www.soros.org/openaccess/read.shtml (accessed 18 July 2016).

Chertkovskaya, E., Watt, P. and Spoelstra, S. (2013), 'Giving notice to employability', *Ephemera: Theory and Politics in Organization*, 13(4): 701–716.

Chesters, G. and Welsh, I. (2006), *Complexity and Social Movements*, London: Routledge.

Christie, N. (1982), *Limits to Pain*, London: Martin Robertson.

CICOPA (2011), 'World Standards of Social Cooperatives, International Organization of Industrial, Artisanal and Service Producers' Cooperatives, Brussels'. Available at: http://www.cicopa.coop/IMG/pdf/world_standards_of_social_cooperatives_en-2.pdf (accessed 18 July 2016).

Clarke, S. (2005), 'The Neoliberal Theory of Society', in A. Saad-Filho and D. Johnston (eds), *Neoliberalism: A Critical Reader*, London: Pluto Press.

Cleaver, H. (1993), 'Theses on the Secular Crisis'. Available at: https://la.utexas.edu/users/hcleaver/secularcrisis.html (accessed 18 July 2016).

Cockburn, C. and Blackburn, R. eds (1969), *Student Power: Problems, Diagnosis, Action*, Harmondsworth, Middlesex: Penguin.

Cohen, S. (1988), *Against Criminology*, New Brunswick, NJ: Transaction Books.

College Herald (1916), quotation, 3(1) May: 2.

Collini, S. (2007), *Absent Minds: Intellectuals in Britain*, Oxford: Oxford University Press.

Collini, S. (2012), *What Are Universities For?* London: Penguin.

Collini, S. (2013), 'Sold Out', *London Review of Books*, 35(20): 3–12.

Collins, C. (2006), '"The Scottish Executive is open for business": The New Regeneration Statement, The Royal Bank of Scotland and the Community Voices Network', *Variant*, 26. Available at: http://www.variant.org.uk (accessed 18 July 2016).

Connell, A. (2015), 'CDE #endweek5blues Rally', *Varsity*. Available at: http://www.varsity.co.uk/news/8303 (accessed 18 July 2016).

Cook, D. (2013), *Realising the Cooperative University*, Manchester: The Cooperative College.
Cooke, B. and Kathari, U. (2001), *Participation: The New Tyranny?* London: Zed books.
Co-operative Congress (1919), 'National Co-operative War Memorial', *Co-operative Congress*, Manchester: Co-operative Union.
Co-operative Union (1919), *General Co-operative Survey*, Manchester: Co-operative Union.
Cornwall, A. (2002), 'Making Spaces, Changing Places: Situating Participation in Development', *IDS Working Paper 170*, Brighton: Institute of Development Studies.
Cowden, S. and Singh, G., Amsler, S., Canaan, J. and Motta, S. eds (2013), *Acts of Knowing: Critical Pedagogy in, Against and Beyond the University*, London: Bloomsbury.
Cocks, J. (2014), *Building Better Relationships: Family Inclusion Strategies Hunter*, Newcastle: FISH Publications.
Cox, L. and Nilsen, A. (2014), *We Make Our Own History: Marxism and Social Movements in the Twilight of Neoliberalism*, London: Pluto Press.
Critchley, P. (1997), Beyond Modernity and Postmodernity, Pt 2: Active Materialism, 1997. Available at: https://mmu.academia.edu/PeterCritchley/Books (accessed 18 July 2016).
Crotty, D. (2015), 'Is It True that Most Open Access Journals Do Not Charge an APC? Sort of. It Depends', *The Scholarly Kitchen*, 26 August 2015. Available at: http://scholarlykitchen.sspnet.org/2015/08/26/do-most-oa-journals-not-charge-an-apc-sort-of-it-depends/ (accessed 18 July 2016).
Crowther, J. (2013), 'The international popular education network: its purpose and contribution', *Rhizome Freirean*, 14, Xátiva, Valencia: Instituto Paulo Freire de España.
Crowther, J., Hemmi, A. and Scandrett, E. (2012), 'Learning environmental justice and adult education in a Scottish community campaign against fish farming', *Local Environment*, 17(1): 115–130.
Crowther, J., Hemmi, A., Martin, I. and Scandrett, E. (2009), 'Real and Virtual Margins of Resistance: The Struggle for Environmental Knowledge and the Contribution of Information and Communication Technologies to Campaigning', in R. Evans (ed.), *Local Development, Community and Adult Learning – Learning Landscapes Between the Mainstream and the Margins*, Magdeburg: Nisaba Verlag.
Crowther, P. (2002), *The Transhistorical Image: Philosophizing Art and Its History*, Cambridge: Cambridge University Press.
Crowther, P. (2009), *The Phenomenology of the Visual Arts (Even the Frame)*, Stanford, CA: Stanford University Press.
Curcio, A. (2014), 'Practicing militant inquiry: Composition, strike and betting in the logistics workers struggles in Italy', *Ephemera: Theory and Politics in Organization*, 14(3): 375–390.
Dalla Costa, M. and James, S. (1972), *The Power of Women and the Subversion of Community*, Bristol: Falling Wall Press.
Davie, G.E. (1961), *The Democratic Intellect: Scotland and Her Universities in the Nineteenth Century*, Edinburgh: University Press.
Davie, G.E. (1990), *The Democratic Intellect*, Edinburgh: Edinburgh University Press.
Davies, B. (2005), 'The (Im)possibility of intellectual work in neoliberal regimes', *Discourses: Studies in the Cultural Politics of Education*, 26(1): 1–14.

Davies, J.S. (2011), *Challenging Governance Theory: From Networks to Hegemony*, University of Bristol: Policy Press.

Davies, W. (2014), *The Limits of Neoliberalism: Authority, Sovereignty and the Logic of Competition*, Thousand Oaks, CA: Sage.

Davis, A. (2003), *Are Prisons Obsolete?* New York: Seven Stories Press.

Dawson, J. (2006), *Ecovillages: New Frontiers for Sustainability*, Schumacher Briefings no. 12, Dartington: Green Books.

Day, S.V., Fleenor, J.W., Atwater, L.E., Sturm, R.E. and McKee, R.A. (2014), 'Advances in leader and leadership development: A review of 25 years of research and theory', *The Leadership Quarterly*, 25(1): 63–82.

De Angelis, M. (2004), 'Separating the doer and the deed: Capital and the continuous character of enclosures', *Historical Materialism*, 12 (2): 57–87.

De Angelis, M. and Harvie, D. (2009), '"Cognitive Capitalism" and the rat-race: How capital measures immaterial labour in British Universities', *Historical Materialism*, 17: 3–30.

de Sousa Santos, B. (2014), *Epistemologies of the South: Justice Against Epistemicide*, Boulder, Colorado: Paradigm Publishers.

Deem, R., Fulton, O., Read, M. and Watson, S. (2001), *New Managerialism and the Management of UK Universities. End of Award Report*, Swindon: Economic and Social Research Council.

Deem, R., Hillyard, S. and Reed, M. (2007), *Knowledge, Higher Education and New Public Managerialism: The Changing Management of UK Universities*, Oxford: Oxford University Press.

Dent, J.J. (1928), *Co-operation and the Working Men's College*, Manchester: Co-operative Union.

DBIS (2011), 'Higher Education: Students at the Heart of the System', London: BIS. Available at: https://www.gov.uk/government/uploads/system/uploads/attachment_data/file/31384/11-944-higher-education-students-at-heart-of-system.pdf (accessed 18 July 2016).

DBIS (2016), 'Success as a Knowledge Economy: Teaching excellence, social mobility and student choice'. Available at: https://www.gov.uk/government/uploads/system/uploads/attachment_data/file/523546/bis-16-265-success-as-a-knowledge-economy-web.pdf (accessed 18 July 2016).

Department of Education and Science National Advisory Council on Art Education (1970), *The Structure of Art and Design Education in the Further Education Sector*, London: Her Majesty's Stationary Office.

DeWalt, B.R. (1994), 'Using indigenous knowledge to improve agriculture and natural resource management', *Human Organization*, 53(2): 123–131.

Dewey, J. (1925), *Experience and Nature*, London: Dover Publications.

Dinerstein, A. (2015), *The Politics of Autonomy in Latin America: The Art of Organising Hope*, London: Palgrave Macmillan.

Directory of Open Access Journals (2014), Journals by Publication Charges. Available at: http://www.doaj.org/doaj?func=byPublicationFeeanduiLanguage=en (accessed 20 January 2014).

Dobash, R.E. and Dobash, R.P. (1992), *Women, Violence and Social Change*, London and New York: Routledge.

Docherty, T. (2011), *For the University: Democracy and the Future of the Institution*, London: Bloomsbury Academic.

Docherty, T. (2015), *Universities at War*, London and Los Angeles, CA: Sage Swifts.

Doherty, T. (2006), *Aesthetic Democracy*, Stanford, CA: Stanford University Press.

Doherty, B and Doyle, T. (2013), *Environmentalism, Resistance and Solidarity: The Politics of Friends of the Earth International*, London: Palgrave Macmillan.

Dopson, Sue, Ferlie, Ewan, McGivern, Gerry, Fischer, Michael D., Ledger, Jean, Behrens, Sonja and Wilson, Sarah (2016), *The Impact of Leadership and Leadership Development in Higher Education: A Review of the Literature and Evidence*, London: Leadership Foundation for Higher Education (Research and development series).

Dunion, K and Scandrett, E (2003), 'Environmental Justice in Scotland as a Response to Poverty in a Northern Nation', in J. Agyeman, R.D Bullard and B. Evans (eds), *Just Sustainabilities: Development in an Unequal World*, 311–322, London: Earthscan.

Duran, E., Firehammer, J. and Gonzalez, J. (2008), 'Liberation psychology as the path toward healing cultural soul wounds, *Journal of Counseling and Development*, 86(3): 288–295.

Durao, F. (2008), *Modernism and Coherence: Four Chapters of a Negative Aesthetics*, Frankfurt: Peter Lang.

Dyer-Witheford, N. (1999), *Cyber Marx: Cycles and Circuits of Struggle in High Technology Capitalism*, Urbana and Chicago: University of Illinois Press.

Eacott, S. (2013), '"Leadership" and the social: Time, space and the epistemic', *International Journal of Educational Management*, 27(1): 91–101.

EduFactory Collective (2009), 'Toward a Global Autonomous University: Cognitive Labor, the Production of Knowledge and Exodus from the Education Factory', *Autonomedia*. Available at: https://libcom.org/library/towards-global-autonomous-university-edu-factory-collective (accessed 18 July 2016).

Enfield, A.H. (1927), *Co-operation: Its Problems and Possibilities*, London: Longmans, Green and Co.

Erikson, J.E. (2001), 'Philosophy and theory', *Journal of Dramatic Theory and Criticism*, 16(1): 143–148.

Estrada, O. (2014) 'The Masked Intellectual: Marcos and the Speech of the Rainforest', in D.A. Castillo and S. A. Day (eds), *Mexican Public Intellectuals*, 197–216, New York: Palgrave Macmillan.

Evans, L., Homer, M. and Rayner, S. (2013), 'Professors as academic leaders: The perspectives of "the Led"', *Educational Management, Administration and Leadership*, 41(5): 674–689.

Eve, M. (2014), *Open Access and the Humanities: Contexts, Controversies and the Future*, Cambridge: Cambridge University Press. Available at: http://dx.doi.org/10.1017/CBO9781316161012 (accessed 18 July 2016).

Fairbrother, S. (1919), quoted in *Co-operative Congress*, Manchester: Co-operative Union.

Family Inclusion Network (2007), *Family Inclusion in Child Protection Practice*, Brisbane, QLD: FIN.

Fanon, F. (1968), *Black Skin, White Masks*, New York: Grove Press.

Federici, S. (1980), 'Wages Against Housework', in E. Malos (ed.), *The Politics of Housework*, 253–261, London: Allison and Busby.

Ferguson, R.S. and Lovell, S.T. (2014), 'Permaculture for agroecology: Design, movement, practice and worldview. A review', *Agronomy for Sustainable Development*, 34(2): 251–274.

Ferguson, R.S. and Lovell, S.T. (2015), 'Grassroots engagement with transition to sustainability: Diversity and modes of participation in the international permaculture movement', *Ecology and Society*, 20(4): 39. http://dx.doi.org/10.5751/ES-08048-200439.

Fischer, M.D., Morris, T. and Dopson, S. (2015), 'Counter-programmatic space and its role in leadership development: A study of 60 Research and Development Series senior

leadership programmes at University of Oxford Saïd Business School', *Asia-Pacific Researchers in Organisation Studies and European Group for Organizational Studies Conference*, Sydney, Australia.
Ford, B. (2010), 'What are conservatoires for? discourses of purpose in the contemporary conservatoire', PhD Thesis, Institute of Education, University of London. Available at: http://ethos.bl.uk/OrderDetails.do?uin=uk.bl.ethos.536511 (accessed 18 July 2016).
Foucault, Michel ([1975] 1991), *Discipline and Punish: The Birth of the Prison*, Harmondsworth: Penguin.
Foucault, Michel (2008), *The Birth of Biopolitics: Lectures at the College de France 1978–1979*, ed. Michel Senellart, trans. Graham Burchell, Basingstoke: Palgrave Macmillan.
Francis, R. (2015), 'A Permaculture Oddysey: 1977 to present', Presentation to IPC-12, London, September 2015.
Freeman, J. (1996), 'The Tyranny of Structurelessness' [online], Available at: http://struggle.ws/pdfs/tyranny.pdf, pp. 1-5 (accessed 2 July 2013).
Freire, P. (1970), *Pedagogy of the Oppressed*, London: Continuum.
Fuchs, C. (2013), 'Open Access Journals and Capitalism: An Interview with Christian Fuchs', *Christian Fuchs*, 24 May 2013. Available at: http://fuchs.uti.at/901/ (accessed 18 July 2016).
Fuller, S. (2005), *The Intellectual: The Positive Power of Negative Thinking*, Cambridge: Icon Books.
Gaia University (2016), Available at: http://www.gaiauniversity.org/ (accessed 18 July 2016).
Gall, G. (2005), *The Political Economy of Scotland. Red Scotland? Radical Scotland?* Cardiff: University of Wales Press.
Gallagher, C. (2011), 'From the Reactive to the Creative', in D. Hancox (ed.), *Fightback: A Reader on the Winter Protest*, 41–45, London: Open Democracy.
Gallagher, S. and Zahavi, D. (2008), *The Phenomenological Mind: An Introduction to Philosophy of Mind and Cognitive Science*, London: Routledge.
Gallant, A. (2014), 'Symbolic interactions and the development of women leaders in higher education', *Gender, Work and Organization*, 21(3): 203–216.
Gelpi, E. (1979), *The Future of Lifelong Education*, Manchester: University of Manchester Press.
Gelpi, E. (1985), *Lifelong Education and International Relations*, London: Croom Helm.
Gill, R. (2009), 'Breaking the Silence, the Hidden Injuries of Neoliberal Academia', in R. Flood and R. Gill (eds), *Secrecy and Silence in the Research Process: Feminist Reflections*, 228–244, London: Routledge.
Giroux, H. (2007), 'Utopian Thinking in Dangerous Times: Critical Pedagogy and the Project of Educated Hope', in M. Cote, R.J.F. Day, and G. de Peuter (eds), *Utopian Pedagogy*, 25–43, Toronto: University of Toronto Press.
Giroux, H. (2011), Occupy Colleges Now: Students as the New Public Intellectuals, *Truthout*, 21 November 2011. Available at: http://www.truth-out.org/news/item/5046:occupy-colleges-now–students-as-the-new-public-intellectuals (accessed 18 July 2016).
Giroux, H. (2013), 'Radical Democracy Against Cultures of Violence', *Truthout*, 17 December 2013. Available at: http://www.truth-out.org/opinion/item/20669-radical-democracy-against-cultures-of-violence (accessed 18 July 2016).
Giroux, H. (2014), *Neoliberalism's War on Higher Education*, Chicago: Haymarket Books.
Goldman, L. (1995), *Dons and Workers: Adult Education Since 1850*, Oxford: Clarendon.

Gonzalez de Allen, G. (2006), 'Enrique Dussel and Manuel Zapata Olivella: An exploration of De-Colonial, Diasporic and Trans-Modern Selves and the politics of recognition', *Worlds and Knowledges Otherwise*, 1(3): 1–11.
Gough, M. (2005), *The Artist as Producer: Russian Constructivism in Revolution*, Berkeley, CA: University of California Press.
Gramsci, A. (1971), *Selections from the Prison Notebooks*, Q. Hoare and G. Nowell Smith (eds), London: Lawrence and Wishart.
Grant, B. (2012), 'Elsevier Abandons Anti-Open Access Bill', *The Scientist*, 28 February 2012. Available at: http://www.the-scientist.com/?articles.view/articleNo/31798/title/Elsevier-Abandons-Anti-Open-Access-Bill/ (accessed 18 July 2016).
Griffin, C. (1983), *Curriculum Theory in Adult and Lifelong Education*, Monograph Collection (Matt - Pseudo).
Gunn, R. (1987), 'Practical reflexivity in Marx', *Common Sense*, 1: 39–41.
Gunn, R. (1989a), 'In defence of a consensus theory of truth', *Common Sense*, 7: 63–81.
Gunn, R. (1989b), 'Marxism and philosophy: A critique of critical realism', *Capital and Class*, 13(1): 1–29.
Gunn, R. (2013), 'Common Sense, Scottish Thought and Current Politics, Richard Gunn: Papers on Political Theory', *Richard Gunn*. Available at: http://www.richard-gunn.com/pdf/scottish_article.pdf (accessed 18 July 2016).
Gunn, R. (2014a), 'Common Sense, Scottish Thought and Current Politics', *Richard Gunn*. Available at: http://www.richard-gunn.com/pdf/scottish_article.pdf (accessed 18 July 2016).
Gunn, R. (2014b), 'New Priorities', *Richard Gunn*. Available at: http://www.richard-gunn.com/pdf/priorities.pdf (accessed 18 July 2016).
Gunn, R. (2015), 'A Note on the Senses: Common Sense from Aristotle to Marx and Beyond', Heathwood Institute and Press. Available at: http://www.heathwoodpress.com/wp-content/uploads/2015/08/A-NOTE-ON-THE-SENSES_Richard-Gunn_Heathwood-Press-2015.pdf (accessed 18 July 2016).
Gunn, R., Smith, R.C. and Wilding, A. (2015), 'Assemblies for democracy: A theoretical framework', *Heathwood Journal of Critical Theory*, 1(1). Available at: https://assembliesfordemocracy.org/2015/07/14/assemblies-for-democracy-a-theoretical-framework-by-richard-gunn-r-c-smith-and-adrian-wilding/ (accessed 18 July 2016).
Gurney, P. (1996) *Co-operative Culture and the Politics of Consumption in England 1870–1930*, Manchester: Manchester University Press.
Haiven, M. (2014), *Crises of Imagination, Crises of Power: Capitalism, Creativity and the Commons*, London: Zed Books.
Haiven, M. and Khasnabish, A. (2014), *The Radical Imagination: Social Movements Research in the Age of Austerity*, London: Zed Books.
Halffman, W. and Radder, H. (2015), 'The academic manifesto: From an occupied to a public university', *Minerva Volume*, 53: 165–187.
Hall, F. (1915), *The Summer School for Co-operators*, Manchester: Co-operative Union.
Hall, F. (1918a), *Further Prospective Developments of Co-operative Education*, Manchester: Co-operative Union.
Hall, F. (1918b), *The Work of a Co-operative Educational Association*, Manchester: Co-operative Union.
Hall, F. (1919), *A Co-operative College*, 5th ed., Manchester: Co-operative Union.
Hall, F. (1923a), *The Necessity for Co-operative Education*, Manchester: Co-operative Union.

Hall, F. (1923b), *The Co-operator's Educational Fellowship*, Manchester: Co-operative Union.

Hall, F. (1928), *The Co-operative College and Its Work*, Manchester: Co-operative Union.

Hall, F. and Wakins, W.P. (1937), *Co-operation*, Manchester: Co-operative Union.

Hall, R. (2014), 'On the abolition of academic labour: The relationship between intellectual workers and mass intellectuality', *tripleC: Communication, Capitalism & Critique*, 12(2): 822–837.

Hall, R. (2015a), 'For a political economy of massive open online courses', *Learning, Media and Technology*, 40(3): 265–286.

Hall, R. (2015b), 'The University and the Secular Crisis', *Open Library of Humanities*, 1(1), p.e6. doi:http://doi.org/10.16995/olh.15.

Hall, R. (2016a), Technology-enhanced learning and co-operative practice against the neoliberal university, *Interactive Learning Environments*. Available at: http://www.tandfonline.com/doi/full/10.1080/10494820.2015.1128214 (accessed 18 July 2016).

Hall, R. (2016b), 'Openness and Power', in M. Peters (ed.), *Encyclopedia of Educational Philosophy and Theory*, 1–6, Springer Singapore. Available at: http://link.springer.com/referenceworkentry/10.1007/978-981-287-532-7_222-1 (accessed 18 July 2016).

Hall, R. and Bowles, K. (2016), 'Re-engineering higher education: The subsumption of academic labour and the exploitation of anxiety', *Workplace: A Journal of Academic Labour*, 28: 30–47.

Hall, R. and Smyth, K. (2016), 'Dismantling the curriculum in higher education', *Open Library of Humanities*, 2(1): e11. doi:http://doi.org/10.16995/olh.66.

Hansard, Series 5 HC (2010), 'Higher Education Funding', 3rd November, 517(64): 924–946. Available at: www.publications.parliament.uk/pa/cm201011/cmhansrd/cm101103/debtext/1011030001.htm#10110358000003 (accessed 18 July 2016).

Hardt, M. and Negri, A. (2000), *Empire*, Cambridge, MA: Harvard University Press.

Hardt, M. and Negri, A. (2005), *Multitude: War and Democracy in the Age of Empire*, London: Penguin Books.

Hardt, M. and Virno, P. (2006), *Radical Thought in Italy: A Potential Politics*, Minneapolis, MN: University of Minnesota Press.

Harney, S. (2002), *State Work: Public Administration and Mass Intellectuality*, Durham: Duke University Press.

Harney, S. (2009), 'Extreme neo-liberalism: An introduction', *Ephemera: Theory and Politics in Organization*, 9(4): 318–329.

Harney, S. and Moten, F. (1998), 'Doing Academic Work', in R. Marin (ed.), *Chalk Lines: The Politics of Work in the Managed University*, 154–180, London: Duke University Press.

Harney, S. and Moten, F. (2013), *The Undercommons; Fugitive Planning and Black Study*, Brooklyn: Minor Comospitions.

Harrison, J.F.C. (1961), *Learning and Living 1790–1960*, London: Routledge and Kegan Paul.

Harvey, D. (2005), *A Brief History of Neoliberalism*, London: Oxford University Press.

Harvey, D. (2006), *Spaces of Global Capitalism: Towards a Theory of Uneven Geographical Development*, London: Verso.

Harvie, D. (2006), 'Value-production and struggle in the classroom', *Capital and Class*, 88: 1–32.

Harvie, J. (2013), *Fair Play*, Basingstoke: Palgrave Macmillan.

Haworth R. and Elmore J. eds (2017), *Out of the Ruins: Emerging Radical Informal Learning Spaces*, Oakland, CA: PM Press.

HEFCE (2013), 'Higher Education in England: Impact of the 2012 Reforms', Report 2013/03, Bristol: HEFCE.

Hegel, G.W.F. (1931), *The Phenomenology of Mind*, 2nd ed., London: Allen and Unwin/ Humanities Press.

Helms, G., French, L., Bradley, L. and the Variant Editorial Group (2016), 'Divergence and Agonism: The different the other and the one who disagrees, Cultural communication and democracy in Scotland', *Variant*. Available at: http://www.variant.org.uk (accessed 19 July 2016).

Hemphill, D. and Leskowitz, S. (2013), 'DIY activists: Self-directed informal learning, communities of practice and radical knowledge-sharing', *Adult Education Quarterly*, 63(1): 57–77.

Henfrey, T. (2010), 'Cultivating Community, Gardening Anthropology: Permaculture, Local Food and Engaged Research', presented at the panel session 'Crisis, Anthropology and the Garden: local resilience and alternative food production', at the 11th biennial conference of the European Association of Social Anthropologists, Maynooth, Ireland, 25th August 2010.

Henfrey, T. (2014), 'Edge, Empowerment and Sustainability: Para-Academic Practice as Applied Permaculture Design', in A. Wardrop and D. Withers (eds), *The Para-Academic Handbook: A Toolkit for Making-Learning-Creating-Acting*, 121–139, London: HammerOn Press.

Henfrey, T. and Brangwyn, B. (2013), *The Transition Research Primer v1.0*, Totnes: Transition Research Network. Available at: www.transitionresearchnetwork.org /transition-research-primer.html (accessed 18 July 2016).

Henfrey, T., and Kenrick, J. (2015), 'Climate, Commons and Hope: The Transition Movement in Global Perspective', supplement to N. Buxton and B. Hayes (eds), *The Secure and the Dispossessed*, London: Pluto Press. Available at: climatesecurityagenda. org/wp-content/uploads/2015/11/018138c_TNI_Climate-Commons-Hope.pdf (accessed 18 July 2016).

Henfrey, T. and Penha-Lopes, G. (2015), *Permaculture and Climate Change: Inspiring Social, Ecological, Economic and Cultural Responses*, East Meon: Permanent Publications.

Henkel, M. (2000), *Academic Identities and Policy Change in Higher Education*, London: Jessica Kingsley Publishers.

HESA (2016), 'Income and Expenditure of Higher Education Providers in 2014/15', Higher Education Statistics Agency. Available at: https://www.hesa.ac.uk/pr229 (accessed 18 July 2016).

Hickey Moody, A. and Page, T. (2015), *Arts Pedagogy and Critical Resistance: New Materialisms*, London: Rowman and Littlefield International.

Hicks, B. (2001), *Philosophy: The Best of Bill Hicks*, Rykodisc.

Hill, D. ed. (2008), *Contesting Neoliberal Education: Public Resistance and Collective Advance*, London: Routledge.

Holloway, J. (2010), *Crack Capitalism*, London: Pluto Press.

Holloway, J. (2016), *In, Against and Beyond Capitalism*, Oakland, CA: PM Press.

Holmwood, J. ed. (2011), *A Manifesto for the Public University,* London and New York: Bloomsbury Academic.

Holmwood, J. (2013a), 'Markets versus Dialogue: The debate over open access ignores competing philosophies of openness', *Impact of Social Sciences*, 21 October 2013. Available at: http://blogs.lse.ac.uk/impactofsocialsciences/2013/10/21/markets-versus -dialogue/ (accessed 18 July 2016).

Holmwood, J. (2013b), 'The neo-liberal knowledge regime, inequality and social critique', *openDemocracy*, 19 July 2013. Available at: http://www.opendemocracy.net/john-holmwood/neo-liberal-knowledge-regime-inequality-and-social-critique (accessed 18 July 2016).

hooks, bell (1990), *Yearning: Race, Gender and Cultural Politics*, Cambridge, MA: South End Press.

Hopkins, R. ed. (2005), 'Kinsale 2021: An Energy Descent Action Plan', Available at: transitionculture.org/wp-content/uploads/KinsaleEnergyDescentActionPlan.pdf (accessed 18 July 2016).

Hopkins, R. (2008), *The Transition Handbook*, Totnes: Green Books.

Hopkins, R. (2011), *The Transition Companion*, Totnes: Green Books.

Hopkins, R. (2013), *The Power of Just Doing Stuff*, Cambridge: UIT/Green Books.

Hopkins, R. (2015), *21 Stories of Transition*, Totnes: Transition Network.

Hoppe, B. and Reinelt, C. (2010), 'Social network analysis and the evaluation of leadership networks', *The Leadership Quarterly*, 21: 600–619.

Hornsey, H. (1919), quoted in *Co-operative Congress*, Manchester: Co-operative Union.

Howell, J., and Pearce, J. (2001), *Civil Society and Development*, Boulder, CO: Lynne Rienner.

Icaza, R. and Vazquez, R. (2013), 'Social struggles as epistemic struggles', *Development and Change*, 44(3): 683–704.

Illich, I. (1973), *Deschooling Society*, Harmondsworth: Penguin.

Informa (2012), Annual Report. Available at: http://www.informa.com/Documents/Investor%20Relations/Corporate%20Governance/Informa%20Annual%20Report%-202012-web.pdf (accessed 18 July 2016).

Integral Permaculture Academy (2016), Available at: http://integralpermaculture.org (accessed 18 July 2016).

International Co-operative Alliance (1995), 'Statement on the Co-operative Identity: Co-operative Principles for the 21st century', International Co-operative Alliance. Available at: www.ica.coop/coop/principles.html (accessed 18 July 2016).

IRHEFSF (2010), 'Securing a Sustainable Future for Higher Education: An Independent Review of Higher Education Funding and Student Finance'. Available at: www.independent.gov.uk/browne-report (accessed 18 July 2016).

Issa, D. (2014), 'Brazil Praxis of empowerment: Mistica and mobilizationin Brazil's landless workers' movement (MST)', in R. Stahler-Sholk, H.E. Vanden and M. Becker (eds), *Rethinking Latin American Social Movements: Radical Action from Below*, 85–100, London: Rowman and Littlefield.

Jacke, D. and Toensmeier, E. (2005), *Edible Forest Gardens: Ecological Vision and Theory for Temperate Climate Permaculture*, White River Junction: Chelsea Green.

Jacoby, R. (2000), *The Last Intellectuals: American Culture in the Age of Academe*, New York: Basic Books.

James, J. (2013), *Transcending the Talented Tenth: Black Leaders and American Intellectuals*, New York: Routledge.

Jarvis, C., Gulati, A., McCririck, V. and Simpson, P. (2013), 'Leadership matters: Tensions in evaluating leadership development', *Advances in Developing Human Resources*, 15(1): 27–45.

Jisc (n.d.), 'Publisher copyright policies and self-archiving', SHERPA/RoMEO. Available at: http://www.sherpa.ac.uk/romeo/ (accessed 18 July 2016).

Johnson, P. (2015), 'The Visible Minority: Nowhere to Be Seen in the Academy', in C. Alexander and J. Arday (eds) *Aiming Higher, Inequality and Diversity in the Academy*, 13–14, London: Runnymede.

Johnson, R. (1993), '"Really Useful Knowledge": Radical Education and Working Class Culture, 1790–1848', in J. Clarke, C. Crichter, and R. Johnson (eds), *Working Class Culture: Studies in History and Theory*, 75–102, London: Hutchinson.
Jones, O. (2011), *Chavs: The Demonization of the Working Class*, London: Verso.
Kamenetz, A. (2010), *DIYU: Edupunks, Edupreneurs and the Coming Transformation of Higher Education*, White River Junction: Chelsea Green Publishing.
Kane, L. (2001), *Popular Education and Social Change in Latin America*, London: Latin America Bureau.
Kautsky, K. (1903), 'The intellectuals and the workers', *Die Neue Zeit*, XXII(4): 125–126.
Kautsky, K. (1946), 'The intellectuals and the workers', *Fourth International*, 7(4): 125–126.
Kelly, R. (2013), I's the University a Factory?', *Mute Magazine*, 10 October 2013. Available at: http://www.metamute.org/editorial/reviews/university-factory (accessed 18 July 2016).
King, E. and Nesbit, P. (2015), 'Collusion with denial: Leadership development and its evaluation', *Journal of Management Development*, 34: 134–152.
Kinman, G. and Wray, S. (2013), 'Higher Stress: A Survey of Stress and Well-Being Among Staff in Higher Education', UCU. Available at: http://www.ucu.org.uk/media/pdf/4/5/HE_stress_report_July_2013.pdf (accessed 18 July 2016).
Klein, N. (2000), *No Logo*, London: Flamingo.
Klein, N. (2008), *The Shock Doctrine: The Rise of Disaster Capitalism*, London: Penguin.
Kunze, I. and Avelino, F. (2015), 'Social Innovation and the Global Ecovillage Network, Research Report', TRANSIT: EU SSH.2013.3.2-1 Grant agreement no: 613169.
Laclau, E. (2015), 'Ideology and Post-Marxism', *Journal of Political Ideologies*, 11(2): 103–114.
Larivière, V., Haustein, S. and Mongeon, P. (2016), 'The Oligopoly of Academic Publishers in the Digital Era', PLOS ONE. 10 June 2016. Available online: http://dx.doi.org/10.1371/journal.pone.0127502 (accessed 18 July 2016).
Larner, W. (2000), 'Neo-liberalism: Policy, ideology, governmentality', *Studies in Political Economy*, 63: 5–26.
Lawrence, S. and Sharma, U. (2002), 'Commodification of education and academic labour: Using the balanced scorecard in a university setting', *Critical Perspectives on Accounting*, 13(5): 661–677.
Laws, W.H. (1915), *The Functions of an Education Committee*, Manchester: Co-operative Union North Western Section.
Lazzarato, M. (1996), 'Immaterial Labour', in M. Hardt and P. Virno (eds), *Radical Thought in Italy: A Potential Politics*, 133–147, Minneapolis, MN: University of Minnesota Press.
Lefebvre, H. (2008), *The Production of Space*, Oxford: Wiley Blackwell.
Leher, R. and Vittoria, P. (2015), 'Social movements and critical pedagogy in Brazil: From the origins of popular education to the proposal of a proposal of a Permanent Forum', *Journal for Critical Education Policy* Studies, 13(3): 145–162.
Lewis, M. (2016), 'Student Loans Mythbusting: The truth about fees, loans and grants for 2015 and 2016 starters', *MoneySavingExpert.Com*. Available online: http://www.moneysavingexpert.com/students/student-loans-tuition-fees-changes#multiThree-tabTwo (accessed 18 July 2016).
Lindenschmidt, J.W. (2004), 'From virtual commons to virtual enclosures: Revolution and counter-revolution in the information age', *The Commoner*, 9: 1–20.
Lockyer, J. (2010), 'Intentional Community Carbon Reduction and Climate Change Action: From Ecovillages to Transition Towns', in M. Peters, S. Fudge and T. Jackson (eds), *Low Carbon Communities: Imaginative Approaches to Combating Climate Change Locally*, 197–215, Cheltenham: Edward Elgar.

Lockyer, J. and Veteto, J eds (2013), *Environmental Anthropology Engaging Ecotopia: Permaculture, Ecovillages and Bioregionalism*, Oxford: Berghahn.

Loke, G. (2015), 'Breaking the Race Inequality Cycle in Higher Education: A Change of Focus Is Needed to Break the Statistical Groundhog Day', in C. Alexander and J. Arday (eds), *Aiming Higher, Inequality and Diversity in the Academy*, 42–44, London: Runnymede.

Lomas, L. (2005), Organisational change and the shifting of the Locus of Power. In: European Conference on Educational Research. Dublin: Educol document, pp. 20. Available at http://www.leeds.ac.uk/educol/documents/143998.doc (accessed 3 March 2010).

London Edinburgh Weekend Return Group (1980), *In and Against The State*, London: Pluto Press.

Lorde, A. (2000), *The Uses of the Erotic: The Erotic as Power*, Tucson: Kore Press.

Loveday, V. (2014), 'Working-class participation, middle-class aspiration? Value, upward mobility and symbolic indebtedness in higher education', *The Sociological Review*, 63(3): 570–588.

Lugones, M. (2006), 'On complex communications', *Hypathia*, 21(3): 75–85.

Lugones, M. (2010), 'Toward a decolonial feminism', *Hypathia*, 25(4): 742–759.

Luhmann, N. (2000), *Art as Social System*, Stanford, CA: Stanford University Press.

Lunghi, A. and Wheeler, S. (2011), *Occupy Everything: Reflections on Why It Is Kicking Off Everywhere*, Brooklyn: Minor Compositions.

Mac Sheoin, T. and Pearce, F. (2014), 'Bhopal and after: The chemical industry as toxic capitalism', *Social Justice*, 41(1–2): 28–48.

Macfarlane, B. (2007), 'Defining and rewarding academic citizenship: The implications for university promotions policy', *Journal of Higher Education Policy and Management*, 29(3): 261–273.

Macfarlane, B. (2013), 'Professors as intellectual leaders: Formation, identity and role', *Studies in Higher Education*, 36(1): 57–73.

MacNamara, L. (2012), *People and Permaculture*, East Meon: Permanent Publications.

MacPherson, I. (2007), *One Path to Co-Operative Studies: A Selection of Papers and Studies*, Victoria: British Columbia Institute for Co-operative Studies.

Maffi, L. ed. (2001), *On Biocultural Diversity*, Washington, DC: Smithsonian Institute Press.

Maldonado-Torres, N. (2007), 'On the coloniality of being: Contributions to the development of a concept', *Cultural Studies*, 21(2): 240–270.

Malos, E. ed. (1980), *The Politics of Housework*, London: Allison and Busby.

Mansbridge, A. (1912), 'Educational Session at Congress', *Co-operative Congress*, 485–490, Manchester: Co-operative Union.

Manzerolle, V., 'The virtual debt factory: Towards an analysis of debt and abstraction in the American credit crisis', *TripleC: Cognition, Communication and Co-operation*, 10(2): 221–236.

Marshall, S. (2012), 'Educational middle change leadership in New Zealand: The meat in the sandwich', *International Journal of Educational Management*, 26(6): 502–528.

Marx, K. (1867), *The Value Form*, Appendix to the 1st German edition of *Capital Volume 1*. Available at: https://www.marxists.org/archive/marx/works/1867-c1/appendix.htm (accessed 10 April 2016).

Marx, K. (1993), *Grundrisse: Foundations of the Critique of Political Economy*, London: Penguin.

Marx, K. (2004), *Capital: A Critique of Political Economy, Vol. I*, London: Penguin Classics.

Maskell, D. and Robinson, I. (2002), *The New Idea of a University*, London: Imprint Academic.
Mathiesen, T. (1974), *The Politics of Abolition*, Oslo: Scandinavian University Books.
Mathiesen, T. (2015), *The Politics of Abolition Revisited*, London: Routledge.
Matthews, D. (2013), 'Inside a Co-operative University', *Times Higher Education*, 29th August 2013. Available at: https://www.timeshighereducation.com/features/inside-a-cooperative-university/2006776.article (accessed 18 July 2016).
Maxey, L. (2009), 'Dancing on a double-edge sword: Sustainability within university corp', *ACME: An International E-Journal for Critical Geographies*, 8(3): 440–453.
McGettigan, A. (2013), *The Great University Gamble: Money, Markets and the Future of Higher Education*, London: Pluto Press.
McGettigan, A. (2014), 'Managerialism, Democracy and the New Political Economy of English Higher Education', *Discover Society*. Available at: http://discoversociety.org/2014/02/15/focus-managerialism-democracy-and-the-new-political-economy-of-english-higher-education/ (accessed 18 July 2016).
McGettigan, A. Financialising the university [online]. Arena Magazine (Fitzroy, Vic), No. 128, Feb/Mar 2014: 39-41. Availability: http://search.informit.com.au/documentSummary;dn=147042592804322;res=IELHSS,ISSN:1039-1010 (accessed 10 March 2017).
McIntosh, A. (2004), *Soil and Soul: People Against Corporate Power*, London: Aurum Press.
McKay, G. (1998), *DIY Culture: Party and Protest in Nineties Britain*, London: Verso Books.
McLaren, P. (1995), *Critical Pedagogy and Predatory Culture: Oppositional Politics in a Postmodern*, London: Routledge.
Menke, C. (1999), *The Sovereignty of Art: Aesthetic Negativity in Adorno and Derrida*, Cambridge, MA: MIT Press.
Mercer, T.W. (1919), 'Co-operative Employés and the Co-operative College', *College Herald* 3(1): 2–3.
Merleau-Ponty, M. (1993), 'Indirect Language and the Voices of Silence', in *The Merleau-Ponty Aesthetics Reader: Philosophy and Painting*, trans. M. Smith, 76–120, Evanston, IL: Northwestern University Press.
Midgely, J. (2014), CommUnity, Speech to Final Event. Unpublished.
Mignolo, W. (2011), 'Epistemic disobedience and the decolonial option: A manifesto', *Transmodernity: Journal of Peripheral Cultural Production of the Luso-Hispanic World*, 1(2): 44–66.
Milburn, K. (2015), 'On Social Strikes and Directional Demands', *weareplanc.org*. Available at: http://www.weareplanc.org/blog/on-social-strikes-and-directional-demands/ (accessed 18 July 2016).
Miller Medina, J.E. (2005), 'The State Machine: Politics, Ideology and Computation in Chile, 1964–1973', unpublished Ph.D. thesis, Massachusetts Institute of Technology.
Miraftab, F. (2004), 'Invited and invented spaces of participation: Neoliberal citizenship and feminists' expanded notion of politics', *Wagadu*, 1: 1–7.
Mirowski, P. (2004), *The Effortless Economy of Science?* Durham, NC: Duke University Press.
Mirowski, P. (2011), *Science-Mart: Privatizing American Science*, Cambridge, MA: Harvard University Press.
Mirza, H.S. (2015), 'Respecting Difference: Widening Participation in Post-race Times', in C. Alexander and J. Arday (eds), *Aiming Higher, Inequality and Diversity in the Academy*, 27–29, London: Runnymede.
Mohanty, T.C. (2003), *Feminism Without Borders: Decolonizing Theory, Practicing Solidarity*, Durham and London: Duke University Press.

Molesworth, M., Nixon, E. and Scullion, R. (2009), 'Having, being and higher education: The marketization of the university and the transformation of the student into consumer', *Teaching in Higher Education*, 14(3): 277–287.
Molesworth, M., Scullion, R. and Nixon, E. (2010), *The Marketisation of Higher Education and the Student as Consumer*, London: Routledge.
Mollison, B. (1979), *Permaculture Two. Practical Design for Town and Country in Permanent Agriculture*, Tyalgum: Tagari.
Mollison, B. and Holmgren, D. (1978), *Permaculture One. A Perennial Agriculture for Human Settlements*, Tyalgum: Tagari.
Morales, A. L. (1998), *Medicine Stories: History, Culture, and the Politics of Integrity.*, Cambridge, MA: South End Press.
Morris, F.A. (2012), 'When ecology goes feral', *Wageningen Journal of Life Sciences*, 59: 7–9.
Morris, R. (1998), *Penal Abolition, the Practical Choice: A Practical Manual on Penal Abolition*, Toronto: Canadian Scholars' Press.
Morrison, J., Rha, J. and Helfman, A. (2003), 'Learning awareness, student engagement and change: A transformation in leadership development', *Journal of Education for Business*, 79(1): 11–17.
Morrow, R. (2015), *Teaching Permaculture Matters*, Blackheath: Mountains Wildfire Press.
Moten, F. and Harney, S. (1999), 'The academic speed up', *Workplace: A Journal for Academic Labour*, 4: 23–28.
Motta, S.C. (2011), 'Notes Towards Prefigurative Epistemologies' in S.C. Motta and A.G. Nilsen (eds), *Social Movements in the Global South: Development, Dispossession and Resistance*, London: Palgrave Macmillan Press.
Motta, S.C. (2013), '"We are the ones we have been waiting for": The feminization of resistance in Venezuela', *Latin American Perspectives*, 40(3): 35–54.
Motta, S.C. (2014), 'Reinventing Revolutions: An 'Other' Politics in Practice and Theory' in R. Stahler-Sholk, H.E. Vanden and M. Becker (eds), *Rethinking Latin American Social Movements: Radical Action from Below*, 21–44, London: Rowman and Littlefield.
Motta, S.C. (2015), 'Becoming Woman: On Exile and Belonging in the Borderlands', in Z. Arashiro and M. Barahona (eds), *Women in Academia Crossing North/South Borders: Gender, Race and Displacement*, 89–116, London: Lexington Books.
Motta, S.C. (2017a), 'Decolonising Critique: From Prophetic Negation to Prefigurative Affirmation', in A. C. Dinerstein (eds), *Social Sciences for an Other Politics: Women Theorising Without Parachutes*, New York and London: Palgrave Macmillan.
Motta, S.C. (2017b) 'Decolonizing Australia's Body Politics: Contesting the Violence of Coloniality of Child Removal' Journal of Resistance Studies 2 (2): 100–133.
Motta, S.C. and Cole, M. (2014), *Constructing Twenty First Century Socialism: The Role of Radical Education*, London: Palgrave Macmillan Press.
Mouffe, C. (2000), *The Democratic Paradox*, London, New York: Verso.
Mouffe, C. (2013), *Agonistics*, London: Verso.
Mountz, A., Bonds, A., Mansfield, B., Loyd, J., Hyndman, J., Walton-Roberts, M., Basu, R., Whitson, R., Hawkins, R., Hamilton, T. and Durran, W. (2015), 'For Slow Scholarship: A Feminist Politics of Resistance through Collective Action in the Neoliberal University', *ACME: An International E-Journal for Critical Geographies*. Available at: http://ojs.unbc.ca/index.php/acme/article/view/1058/1141 (accessed 18 July 2016).
Mukherjee, S., Scandrett, E., Sen, T. and Shah, D. (2011), 'Generating Theory in the Bhopal Survivors' Movement', in S.C. Motta and A.G. Nilsen (eds), *Social Movements in the Global South: Dispossession, Development and Resistance*, 150–177, Basingstoke: Palgrave Macmillan.

NACAE (1970), *The Structure of Art and Design Education in the Further Education Sector*, London: HMSO.
Naidoo, R. (2016), 'Higher education is trapped in a competition fetish', University World News, 15 April 2016, 409. Available at: http://www.universityworldnews.com/article.php?story=20160413131355443 (accessed 18 July 2016).
Naidoo, R., Shankar, A. and Ekant, V. (2011), 'The consumerist turn in higher education: Policy aspirations and outcomes', *Journal of Marketing Management*, 27 (11/12): 1142–1162.
Narayan, S and Scandrett, E. (2014), 'Science in community environmental struggles: Lessons from community environmental monitors, Cuddalore, Tamil Nadu', *Community Development Journal*, 49(4): 557–572.
Neary, M. (2011), 'The Social Science Centre: A Radical New Model for Higher Education', *Open Democracy UK*. Available at: https://www.opendemocracy.net/ourkingdom/mike-neary/social-science-centre-radical-new-model-for-higher-education (accessed 18 July 2016).
Neary, M. (2012), 'Teaching Politically: Policy, Pedagogy and the New European University', *The Journal for Critical Education Policy Studies*, 10(2): 233–257. Available at: http://www.jceps.com/PDFs/10-2-08.pdf (accessed 18 July 2016).
Neary, M. (2012), 'The University as a Form of Social Knowing', in M. Neary, H. Stevenson and L. Bell (eds), *Towards Teaching in Public: Reshaping the Modern University*, 144–164, London, Continuum International Publishing Group.
Neary, M and Amsler, S. (2012), 'Occupy: A new pedagogy of space and time?', *Journal for Critical Education Policy Studies*, 10(2): 106–138.
Neary, M. and Saunders, G. (2011), 'Leadership and Learning Landscapes: The Struggle for the Idea of the University', *Higher Education Quarterly*, 65(4): 333–352.
Neary, M. and Saunders, G. (2016), 'Student as producer and the politics of abolition: Making a new form of dissident institution? *Critical Education*, 7(5): 1–23.
Neary M. and Winn J. (2009), 'The Student as Producer: Reinventing the Student Experience in Higher Education', in L. Bell, H. Stevenson, and M. Neary (eds), *The Future of Higher Education: Policy, Pedagogy and the Student Experience*, 126–138, London: Continuum.
Neary M. and Winn J. (2012), 'Open Education: Commons, Commonism and the New Commonwealth', *Ephemera: Theory and Politics in Organization*, 12(4): 406–422.
Neary, M. and Winn, J. (2016), 'Beyond Public and Private: A Framework for Co-operative Higher Education', Co-operative Education Conference 2016, 21–22nd April 2016, Manchester. Available at: http://eprints.lincoln.ac.uk/23051/ (accessed 18 July 2016).
Newfield, C. (2010), 'The structure and the silence of the cognitariat', *Eurozine*, 5 February 2010. Available at: http://www.eurozine.com/articles/2010-02-05-newfield-en.html (accessed 18 July 2016).
Newfield, C. (2013), *Unmaking the Public University: The Forty Year Assault on the Middle Class*, Cambridge: Harvard University Press.
Neylon, C. (2013), '@d_mainwaring....I've also been described as "neo liberal" (alongside uber capitalist) and "Marxist" in the past year which is fun...', @*CameronNeylon*, 9 December 2013. Available at: https://twitter.com/CameronNeylon/status/410035300388597760 (accessed 18 July 2016).
Nicolau, I. (2013), 'Historical evolution of the death penalty abolition as a fundamental human right, *Contemporary Readings in Law and Social Justice*, 5(2): 278–283.

Nilsen, A.G. and Cox, L. (2013), 'What Would a Marxist Theory of Social Movements Look Like?', in C. Barker, L. Cox, J. Krinsky and A.G. Nilsen (eds), 63–82, *Marxism and Social Movements*, Leiden: Brill.

Noble, T. and Pym, F. (1970), 'Collegial authority and the receding locus of power', *The British Journal of Sociology*, 21(4): 431–445.

Nolan, S. Massebiaux, E.P. and Gorman, T. (2013), 'Saving jobs, promoting democracy: Worker co-operatives', *Irish Journal of Sociology*, 21(2): 103–115.

Orr, L., Scandrett, E. and Whiting, N. (2013), 'An educational approach to gender justice', *Concept*, 4(1): 1–4.

Osborne, P. (1996), *A Critical Sense: Interviews with Intellectuals*, London: Routledge.

Park, J. (2008), 'An Interview with Frances Pinter of Bloomsbury Academic', *Creative Commons*, 20 October 2008. Available at: http://creativecommons.org/weblog/entry/10100 (accessed 18 July 2016).

Pearce, J. (2008), '"We Make Progress Because We Are Lost": Critical Reflections on co-producing Knowledge as a methodology for researching Non-Governmental Public Action', NGPA Working Paper Series, London School of Economics.

Pearce, J. (2012), 'Power in Community: A Research and Social Action Scoping Review'. Available at: http://www/ahrc.ac.uk/Funding-Opportunities/Pages/Connecte-Communities-Scoping-Studies-and-Research Reviews.aspx (accessed 18 July 2016).

Pearce, J. (2013), 'Power and the twenty first century activist: From the neighbourhood to the square', *Development and Change*, 4(33): 639–663.

Pearce, J. and Milne, E.J. (2010), *Participation and community on Bradford's traditionally 'white' estates. A community research project*, York: Joseph Rowntree Foundation.

Pearce, J., Howard, J. and Bronstein, A. (2010), 'Learning from Latin America: Organising for social transformation', *Community Development Journal*, 45(3): 265–275.

Pearce, J., Pearson, M. and Cameron, S. (2007), 'The Ivory Tower and Beyond: The University of Bradford at the Heart of Its Communities'. Unpublished.

People's Political Economy (PPE), '2013 Inaugural Report: From foundations to future'. Available at: https://agentofhistory.files.wordpress.com/2015/08/ppe-report-2013.pdf (accessed 18 July 2016).

Pepper, C. and Giles, W. (2015), 'Leading in middle management in higher education', *Management in Education*, 29(2): 46–52.

Pirie, I. (2009), 'The political economy of academic publishing', *Historical Materialism*, 17: 31–60.

Posner, R. (2003), *Public Intellectuals: A Study of Decline*, Cambridge: Harvard University Press.

Postone, M. (1993), *Time, Labor and Social Domination*, Cambridge: Cambridge University Press.

Radice, H. (2013), 'UK higher education under neoliberalism', *ACME: An International E-Journal for Critical Geographies*, 12(3): 407–418.

Rae, W.R. (1904), *How Best Can Co-operative Societies Utilise Their Educational Funds in View of the Educational Facilities Now Provided by Municipal and Local Authorities*, Manchester: Co-operative Union.

Rae, W. R. (1909) 'Inaugural Address', *Co-operative Congress*, 20–35, Manchester: Co-operative Union.

Rancière, J. (2006), *The Politics of Aesthetics*, London: Continuum.

Rancière, J. (2010), *Dissensus: On Politics and Aesthetics*, London: Continuum.

Ranciere, J. (2012), *Proletarian Nights*, Verso: London and New York.

Ranciere, J. (2015), *Dissensus: On Politics and Aesthetics*, Bloomsbury Academic

Ratcliffe, R. (2013), 'Students Occupy Sussex University in Protest Against Privatisation', *The Guardian*, 8 February 2013. Available at: http://www.theguardian.com/education/2013/feb/08/students-occupy-sussex-university-in-protest-against-privatisation (accessed 18 July 2016).

Readings, B. (1997), *The University in Ruins*, Cambridge: Harvard University Press.

Reay, D., Crozier, G. and Clayton, J. (2009), '"Fitting in" or "standing out": Working-class students in UK higher education', *British Educational Research Journal*, 32(1): 1–18.

Redfern, P. (July 1939) 'Education Past and Present', *Co-operative Review*, 13(7): 218–220.

Reid, D. (2012), 'Introduction', in J. Ranciere (2012), *Proletarian Nights*, xiii–xxxv, Verso: London and New York.

Research and Destroy (2009), 'Communique from an Absent Future,' *After the Fall*, Berkeley: Little Black Cart, 7–11. Available at: http://libcom.org/library/communique-absent-future (accessed 18 July 2016).

Ridley, D. (2016), 'On Practicing What You Preach', *Citizen Sociology*, 9 February 2016. Available at: https://citizensociology.wordpress.com/2016/02/09/on-practicing-what-you-preach/ (accessed 18 July 2016).

Ridley-Duff, R. and Bull, M. (2014), 'Solidarity co-operatives: An embedded historical communitarian pluralist approach to social enterprise development?' (Keynote to RMIT Research Colloquium), in: 2014 Social Innovation and Entrepreneurship Research Colloquium, Melbourne, RMIT Building 80, 26th–28th November 2014. Available at: http://shura.shu.ac.uk/9890/ (accessed 14th July 2016).

Robbins L.C. (1963), *Higher Education: Report of the Committee Appointed by the Prime Minister Under the Chairmanship of Lord Robbins*, 1961–1966, London: HMSO.

Roberts, D. (2012), 'Prison, foster care and the systemic punishment of black mothers,' *UCLA Law Review*, 59(6): 1476–1500.

Robin, C. (2016), 'From the Talmud to Judith butler: Audiences as Co-Creators with – and of – the public intellectual', *Corey Robin*. Available at: http://coreyrobin.com/2016/07/02/from-the-talmud-to-judith-butler-audiences-as-co-creators-with-and-of-the-public-intellectual/ (accessed 18 July 2016).

Robinson, S. and Paten, J. (2008), 'The question of genocide and indigenous child removal: The colonial Australian context', *Journal of Genocide Research*, 10(4): 501–518.

Roggero, G. (2011), *The Production of Living Knowledge, the Crisis of the University and the Transformation of Labour in Europe and North America*, Philadelphia, PA: Temple University Press.

Rogowski, S. (2015), 'From child welfare to child protection/safeguarding: A critical practitioner's view of changing conceptions, policies and practice', *Practice* 27(2): 97–112.

Rolfe, G. (2013), *The University in Dissent*, Abingdon: SRHE and Routledge.

Rose, G. (1995), *Hegel Contra Sociology*, London: Athlone Press.

Said, E. (1993), *Representations of the Intellectual: The 1993 Reith Lectures*, London and Sydney: Vintage.

Saks, M. (2003), 'The Limitations of the Anglo-American sociology of the professions: a critique of the current neo-Weberian orthodoxy', *Knowledge, Work and Society*, 1: 11–31.

Salmon, A. (2011), 'Aboriginal mothering, FASD prevention and the contestations of neoliberal citizenship', *Critical Public Health*, 21(2): 165–178.

Sandoval, C. (2000), *Methodology of the Oppressed*, Minneapolis: University of Minnesota Press.

Santos, B. da Sousa (2014), *Epistemologies of the South: Justice Against Epistemicide*, London: Taylor and Francis.

Sarangi, S. (2009), 'Global industrial disaster, National State failure and local self-provision of Health Care', *Global Social Policy*, 9(3): 316–318.

Saunders, G. (Forthcoming), 'Working With Groups Who Provide Alternative Forms of Higher Education', Ph.D Thesis, Lincoln University.

Sayre, G.M., (2005) 'The crisis in scholarly publishing: Demystifying the fetishes of technology and the market', *Profession*, 52–58.

Scandrett, E. (2007), 'Environmental justice in Scotland: Policy, pedagogy and praxis', *Environmental Research Letters*, 2(4). Available at: http://iopscience.iop.org /article/10.1088/1748-9326/2/4/045002/pdf (accessed 18 July 2016).

Scandrett, E. (2014), 'Popular Education methodology, activist academics and emergent social movements: Agents for Environmental Justice', *Interface: A Journal for and about Social Movements*, 6(1): 327–334.

Scandrett, E. and Mukherjee, S. (2011), 'Globalisation and abstraction in the Bhopal survivors' movement', *Interface: A Journal for and about Social Movements*, 3(1): 195–209.

Scott, P. (2013), 'The Coalition Government's Reform of Higher Education: Policy Formation and Political Process', in C. Callender and P. Scott (eds), *Browne and Beyond: Modernizing English Higher Education*, London: Institute of Education Press.

Scott, G. and Mooney, G. (2009), 'Poverty and social justice in the devolved Scotland: Neoliberalism meets social democracy?', *Social Policy and Society*, 8(3): 379–389.

Scott, J. (1998), *Seeing Like a State: How Certain Schemes to Improve the Human Condition Have Failed*, New Haven: Yale University Press.

Scottish Government (2010), *Building a Smarter Future – Towards a Sustainable Scottish Solution for the Future of Higher Education*, Edinburgh: Crown. Available at: http:// www.gov.scot/Resource/Doc/335256/0109656.pdf (accessed 18 July 2016).

Sears, E., Warburton-Brown, C., Remiarz, T., and Ferguson, R.S. (2013), 'A social learning organisation evolves a research capability in order to study itself', Poster presentation at the Tyndall Centre Radical Emissions Reduction Conference, London, UK, 10th–11th December 2013.

Serewizc, L. (2015), 'In the UK Political Philosophy is a Crime', *Philosophical Politics*, 15 December 2015. Available at: https://goo.gl/A8yNjf (accessed 18 July 2016).

Seyfang, G., and Smith, A. (2007), 'Grassroots Innovations for Sustainable Development: Towards a new research and policy agenda', *Environmental Politics*, 16 (4): 584–603.

Shattock, M. (2006), *Managing Good Governance in Higher Education*, Maidenhead: Open University Press.

Shattock, M. (2008), 'The change from private to public governance of British higher education: Its consequences for Higher Education policy making 1980–2006', *Higher Education Quarterly*, 62(3): 181–203.

Shattock, M. (2013), 'University governance, leadership and management in a decade of diversification and uncertainty', *Higher Education Quarterly*, 7(3): 217–233.

Shukaitis, S (2010), 'Sisyphus and the labour of imagination: Autonomy, cultural production and the antinomies of worker self-management', *Affinities: A Journal of Radical Theory, Culture and Action*, 4(1): 57–82.

Simmonds, D. and Tsui, O. (2010), 'Effective design of a global leadership programme', *Human Resource Development International*, 13(5): 519–540.

Sitrin, M. (2014), 'Horizontal Paradigms – Cuba Style', *ZNet*, 9 November 2014. Available at: https://zcomm.org/znetarticle/horizontal-paradigms-cuba-style/ (accessed 18 July 2016).

Slaughter, S. and Rhoades, G. (2009), *Academic Capitalism and the New Economy: Markets, State and Higher Education*, Baltimore, MD: John Hopkins University Press.

Sloane, M. (2016), Dialogue over dissemination: Unlocking the potential of knowledge exchange through creative collaboration, *LSE Blogs*, 13 June 2013. Available at: http://blogs.lse.ac.uk/impactofsocialsciences/2016/06/13/dialogue-over-dissemination-unlocking-the-potential-of-knowledge-exchange-through-creative-collaboration/ (accessed 18 July 2016).

Smith, R. (2013), *Scottish Code of Good Higher Education Governance*, Edinburgh: The Scottish Government. Available at: http://www.scottishuniversitygovernance.ac.uk/wp-content/uploads/2013/07/Scottish-Code-of-Good-HE-Governance.pdf (accessed 18 July 2016).

Social Science Centre (2013), 'An Experiment in Free co-operative Higher Education', *Radical Philosophy*, 182. Available at: https://www.radicalphilosophy.com/news/an-experiment-in-free-co-operative-higher-education (accessed 18 July 2016).

Social Science Centre (2014), http://socialsciencecentre.org.uk (accessed 18 June 2014).

Somerville, P. (2007), 'Co-operative identity', *Journal of Co-operative Studies*, 40(1): 5–17.

Somerville, P. and Saunders, G. (2013), 'Beyond Public and Private: The Transformation of Higher Education', University of Lincoln. Available at: http://josswinn.org/wp-content/uploads/2013/11/Somerville-and-Saunders-2013-Beyond-public-and-private.pdf (accessed 18 July 2016).

Sperlinger, T. (2014), 'Is a Co-operative University Model a Sustainable Alternative?' *The Guardian*, 26 March 2014. Available at: http://www.theguardian.com/higher-education-network/blog/2014/mar/26/free-university-cooperative-model-sustainable-alternative (accessed 18 July 2016).

Spivak, G.C. (2012), *An Aesthetic Education in the Era of Globalization*, Cambridge, MA: Harvard University Press.

Springer, S., Birch, K. and MacLeavy, J. eds (2016), *Handbook of Neoliberalism*, London: Routledge.

Stallman, R. (2010), 'Why Software Should Be Free', in R. Stallman, *Free Software, Free Society: Selected Essays of Richard Stallman*, 43–56, Boston, MA: Free Software Foundation.

Stedile, J. (2003), 'Brazil's social movements', *ZNet*, 22 October 2003. Available at: https://zcomm.org/znetarticle/brazils-social-movements-by-joao-pedro-stedile/ (accessed 18 July).

Suber, P. (2012), *Open Access*, Cambridge, MA: MIT Press. Available at: http://bit.ly/oa-book (accessed 18 July 2016).

Summer Schools (1916) 'Official report of co-operative summer schools, 1915', *College Herald*, 3(1): 4.

Tapper, T. and Salter, B. (2003), 'Interpreting the process of change in higher education: The case of the research assessment exercises, *Higher Education Quarterly*, 57(1): 4–23.

Tarlau, R. (2013), 'The social(ist) pedagogies of the MST: Towards new relations of production in the Brazilian countryside', *Education Policy Analysis Archives*, 21(4):1–27.

Tawney, R. H. (1912) *Education and Social Progress*, Manchester: Co-operative Union.

Taylor, R., Rockhill, K. and Fieldhouse, R. (1985) *University Adult Education in England and the USA*, London: Croom Helm.

Tent City University (2012), 'Welcome to Tent City University'. Available at: https://web.archive.org/web/20150924003042/http://tentcityuniversity.org/ (accessed 18 July 2016).

Terranova, T. (2004), *Network Culture: Politics for the Information Age*, London: Pluto Press.
The British Permaculture Association (2016), Research. Available at: https://www.permaculture.org.uk/research (accessed 18 July 2016).
Thistlewood, D. (1992), *Histories of Art and Design Education: Cole to Coldstream*, Harlow: Longman.
Thomas, J. (1939) 'Education outlook', *Co-operative Review* 13(7): 198–201.
Thompson, E. P. (ed., 1970), *Warwick University Ltd: Industry, Management and the Universities*, Harmondsworth: Penguin.
Thompson, J. and Bekhradnia, B. (2011), *Students at the Heart of the System. An Analysis of the Higher Education White Paper*, Oxford: HEPI.
Thorpe, R. (2007), 'Family inclusion in child protection practice: Building bridges in working with (not against) families', *Communities, Children and Families Australia*, 3(1), 4–10.
Toledo, V. (2001), 'Biocultural diversity and local power in Mexico: Challenging globalization', in L. Maffi (ed.), *On Biocultural Diversity*, 472–488, Washington, DC: Smithsonian Institute Press.
Tomlinson, M. (2014), 'Exploring the Impact of Policy Changes on Student Attitudes and Approaches to Learning in Higher Education', Higher Education Academy. Available at: http://www.heacademy.ac.uk/assets/documents/research/Exploring_the_impact_of_policy_changes_student_experience.pdf (accessed 18 July 2016).
Transition Research Network (2016), Available at: http://www.transitionresearchnetwork.org/ (accessed 18 July 2016).
Turnbull, S. and Edwards, G. (2005), 'Leadership development for organizational change in a new UK university', *Advances in Developing Human Resources*, 7(3): 396–413.
UCAS (2015), 'Number of Students Applying to UK Universities and Colleges Rises by 2%', UCAS. Available at: https://www.ucas.com/corporate/news-and-key-documents/news/number-students-applying-uk-universities-and-colleges-rises-2 (accessed 18 July 2016).
UCAS (2016), 'Deadline Applicant Statistics 2016', UCAS. Available at: https://www.ucas.com/sites/default/files/mr_january_160115.pdf (accessed 18 July 2016).
UCU (2013), 'Over Half of Universities and Colleges Use Lecturers on Zero Hours Contracts'. Available at: http://www.ucu.org.uk/6749 (accessed 18 July 2016).
UCU (2016), 'Precarious work in higher education: a snapshot of insecure contracts and institutional attitudes'. Available at: https://www.ucu.org.uk/media/7995/Precarious-work-in-higher-education-a-snapshot-of-insecure-contracts-and-institutional-attitudes-Apr-16/pdf/ucu_precariouscontract_hereport_apr16.pdf (accessed 18 July 2016).
UCU (2016), 'Report Reveals University Heads' Pay Rises and Perks', UCU. Available at: https://www.ucu.org.uk/article/8096/Report-reveals-university-heads-pay-rises-and-perks (accessed 18 July 2016).
Undercommoning (2016), 'Undercommoning: Revolution Within, Against and Beyond the University'. Available at: http://undercommoning.org/undercommoning-within-against-and-beyond/ (accessed 18 July 2016).
University for Strategic Optimism (2011), *Undressing the Academy, or The Student Handjob*, London: Minor Compositions.
University of Utopia (n.d.), 'Anti-Curricula: A Course of Action'. Available at: http://www.universityofutopia.org/sharing/outside (accessed 18 July 2016).
Van Den Hemel, E. (2008), 'Included but not belonging: Badiou and Ranciere on human rights', *Krisis: Journal for Contemporary Philosophy*, 3: 16–30.

Van Meer, K. (2009), 'What is Militant and Co-research?' Available at: https://teamcolors.wordpress.com/2009/06/08/workshop-what-is-militant-research/ (accessed 18 July 2016).

Veletsianos, G. and Kimmons, R. (2012), 'Assumptions and challenges of open scholarship', *The International Review of Research in Open and Distance Learning*, 13(4): 166–189.

Vernon, K. (2011) 'Values and Vocation: Educating the Co-operative Workforce, 1918–1939, in A. Webster, A. Brown, D. Stewart, J.K. Walton and L. Shaw (eds) *The Hidden Alternative: Co-operative Values, Past, Present and Future*, 37–58, Manchester: Manchester University Press.

Vincent, N. and Wickham, C. (2013), 'Debating Open Access: Introduction', in N. Vincent and C. Wickham (eds), *Debating Open Access*, 4–12, London: British Academy.

Virno, P. (1996), 'Virtuosity and Revolution', in M. Hardt and P. Virno (eds, trans. E. Emery), *Radical Thought in Italy: A Potential Politics*, 190–201, Minneapolis: University of Minnesota Press.

Virno, P. (2001), *General Intellect*. Available at: http://www.generation-online.org/p/fpvirno10.htm (accessed 14th July 2016).

Virno, P. (2004), *A Grammar of the Multitude: For an Analysis of Contemporary Forms of Life*, Cambridge, MA: Semiotext (e).

Vittoria, P. (2015a), in conversation with J. Canaan and M. Neary, 15 October 2015.

Vittoria, P. (2015b), Talk, Lincoln University, 15 October 2015.

Von Prondzynski, F., Brotherstone, T., Macwhirter, I., Parker, R. and Simpson, A.F. (2012), *Report of the Review of Higher Education Governance in Scotland, Edinburgh: The Scottish Government*. Available at: http://www.gov.scot/resource/0038/00386780.pdf (accessed 18 July 2016).

Voss, B. (2013), 'Massive Open Online Courses (MOOCs): A Primer for University and College Board Members'. Available at: http://agb.org/sites/default/files/legacy/report_2013_MOOCs.pdf (accessed 18 July 2016).

Wainwright, H. (1994), *Arguments for a New Left: Answering the Free-Market Right*, Oxford: Blackwell.

Walsall Co-operative Society (1919) 'Resolution', in *Co-operative Congress Report*, ed A. Whitehead, Manchester: Co-operative Union.

Wanggren L. and Milatovic M. (2015), 'Introduction: Education, intersectionality and social change', *Journal of Feminist Scholarship*, 7/8. Available at: http://www.jfsonline.org/issue7-8/articles/wanggrenmilatovic/ (accessed 18 July 2016).

Warner, M. (1995), *From the Beast to the Blonde: On Fairy Tales and Their Tellers*, New York: The Noonday Press.

Warner, M. (2015), 'Learning My Lesson: Marina Warner on the Disfiguring of Higher Education', *London Review of Books*, 37 (6): 8–14. Available at: http://www.lrb.co.uk/v37/n06/marina-warner/learning-my-lesson (accessed 18 July 2016).

Waugh, C. (2009), '*Plebs*': *The Lost Legacy of Independent Working-Class Education*, Sheffield: Post-16 Educator.

Weeks, K. (2011), *The Problem with Work: Feminism, Marxism, Antiwork Politics and Postwork Imaginaries*, Durham, NC: Duke University Press.

Weller, M. (2014), *The Battle for Open: How openness won and why it doesn't feel like victory*, Ubiquity Press. Available at: http://www.ubiquitypress.com/site/books/detail/11/battle-for-open/ (accessed 18 July 2016).

West, C. (1990), 'The New Cultural Politics of Difference', in R. Ferguson, M. Gever, T.T. Minh-ha and C. West (eds), *Out There: Marginalization and Contemporary Cultures*, 19–32, Cambridge: MIT Press.

Western S. (2008), *Leadership: A Critical Text*, London: SAGE.
White, M. (2007), *Maps of Narrative Practice*, New York: WW Norton and Company.
Williams, J. (2006), 'The Pedagogy of Debt', *College Literature*, 33(4): 155–169.
Williams, J. (2009), 'The Pedagogy of Debt,' in Edufactory Collective (eds), *Towards a Global Autonomous University*, 89–96, Brooklyn: Autonomedia.
Williams, J. (2012), 'Deconstructing Academe: The Birth of Critical University Studies', *Chronicle of Higher Education*. Available at: http://chronicle.com/article/An-Emerging-Field-Deconstructs/130791/ (accessed 18 July 2016).
Williams, J. (2013), *Consuming Higher Education: Why Learning Can't Be Bought*, London: Bloomsbury Academic.
Williams, J. and Roberts, D. (2016), 'Academic Integrity: Exploring Tensions Between Perception and Practice in the Contemporary University', *The Society for Research into Higher Education*, 30 June 2016. Available at: http://www.srhe.ac.uk/downloads/WILLIAMSJoannaROBERTSDavid.pdf (accessed 18 July 2016).
Willis, P. (1982), *Learning to Labour: How Working Class Kids Get Working Class Jobs*, New York: Columbia University Press.
Wilson, J. F., Webster, A. and Vorberg-Rugh, R. (2013) *Building Co-operation: A Business History of the Co-oprative Group, 1863–2013*, Oxford: Oxford University Press.
Wink, W. (2000), *The Powers That Be*, New York: Bantam Doubleday.
Winn, J (2013a), 'Co-operative Universities: A bibliography', *Joss Winn*, 21 November 2013. Available at: http://josswinn.org/2013/11/21/co-operative-universities-a-bibliography/ (accessed 18 July 2016).
Winn, J. (2013b), 'Helplessness', *Joss Winn*, 7 July 2013. Available at: http://josswinn.org/2013/07/helplessness/ (accessed 18 July).
Winn, J. (2014), 'Is an Open Access journal article a commodity?' *Joss Winn*, 2 February 2014, Available at: http://josswinn.org/2014/02/is-an-open-access-journal-article-a-commodity/ (accessed 18 July).
Winn, J (2015a), 'The co-operative university: Labour, property and pedagogy', *Power and Education*, 7(1): 39–55.
Winn, J (2015b), 'Writing about academic labour', *Workplace: A Journal for Academic labor*, 25: 1–15. Available at: http://ices.library.ubc.ca/index.php/workplace/article/view/185095/185275 (accessed 18 July 2016).
Winn, J. (2015c), 'Open education and the emancipation of academic labour', *Learning, Media and Technology*, 40: 385–404. Available at: http://dx.doi.org/10.1080/17439884.2015.1015546 (accessed 18 July).
Winn, J. (2016a), 'HE White Paper, the HERB and Co-operative Higher Education', *Joss Winn*, 22 June 2016. Available at: http://josswinn.org/2016/05/19/website-for-co-operative-leadership-for-higher-education/ (accessed 18 July 2016).
Wise, A. (2013), 'Evidence to House of Commons Select Committee Inquiry', *Inquiry into Open Access. Fifth Report of Session 2013–2014*, Ev1–Ev11, London: House of Commons.
Wolf, A. (2015), *Heading for the Precipice: Can Further and Higher Education Funding Policies be Sustained?* London: Policy Institute, King's College.
Woodin, T. (2007), 'Working class education and social change in nineteenth and twentieth century Britain', *History of Education* 36(4/5): 483–496.
Woodin, T. (2011), 'Co-operative Education in the Nineteenth and early Twentieth Centuries: Context, Identity and Learning', in T. Webster, A. Brown, D. Stewart, J.K. Walton and L. Shaw (eds) *The Hidden Alternative: Co-operative Values, Past, Present and Future*, 78–95, Manchester: Manchester University Press.

Woodin, T. (2012), 'Co-operative schools: Building communities in the twenty first century', *Forum*, 54(2): 327–339.

Woodin, T., ed. (2015), *Co-operation, Learning and Co-operative Values*. London: Routledge.

Woodin, T. (2017), 'Co-operative Education, Neoliberalism and Historical Perspectives: The Dilemmas of Building Alternatives', in Rudd, T. and Goodson, I. F. (eds) *Negotiating Neoliberalism: Developing Alternative Educational Visions*, 117–128, Rotterdam: Sense Publishers.

Woolf, L. (1914), *Education and the Co-operative Movement*, London: Women's Co-operative Guild.

Wright, S. (2002), *Storming Heaven: Class Composition and Struggle in Italian Autonomist Marxism*, London: Pluto Press.

Wright, S., Greenwood, D. and Boden, R. (2011), 'Report on a field visit to Mondragón University: A cooperative experience/experiment,' *Learning and Teaching*, 4(3): 38–56.

Wyness, G. (2013), 'As Easy as AAB: The Impact of the Quasi-Market on Institutions, Student Numbers and the Higher Education Sector', in C. Callender and P. Scott (eds) *Browne and Beyond: Modernizing English Higher Education*, London: Institute of Education Press.

Yeo, S. (1988), *New Views of Co-operation*, London: Routledge.

Yeo, S. (2014), 'The Co-operative University: Transforming Higher Education,' in T. Woodin, ed., *Co-operation, Learning and Co-operative Values*, London: Routledge.

Zembylas, M. (2006), 'Witnessing in the classroom: The ethics and politics of affect', *Educational Theory*, 56(3): 305–324.

Ziai, A. (2013), 'Boaventura de Sousa Santos, interviewed', *Development and Change*, 44(3): 727–738.

Zibechi, Raul (2013), 'Autonomous Zapatista Education: The Little Schools of Below', *Upside Down World*, 27 August 2013. Available at: http://upsidedownworld.org/main/mexico-archives-79/4427-autonomous-zapatista-education-the-little-schools-of-below (accessed 18 July 2016).

Zoller H.M. and Fairhurst G.T. (2007), 'Resistance leadership: The overlooked potential in critical organization and leadership studies', *Human Relations*, 60(9): 1331–1360.

Index